TEACH YOURSELF BOOKS

WINDOWS

WINDOWS

Diane Saxon

TEACH YOURSELF BOOKS

Long-renowned as the authoritative source for self-guided learning – with more than 30 million copies sold worldwide – the *Teach Yourself* series includes over 200 titles in the fields of languages, crafts, hobbies, sports, and other leisure activities.

British Library Cataloguing in Publication Data
Saxon, Diane
  Windows
  I. Title II. Saxon, Stephen
  005.4

Library of Congress Catalog Card Number: 93-85130

First published in UK 1994 by Hodder Headline Plc, 338 Euston Road, London NW1 3BH

First published in US 1994 by NTC Publishing Group, 4255 West Touhy Avenue, Lincolnwood (Chicago), Illinois 60646 – 1975 U.S.A.

Copyright © 1994 Diane Saxon and Stephen Saxon

In UK: All rights reserved. No part of this publication may be reproduced or transmitted in any form or by any means, electronic or mechanical, including photocopy, recording, or any information storage and retrieval system, without permission in writing from the publisher or under licence from the Copyright Licensing Agency Limited. Further details of such licences (for reprographic reproduction) may be obtained from the Copyright Licensing Agency Limited, of 90 Tottenham Court Road, London W1P 9HE.

In US: All rights reserved. No part of this book may be reproduced, stored in a retrieval system, or transmitted in any form, or by any means, electronic, mechanical, photocopying, or otherwise, without prior permission of NTC Publishing Group.

Typeset by Rowland Phototypesetting Ltd, Bury St Edmunds, Suffolk.
Printed in England by Cox & Wyman Ltd, Reading, Berkshire.

Second edition 1992
Impression number   14 13 12 11 10 9 8 7 6 5 4 3 2
Year   1999 1998 1997 1996 1995 1994

CONTENTS

1	**Introduction**	1
	About this book	1
	Conventions	2
	The companion disk	3
	Using the companion disk	3
	About Windows	4
	Background	4
	Windows 3.0	5
	Windows 3.1	5
	Choosing a Computer to run Windows	6
	What does Windows offer?	6
	What of the future?	9
2	**Getting started**	10
	Loading Windows	10
	From the DOS prompt	10
	From the DOS shell	10
	Program Manager	12
	The Program Manager window	13
	Features of the Program Manager window	16
	Exiting from Windows	18
3	**Fun with the mouse**	20
	Using a mouse	20
	Mouse types	21

Mouse techniques	22
Practice tasks	23
Windows tutorial	25
Mouse lesson	26
Windows lesson	27

4 Fun with games — 29
- Solitaire — 30
- Minesweeper — 38
- Reversi — 41

5 Fun with the desktop — 44
- Customising Program Manager — 44
  - Moving windows — 46
  - Sizing windows — 46
  - Saving changes — 47
- Customising the desktop — 48
  - Changing colours — 48
  - Wallpapers and screen savers — 50
    - Wallpapers — 50
    - Screen savers — 52
    - Customising the screen saver — 53

6 Fun with Paintbrush — 55
- Drawing lines — 57
  - The line tool — 57
  - Changing line thickness — 57
- Selecting colours — 57
- The eraser tools — 58
- Clearing the drawing — 59
- Drawing shapes — 60
  - The box tools — 60
  - The circle tools — 61
  - The rounded corner box tools — 61
  - The polygon tools — 61
  - The curved line tool — 62
- Saving — 63
- Printing — 64
- The brush tool — 64
  - Changing brush shape — 65
- The airbrush tool — 65
- The roller tool — 66

The text tool	66
Correcting mistakes	68
Selecting parts of a picture	68
Moving	69
Copying	69
Deleting	69
Exiting from Paintbrush	69
Opening a picture	69
Practice tasks	71
Home sweet home	71
From MENUS to menus!	72

7 Using Write — 74

Entering text	75
Saving your document	76
Correcting the text	76
Selecting sections of text	77
Mouse methods	77
Keyboard methods	78
Changing styles	78
Printing	80
Tabs	81
Inserting pictures into documents	82
Exiting from Write	82

8 Fun with fonts — 84

What is a font?	84
Why should I use different fonts?	85
Where can I use fonts in Windows	85
Using Fonts in Paintbrush	85
Using Fonts in Write	87
TrueType fonts	87
Installing a new font	87

9 Using Cardfile — 91

Entering information	92
Entering the Index Line	92
Adding cards	93
Deleting cards	94
Saving the Cardfile	94
Searching the file	95
Adding pictures to a Cardfile	96

	Printing a Cardfile	98
	Printing Index Lines	98
	Practice task – Animal corner!	98
10	**Windows Calendar**	102
	Entering details for the current day	103
	Entering details for a different date	104
	Viewing a complete month	105
	Saving the Calendar file	106
	Special times	106
	Setting the alarm	107
	Opening a Calendar file	108
	Printing the Calendar file	108
	Exiting from Calendar	109
11	**Windows Calculator**	110
	Standard Calculator	111
	Scientific Calculator	113
	Using the Clipboard	114
12	**Fun with sound**	116
	Choosing a sound card	117
	Sound in Windows	118
	Loading a sound file	119
	Special effects	119
	Mixing sounds	120
	Saving the sound file	122
	Embedding a sound	122
	Recording sound samples	123
13	**Projects**	125
	Project 1 Design a business card	125
	Project 2 Christmas card mailing list	127
	Project 3 SuperTex 3	128
	Project 4 ID Cards	133
	Project 5 Deserted!	135
14	**Fun with the companion disk**	137
	IconWorks icon editor	137
	Loading IconWorks	138
	Editing an icon	139
	Saving an icon	140

Loading an icon	141
Adding an icon to Program Manager	142
Dominoes	143
How to play Dominoes	143
Loading Dominoes	144
The playing board	144
Starting a game	145
Hangman	146
How to play Hangman	147
Loading Hangman	147
Starting a game	148
Checkers	150
How to play Checkers	150
Loading Checkers	150

REFERENCE SECTION 153

15 Program Manager 154

Program Manager	154
Opening a window	155
Features of the Program Manager window	155
Working with application windows	159
Maximising a window	159
Restoring a window	159
Minimising a window	159
Switching between windows	160
Closing an application window	160
Working with group windows	160
Arranging windows	161
Switching between group windows	162
Maximising a group window	163
Restoring a group window	163
Minimising a group window	163
Sizing a group window	164
Moving a group window	164
Closing a group window	164
Arranging icons in a group	164
Creating program groups	165
Deleting a program group	166
Adding a new item to a group	166
Loading and running programs	168
Running non-Windows appliations	168

	Properties	169
	Changing icons	169
	Saving changes	170
	Exiting from Windows	170
16	**Windows Help**	**173**
	Accessing Help	173
	Windows Tutorial	174
	The 'About' Dialog box	174
	Windows Help contents	175
	Printing Help screens	176
	Help options	177
	Glossary	177
	Searching in Help	178
	Help history	179
	Context sensitive help	179
17	**File Manager**	**181**
	Data storage	181
	Starting File Manager	183
	Changing views	184
	Changing directory	184
	Displaying file information	185
	Arranging files	186
	Returning to higher levels	186
	Changing drives	186
	Saving options	187
	Creating directories	187
	File operations	188
	Selecting files	188
	Moving files	188
	Moving by dragging	188
	Moving using menus	189
	Opening more than one directory	190
	Copying files and directories	191
	Copying by dragging	191
	Copying using menus	191
	Copying to the Clipboard	191
	Searching for files and directories	192
	Renaming files	193
	Deleting files	193
	Formatting floppy disks	194

Creating a system disk	195
Copying floppy disks	195
Starting programs from File Manager	196
Drag and drop printing	197
Exiting from File Manager	197

18 Control Panel 198
Colours	198
Changing colour schemes	199
Creating your own colours	200
Fonts	201
Installing new fonts	202
TrueType setting	202
Removing fonts	203
Ports	203
Mouse	204
Desktop	205
Patterns	206
Screen savers	206
Setting passwords	206
Wallpaper	207
Sizing grid	208
Icons	208
Keyboard	208
Printers	208
International	210
Date and time	211
386 Enhanced	211
Drivers	212
Sound	212

19 Main window 214
Print Manager	214
Printing documents	214
Print Manager menu options	216
Installing a printer	217
Printer setup options	218
Closing Print Manager	219
Windows Setup	219
Changing system settings	220
Setting up applications	220
Adding or removing components	221

	MS-DOS Prompt	222
	Clipboard Viewer	223
	Saving Clipboard files	223
20	**Accessories 1 – Paintbrush**	**226**
	Starting a new file	227
	Opening an existing file	227
	The Paintbrush toolbox	227
	Saving the file	229
	Printing	229
	Changing printing size	229
	Changing the appearance of the picture	230
	Changing line thickness	230
	Selecting colours	230
	Editing colours	231
	Changing brush shape	231
	Changing the appearance of text	232
	Editing the picture	233
	Editing tools	233
	Moving picture elements	234
	Copying picture elements	234
	Deleting picture elements	234
	The Pick menu	234
	Document management	235
	Changing drawing size	235
	Page setup	235
	Changing margins	236
	Changing page view	237
	Exiting from Paintbrush	237
21	**Accessories 2 – Write**	**239**
	Starting a new document	239
	Opening an existing document	240
	Entering text	240
	Cursor movement	240
	Saving	241
	Printing	241
	Correcting the text	242
	Selecting text	242
	Mouse methods	242
	Keyboard methods	243
	Cut and paste	243

Character formatting	244
Printing styles	244
Fonts	244
Paragraph formatting	245
Text alignment	246
Spacing	246
Indents	246
Inserting page breaks	247
Inserting manual page breaks	247
Using the Repaginate option	247
Document layout	248
Headers	249
Footers	249
The ruler line	250
Tabs	250
Clearing tab stops	251
Page layout	251
Search and replace	252
Search	252
Replace	253
Go To option	254
Inserting pictures and objects into Write documents	254
Exiting from Write	255

22 Accessories 3 – Notepad, Clock, Calendar and Calculator 257

Notepad	257
Starting a new file	258
Opening an existing file	258
Entering text	258
Saving the file	259
Printing a file	259
Adding date and time	259
Changing the page setup	260
Adding a header	260
Adding a footer	260
Changing margins	260
Searching	261
Exiting from Notepad	261
Clock	261
Displaying Clock on the desktop	262
Exiting from Clock	262

Calendar	263
Entering details	263
Removing entries	263
Changing the time interval	264
Changing the view	265
Changing to a different date	265
Saving the file	266
Opening an existing file	266
Starting a new file	266
Printing a file	266
Adding a header	267
Adding a footer	267
Changing margins	267
Special times	267
Setting the alarm	268
Defining special days	268
Exiting from Calendar	269
Calculator	269
Standard calculator	269
Scientific calculator	271
Statistics	271
Using the Clipboard	273
23 Accessories 4 – Cardfile and Terminal	274
Cardfile	274
Starting a new file	275
Opening an existing file	276
Entering information	276
Moving through the cards	276
Changing view	277
Adding a new card	277
Editing the Index Line	277
Deleting a card	277
Duplicating a card	278
Saving the file	278
Printing a file	278
Adding a header	278
Adding a footer	279
Changing margins	279
Searching	279
Merging Cardfiles	280
Adding pictures	281

Auto dialling telephone numbers	282
Exiting from Cardfile	282
Terminal	282
Setting up the communications parameters	284
Transferring data	285
Exiting from Terminal	286

24 Accessories 5 – Character Map, Sound Recorder, Media Player and Recorder — 287

Character Map	287
Viewing symbols	288
Copying symbols	288
Closing Character Map	289
Sound Recorder	289
Loading a sound file	290
Special effects	290
Editing the sample	291
Deleting part of a file	291
Inserting files	291
Mixing files	292
Embedding a sound	292
Saving a sound file	292
Recording your own samples	293
Exiting from Sound Recorder	293
Media Player	293
Exiting from Media Player	294
Recorder	294
Creating a macro	295
Running the macro	296
Exiting from Recorder	296

25 Installing Windows — 298

Installing Windows	298
Optimising your system	299
Processor speed	299
Memory	300
Disk storage	301
Running Windows	301
Real mode	301
Standard mode	302
386 Enhanced mode	302
Using swap files	302

Application swap files	302
386 Enhanced swap files	302
Setting up swap files	302

Appendix 1 – Keyboard equivalents or shortcut keys 306
Appendix 2 – Choosing a computer to run Windows 308

Glossary 312

Acknowledgements

A number of products are referred to in this book. The names of such products may be registered trademarks and are acknowledged as being the property of their owners. As many trademarks and owners as possible are listed below.

AdLib Inc.: AdLib
Adobe: Postscript
Aldus: PageMaker
Apple Corporation: Lisa and Macintosh
Borland: dBASE III PLUS, dBASE IV
Computer Peripherals Inc: MaestroPro
Digital Research: GEM
Epson: printer standards
Hewlett Packard: laser printer standards
IBM: PC, XT, AT
Intel: Pentium
Lotus: 1-2-3
Micrographx: Windows Draw
Microsoft: MS-DOS, Windows, LAN Manager, Word, Excel, Microsoft Mouse, Microsoft Soundkit, Visual Basic
Mossburn Graphics: animals and famous faces clip art files
WestPoint Creative Labs Inc.: SoundBlaster

Using the companion disk

The companion disk supplied with the disk and book pack is used at various points throughout the book. We suggest that you make a backup copy of the disk on another floppy disk. Use the copy for the tasks in the book and keep the original in a safe place.

Before you start to make the copy, it is always a good idea to 'write protect' the disk that you are copying to stop it being overwritten by mistake. For those new to computing, the write protect tab is the black plastic tab at the bottom left hand corner of the disk. The tab should be pushed downwards so that it reveals a small hole in the disk casing.

From DOS

- Insert the companion disk.
- Type DISKCOPY A: A:

You will be prompted to insert the disks as required. Note that the **source** disk is the companion disk supplied with the book and the **target** disk is the one you are using for the copy.

From DOS-shell

- Insert the companion disk.
- Double click on the [DISK UTILITIES] option at the bottom of the screen.

- Double click on the DISK COPY option.
- Enter A: A: in the entry box which you are given.

You will be prompted to insert the disks as required. Note that the **source** disk is the companion disk supplied with the book and the **target** disk is the one you are using for the copy.

From Windows

This option is only recommended for people who know how to use the basic features of Windows.

- Double click on the File Manager icon.
- Insert the companion disk.
- Click on the DISK menu.
- Click on the COPY DISK option.
- Choose A: in both of the list boxes.

You will be prompted to insert the disks as required. Note that the **source** disk is the companion disk supplied with the book and the **target** disk is the one you are using for the copy.

1
INTRODUCTION

Windows is probably the biggest change in personal computing since the appearance of the first IBM personal computer in 1980. Windows has enabled users who know little about computers or the way they work to produce effective output much faster than was previously possible. Recent years have seen an explosion in the use of Windows and the software available for Windows. Computer users are now able to integrate applications and features such as graphics, sound and video which would have seemed impossible only a short while ago. This first chapter looks at the development of the Windows environment and the advantages it offers the user. The implications in terms of hardware and some disadvantages of using Windows are also considered. The chapter also introduces the reader to the approach and conventions used in the book.

About this book

This book is an introduction to the use of Windows on a personal computer. The book is suitable both for beginners and those with some experience of Windows. The aim of the book is to build up the necessary knowledge in a relevant and interesting way through the use of practical examples, and then to provide further reference information on specific topics. The book is divided into two main sections. The first section comprises a series of practical chapters which are designed quickly to build up your skills in using different parts of Windows. The second part of the book, starting from chapter 15, is made up of reference material which will be invaluable for dipping into when you are more experienced or need to check a particular operation.

The minimum requirements for the use of the book are a computer suitable for running Windows, a mouse, and the Windows package. A printer is obviously useful if you wish to produce printed copies of your work but is not essential. In this book, you learn through practical tasks, acknowledged as one of the best ways to learn and retain a skill. The book starts with an introductory chapter on Windows and computers in general. The use of the package is then built up gradually throughout the first part of the book in which various activities are used to consolidate and extend your skills. Each chapter is richly illustrated by screen dumps or pictures of the screens as they will look as you are working through the chapter.

Conventions

Text in **bold** type	used for new words the first time they are introduced
Text in *italic* type	indicates practice activities
Text in this typeface	indicates text to be typed in
Text in CAPITALS	used for directory and file names
Text in SMALL CAPITALS	used for menu names and options
`386`	only works in 386 Enhanced mode
3.0 only	applies to Windows version 3.0
3.1 only	only available in Windows 3.1 or 3.11
	indicates the companion disk is required

INTRODUCTION

 used for keyboard methods. Keys are shown with initial capital letters as in Page Down

 indicates a sound card is required

 denotes practice exercises

 indicates points to note

 indicates hints and tips

denotes chapter summary

The companion disk

The companion disk to the book contains some of the text and graphics for the practice tasks and projects. Where the information is contained on the companion disk, this will be indicated at the appropriate points in the text. In addition, the disk has three full-featured Windows games: Dominoes, Hangman and Checkers. The disk also contains some extra fonts and clip art pictures relevant to the text. An icon editor, IconWorks, is supplied on the companion disk for you to use to create your own icons.

Using the companion disk

The files on the companion disk can all be opened from the floppy disk supplied. If you then change the files and save them on to the same disk, the changes you have made will overwrite the information on the files and they will be permanently changed. This can be avoided by making a copy disk. Refer to the page on using the companion disk at the start of the book for details of how to do this.

About Windows

Background

Windows is a **Graphical User Interface** (GUI) which aims to make the computer easier to work with by using **windows, icons**, a **mouse** and a **pointer** to load applications and work within them. The icon is a picture representing an application or program. Icons for related applications are grouped into a window on the screen. All applications which are designed to run under Windows make use of the same screen features, layout and help facilities. This makes it easier for users to learn new programs.

The initial letters of the four words Windows, Icon, Mouse, Pointer spell out the word WIMP and this type of environment used to be known as the WIMP environment! Fortunately, this term has gone out of fashion, and most users are much happier with the current term GUI. The WIMP approach to personal computing was pioneered in the early 1980s by the Apple Corporation with their Lisa and Macintosh range of personal computers. These computers were much more user-friendly than other personal computers available at the same time which used the Microsoft Disk Operating System (DOS) to make them work. Users had to know a certain number of basic DOS commands in order to run programs, create files of information on their disks and keep their disks tidy. The WIMP approach changed all this so that programs could be started by clicking the mouse on a picture representing the program. Files could be created just as easily, with any name the user fancied. Files were stored in folders, which made keeping the disk tidy much easier, and files that were no longer wanted were thrown into a trash can!

The first GUI for the DOS based computer was the GEM package from Digital Research Inc. which was very popular in the mid-1980s and was supplied as standard with many computers. All the programs on the PC could be run from within GEM, and a number of excellent packages were designed which made extensive use of this environment. In addition, GEM simplified the processes of creating, copying and deleting files on the disk. Windows was introduced around the same time. Its popularity soared with the introduction of Windows 3.0 in 1990, which offered a greatly increased range of functions over the previous versions.

INTRODUCTION

Windows 3.0

Windows 3.0 offered significant improvements over version 2, notably the ability to use **extended memory** and run more than one program at the same time, the inclusion of one-line help facilities, a much improved screen display and new games, Solitaire and Reversi. Windows 3.0 is the last version which can be run on the older PC and XT class of computers.

Windows 3.1

Windows 3.1 appeared in 1992 with an enhanced range of programs and functions, the most important of which were a much improved File Manager, better control of printing, TrueType fonts, and improved multi-media facilities to include sound, graphics, animation and video. Version 3.1 also provided object linking and embedding, which is a powerful way to transfer and share information between Windows programs. In addition, there were improvements to the way programs ran within Windows, more control over the desktop, better memory usage and many general improvements in the overall performance and efficiency of the package. Windows 3.1 for Workgroups appeared in 1993. It was aimed at Windows users on a network and included MS Mail to send mail electronically around the network. This version was closely followed by Windows 3.11 for Workgroups which improved the performance of Windows on the network, included built in fax software and Microsoft Schedule+. All these facilities mean that it is very easy to share information among the users of the network.

If you bought Windows or your computer after 1992 you are likely to have Windows version 3.1. Many earlier users have upgraded to version 3.1 to take advantage of the new features. Version 3.1 is now easily the most popular version and this popularity is reflected in the book which mainly uses screen pictures from version 3.1. At the time of going to press version 3.11 was not yet widely used. If you are using a different version you may sometimes find that your screen does not look the same as that shown in the book. The functions which are different or not available in version 3.0 are indicated at the appropriate points in the text. Version 3.11 has Schedule+ instead of Calendar. Apart from this all features of 3.1 also apply to version 3.11.

Choosing a Computer to run Windows

Using Windows and Windows applications to the full places heavy demands on your computer system. To run Windows efficiently requires a powerful computer with a large amount of hard disk space. The technical information for the hardware can be found in Appendix 2, Choosing a computer to run Windows. Many computers are now sold as 'Windows ready' systems with the necessary speed and memory and with Windows pre-loaded. If you are buying one of these you can be reasonably sure that it will have all the necessary features to run Windows. It would still be worth your while checking that the computer has the necessary power and sufficient disk space for the applications you intend to use.

What does Windows offer?

The Windows environment offers many facilities which were difficult or impossible to achieve with individual DOS based applications. Probably the most notable of these are the ability to run more than one program at the same time and to switch easily between them, and the way in which information can be transferred and shared between packages with a few clicks of the mouse. The advantages and disadvantages of using Windows are discussed below.

Advantages

Uniform appearance	All applications in Windows look and feel the same and use many of the same techniques, making it easier for users to learn different applications.
Ease of use	All Windows applications make full use of the mouse and have pull down menus, built-in help and dialog boxes.
Mouse support	All operations within Windows applications can be accomplished using the mouse.
Excellent built-in help	All Windows applications contain extensive built-in help with features such as browsing and searching for ease of use.
Visually attractive	The basic window and icon layout is clear, colourful and easy to work with.
Share information	Information from one application can be

INTRODUCTION

between applications	easily transferred to any other or others by placing it into a common area known as the Clipboard.
Excellent range of accessories	The Windows package includes many useful accessories, such as a calculator, notepad, and word processor.
Wide range of fonts	Windows 3.1 includes a number of fonts known as TrueType fonts because of their ability to print exactly as shown on the screen. Using these fonts will produce quality output on many types of printers. Extra fonts can also be purchased to add variety to the printed work.
Excellent graphics	Windows was designed to handle graphics. It offers versatility in transferring files between graphics programs. Most of the best graphics packages are now Windows based software. A vast range of clip art is available.
Ability to multi-task	Many different applications can all be run at the same time.
Expanding software base	Windows software is the biggest growth area in current computer development. There are more and more Windows packages coming onto the market.
Many games available	Two games are supplied with Windows, and many more can be purchased in games packs from Microsoft and from other sources.
Data links between applications	Files can be set up so that if data is changed in one application, it will be automatically changed in the linked application.
Network support	Windows 3.1 supports all standard network software and improves access to network functions.
Market leader	Microsoft is the originator of MS-DOS and Windows and is currently the world's top software development company. It has developed a number of other leading packages such as Word, Excel and LAN Manager.
Multi-media capabilities	Windows 3.1 has facilities for sound editing and recording, and can be used for multi-

media output. Extra hardware is required to realise these capabilities.

Disadvantages

Hardware requirements

Windows requires you to have at least a fast 286 computer and lots of free disk space. Each new application seems to need a faster machine and more disk space so you constantly find yourself upgrading hardware. Refer to Appendix 2 for more technical information on hardware requirements.

Cost

The hardware needed to get the best out of Windows is near the top of the range and therefore expensive.

Large data files

Files created in Windows are far larger than their DOS equivalents, particularly if the files contain graphic elements. They therefore need more disk space to store them.

Uniformity

All Windows applications look and feel the same. There is less variety than there used to be with DOS packages developed by different companies and some users will find this boring! Windows basic colours can be livened up with backgrounds and screen savers. Chapter 5 gives details of customising the screen display.

Monopoly

Microsoft almost completely dominates the Windows market. It produces most of the leading packages and continues to upgrade its products at an ever increasing rate. If you are to stay up to date with the latest developments you have little option but to upgrade your software. The upgraded software is invariably bigger and better but needs a bigger and better computer to run it on!

Not real computing!

Windows makes everything seem easy and does not really teach the user anything about DOS, the computer commands or hard disk management.

INTRODUCTION

What of the future?

Windows for Workgroups was released in 1993. The end of that year saw the release of Windows for Workgroups 3.11 which is seen by Microsoft as a replacement for Windows 3.1 for all users, not just those using computer networks. Version 3.11 uses new technology to speed up the processes of loading and switching between applications and reading and writing data on your hard disk. In addition, it includes electronic mail and fax facilities and a scheduling aid. To run version 3.11 you will need more memory in your computer and a larger hard disk as this version requires more disk space.

Windows NT (New Technology) is the latest Windows product. This version signals a move away from DOS and the type of processors used in PCs and is designed to enable Windows to run on many different types of computers. Windows NT is aimed at larger commercial users running powerful computer networks, and offers full network support with fast data transfer and special features to ensure security of data. Users will need to have top of the market file server hardware, as the product requires 100 MB or more of disk space and a minimum of 8 MB of memory. Also expected is a new release of Windows, version 4, which is being heralded as a full operating system, able to operate without needing to use DOS. At the time of going to press, no launch date has been announced and little or no information is available on the features it will offer.

Summary

This chapter has discussed the following topics:

- the developments of Windows computing;
- the conventions used in this book;
- contents and use of the companion disk;
- the advantages and disadvantages of using Windows;
- future developments.

2
— GETTING STARTED —

This chapter shows you how to load the Windows program, introduces the Windows desktop, and describes some of the basic components which are always present in Windows. From now on, you will need to have access to the Windows program. Chapter 25 contains instructions for installing Windows on your computer and assistance with setting Windows up to get the best performance from your hardware.

Loading Windows

From the DOS prompt

Type WIN at the prompt and press the Enter key. Windows should now load. If a message, Bad command or filename, is displayed, this indicates there is a problem with the installation or setting up of Windows on your computer. Please refer to chapter 25 for assistance in installing the system.

From the DOS shell

DOS shell is a utility program supplied with MS-DOS version 4 and above which provides a means of loading and running programs without a

GETTING STARTED

detailed knowledge of DOS commands. The computer is normally set up so that DOS shell is loaded automatically each time the computer is switched on. DOS shell can be operated using keys or a mouse. The instructions in this chapter use the mouse. The MS-DOS 6 shell screen is shown in figure 2.1.

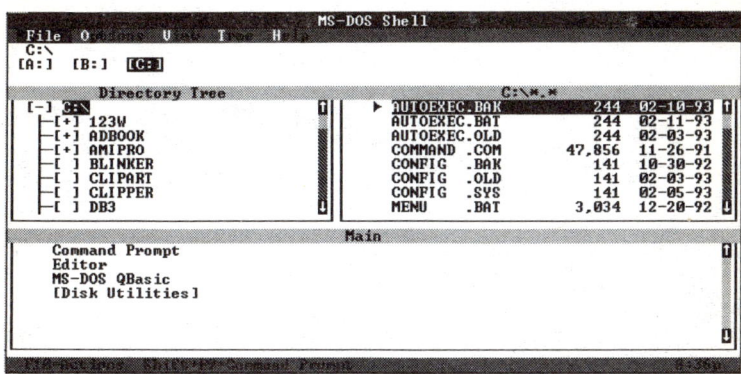

Figure 2.1

The DOS shell screen has a Directory Tree window and another window next to it which shows the files that are in the selected directory. In the lower part of the screen there is a third window called **Main** which will show:

Command Prompt
Editor
MS-DOS QBasic
[Disk Utilities]

These are all programs that are supplied with MS-DOS. There may also be other program names in the Main window, depending on how your computer has been set up.

If the Main window contains the Windows option

If Windows is listed in the Main window in the lower part of the screen, **double click** (press on the left mouse button twice in quick succession) on the Windows option. Windows should now load. If Windows does not load, this indicates a problem with the installation or setting up of Windows on your computer. Refer to chapter 25 for assistance in installing the system.

WINDOWS

If the Main window does not contain the Windows option

If Windows is not an option in the Main window, pull down the FILE menu by pressing the left mouse button once on the FILE heading. This will pull down the File menu box. Click on the RUN option from this menu. The screen should now be as shown in figure 2.2.

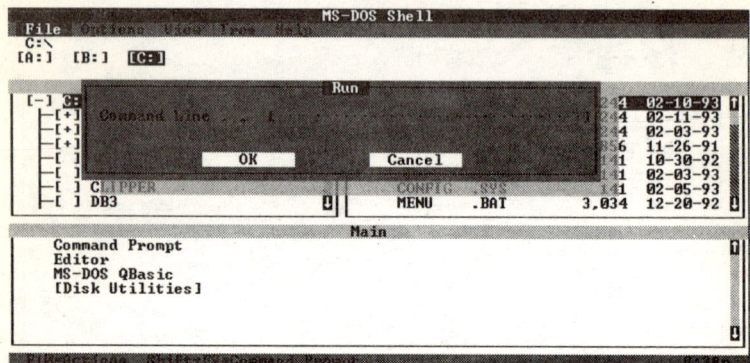

Figure 2.2

In the box type WIN and press Enter. Windows should then load, and you should see the loading screen, as in figure 2.3. If Windows does not load, this indicates a problem with the installation or setting up of Windows on your computer. Refer to chapter 25 for assistance in installing the system.

Program Manager

While Windows is loading, the loading screen is displayed. Figure 2.3 shows 3.0, 3.1 and 3.11 loading screens.

Version 3.0   Version 3.1   Version 3.11

Figure 2.3

GETTING STARTED

In a short while, the loading screen will be replaced by Windows Program Manager. Program Manager will either appear as a screen full of icons similar to that shown in figure 2.5, or as a blank screen with an icon in the corner as shown in figure 2.4. If Program Manager appears as an icon, then the Program Manager window has to be opened before you can start using Windows. This can be done in either of the following ways:

- Double click on the text under the Program Manager icon

or
- Hold down Alt and press Enter, then press Enter again.

Figure 2.4

If the pointer changes to an hour glass symbol, this means that you should wait until the action has been completed. You will see this symbol many times when working in Windows. If your computer is not very fast or has little free memory, the hour glass will be present on the screen for what can seem a very long time!

The Program Manager Window

Figure 2.5 shows a Windows 3.0 Program Manager window.

— 13 —

WINDOWS

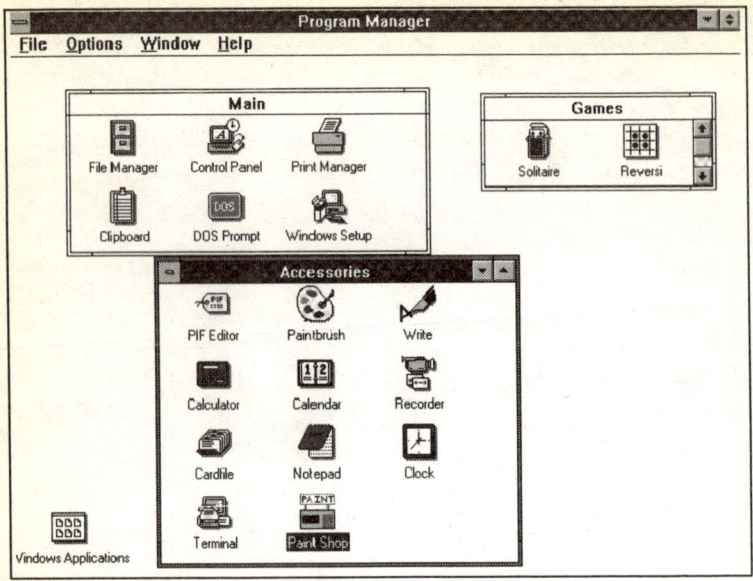

Figure 2.5

The desktop is currently displaying Windows Program Manager. Program Manager is used to load and run other programs and applications. The screen area occupied by Windows is called the **desktop**. Each separate area on the desktop is a **window**. Windows can be sized and moved around the desktop to suit the requirements of individual users. The number and content of the windows on the desktop will be different according to the software applications installed on the computer.

Inside Program Manager the icons, which represent applications, are arranged into different **groups**. In the standard Windows installation the groups which are set up are:

Main   contains the important programs which are required for Windows to run.

Games   contains two Windows games.

3.1 only

Startup   This group, which is supplied only with Windows 3.1, contains any applications to be automatically run when Windows is started.

— 14 —

GETTING STARTED

Accessories   contains a number of useful programs which aid many tasks in Windows.

3.1 only

Applications   contains any programs which Windows identified at installation (see chapter 25).

Network (version 3.11 only)   contains programs for use on the network. This group is shown in figure 2.6

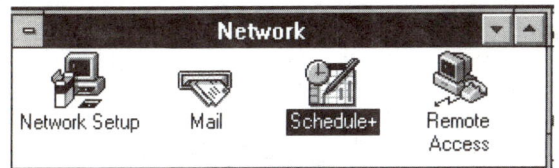

Figure 2.6

Each group contains **icons** representing the programs in that group. Icons can be moved between different groups and new icons can be added to groups. A new icon would be needed for any new programs which you wanted to use within Windows. This can be done for both Windows programs and non-Windows programs.

The Program Manager window can contain many groups such as those shown in figure 2.7.

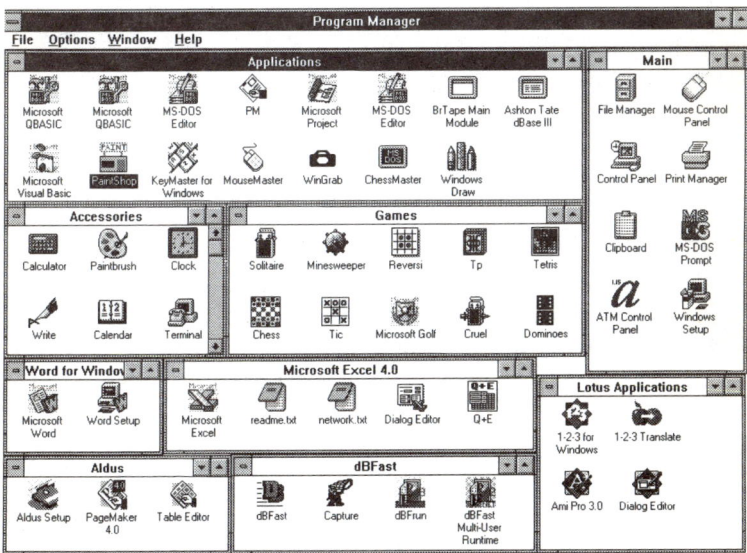

Figure 2.7

— 15 —

WINDOWS

Features of the Program Manager window

The basic components of the Program Manager window are shown in figure 2.8.

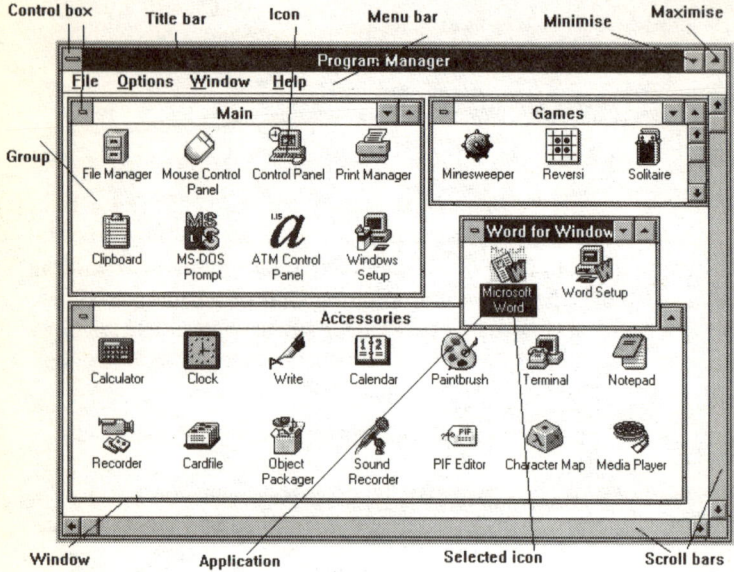

Figure 2.8

Title Bar

The **Title Bar** is the name given to the top line of the window. This line is coloured blue on a colour monitor and a different shade of grey on a mono monitor. The Title Bar tells you the program that is currently in use. The Title Bar in figure 2.8 shows Program Manager.

Program group

Icons can be arranged in separate groups for different types of programs. You can create your own groups or use the standard groups supplied with Windows. Windows applications create their own window and program group as part of the installation process.

— 16 —

Menu Bar

| <u>F</u>ile | <u>O</u>ptions | <u>W</u>indow | <u>H</u>elp |

Figure 2.9

In nearly all Windows programs there is a Menu Bar across the top of the screen, similar to that shown in figure 2.9. This enables menus to be 'pulled down' to accomplish various commands and operations within the program you are using. Many menu options have shortcuts using the keyboard.

Minimise button

The Minimise button is the arrow pointing downwards at the top right hand corner of the window. It is used to remove the window from the screen, usually to perform another task using a different part of Windows or another program. The minimised program appears as an icon at the bottom of the screen. This area is known as the icon bar. The program will continue to run when it is minimised and no data will be lost.

Maximise button

The Maximise button is the arrow pointing upwards at the top right hand corner of the window. It is used to make the program window occupy the whole screen so that more of the data can be seen and there is more space to work in.

Restore button

If the Maximise button has been clicked, there will be a Restore button in its place. If this Restore button is clicked, the window will return to the size it was before it was maximised.

Control Menu box

The Control Menu box is the grey box in the top left of the window. It is used to exit from a program and provides another way of maximising and minimising the window. To open the Control Menu box, click on the box with the left hand mouse button. The Control Menu box can also be opened by holding down the Alt key and pressing the SpaceBar.

The Control Menu is shown in figure 2.10.

Figure 2.10

Exiting from Windows

There are a number of ways to exit from Windows.

- Click on FILE with the mouse to pull down the File menu then click on EXIT.

or
- Click on the Control Menu box at the top left hand corner of the Program Manager window to display the Control Menu. Click on the CLOSE option.

or
- Double click on the Control Menu box at the top left hand corner of the Program Manager window.

or
- Hold down Alt and press F for the FILE menu. Press X for EXIT.

or
- Hold down Alt and press F4.

All these methods will display the Exit Windows box as shown in figure 2.11.

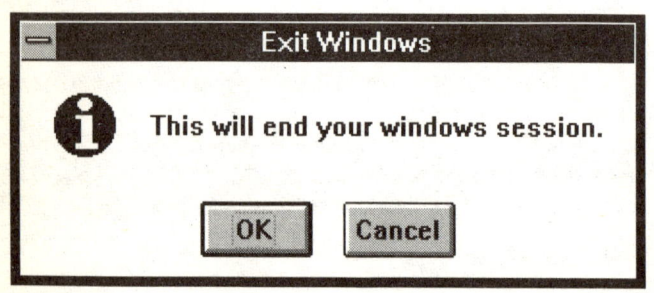

Figure 2.11

GETTING STARTED

Figure 2.11 shows the Windows 3.1 Exit Windows box. Windows 3.0 has a slightly different box, but this makes little difference at this stage. The Exit Windows box is an example of a Windows **dialog box**. Dialog boxes are used extensively throughout Windows to pass information from Windows to the user, or to allow the user to select an option. Dialog boxes always have at least one button, and often more. In this case, there are two buttons, the OK button and the Cancel button. The option is selected by clicking the required button. As you might expect, clicking OK confirms the selection, clicking Cancel cancels the selection.

A dialog box can also be used with key presses instead of the mouse if required. One of the buttons in the dialog box will have a dark outline. This indicates that it is the default choice. This option can be selected by pressing the Enter key. The other options can be selected by pressing the Tab key until the required button is highlighted and then pressing the Enter key to select.

Click on OK or press Enter to confirm that you wish to exit from Windows. If you have any active applications which have unsaved data, Windows will remind you of this and ask whether the data is to be saved before exiting. You will be returned to DOS or DOS shell in the same position as when Windows was loaded.

Practise loading and closing Windows using the different methods given in the chapter. Try to use a mixture of mouse and keyboard methods.

Summary

This chapter has

- shown how to load the Windows program;
- introduced the basic features of the Windows screen;
- introduced some of the terms used in Windows;
- introduced Windows dialog boxes;
- shown you the various ways of exiting from Windows.

3
FUN WITH THE MOUSE

Mastering mouse techniques early on is very important as Windows makes full use of the mouse. This chapter looks at the various mouse types and the way the mouse is used within Windows. The basic skills are introduced and practice activities provided. The chapter then explores the Windows tutorial.

Using a mouse

Figure 3.1

For the purposes of this book, a mouse is a pointing device attached to the computer, as shown on the left of figure 3.1. Moving the mouse around the desk or mouse mat causes a pointer to move around the screen. The mouse provides another way of operating a program. It partly or completely replaces key presses from the keyboard, removing the need to learn commands to operate software packages and therefore making them easier to use. You need a mouse to get the best out of Windows.

Mouse types

One-button mouse

Figure 3.2

The single button mouse, shown in figure 3.2, is used by the Apple Macintosh. It has only one button and so double clicking is used for a number of tasks. This type of mouse was never used in the PC market and there are none available for or supported by Windows.

Two-button mouse

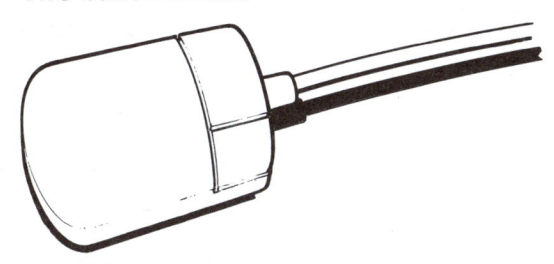

Figure 3.3

The two button rodent shown in figure 3.3 is probably the most commonly used in the PC market and, not surprisingly, is the Windows standard mouse because it was introduced by Microsoft. Many two button mice carry the Microsoft logo. The left-hand button is used more than the smaller right hand button. The success and influence of the Windows environment has encouraged other software manufacturers to include mouse support in their packages. If a program can use a mouse, the Microsoft mouse is always supported.

Three-button mouse

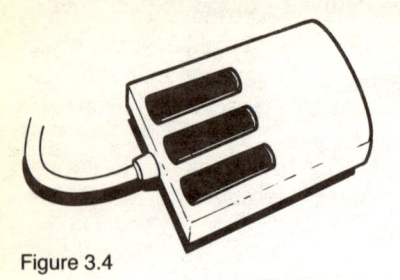

Figure 3.4

Mice with three buttons, like that shown in figure 3.4, are also used for the PC market, but are now less common than two-buttoned mice. Windows also supports the three-buttoned mouse. The left and right buttons have the same action as on the two buttoned mouse. The middle button is an extra feature which can be very useful in some programs. It is especially useful for playing Minesweeper!

Mouse techniques

Moving

Moving the mouse causes the pointer on the screen to move in the same direction as the mouse.

Clicking

Clicking is used to pull down menus and select objects on the screen. The mouse pointer should be moved so that it points to the required menu or object and the left mouse button pressed and released. This technique is used very frequently within Windows and so should be mastered early.

Double clicking

Double clicking is used to open and start applications. The mouse pointer should be moved so it points to the required object and the left mouse button pressed and released twice in quick succession. Double clicking is the most difficult mouse technique to master. It may take quite a bit of practice before you can click at the right speed, so don't worry if you are finding it difficult at this stage. The usual problem is that you are not clicking quickly enough.

FUN WITH A MOUSE

Dragging

Dragging is used to draw objects on the screen or to move from one part of the screen to another. The pointer should be moved over the object which is to be dragged, and the left mouse button pressed and held down. The mouse is then moved with the button still pressed. As the mouse is moved, the pointer will disappear and the object being dragged will be moved around the screen. The object can then be moved to its new position, and the left mouse button released. The object will then remain in its new position.

Mouse techniques practice tasks

The following exercises will give you some practice in using the mouse and trying out the different techniques.

- *Check that the Program Manager desktop is displayed on the screen. If it isn't, double click on the Program Manager icon at the bottom of the screen.*
- *Move the mouse so that the pointer points to any of the icons in the Program Manager window. Keep the pointer over the icon you have chosen and click with the left mouse button.*
- *This should cause the writing underneath the icon to change colour. This colour change indicates that the icon has been highlighted or selected. If the writing does not change colour, try again.*
- *Double click the left hand mouse button on the highlighted text bar to open the selected application. This opens a window, with the title bar showing the name of the selected application.*
- *Now move the pointer to the downward pointing arrow in the top right-hand corner of this new window. Click the left mouse button. This will cause the window to disappear from the screen and appear as a small icon at the bottom of the screen. Remember that this means the application has been minimised. The icons at the bottom may not be visible if the desktop has another open window. The icons will be hidden behind this window.*
- *If the Program Manager window is still on the screen, repeat the last action with the Program Manager window so it is minimised.*
- *Check that both windows have now disappeared and there are two icons at the bottom of the screen.*
- *Next move the pointer onto the grey background area of the screen. Double click the left-hand mouse button in this area.*

— 23 —

- *This should cause the Windows Task List box to appear as shown in figure 3.5. If the Task List does not appear, it is usually because the mouse clicks were not fast enough. Double clicking is a technique which requires a little practice to get the speed right. In figure 3.5, Program Manager and Paintbrush were open, so those were the programs displayed in the Task List.*

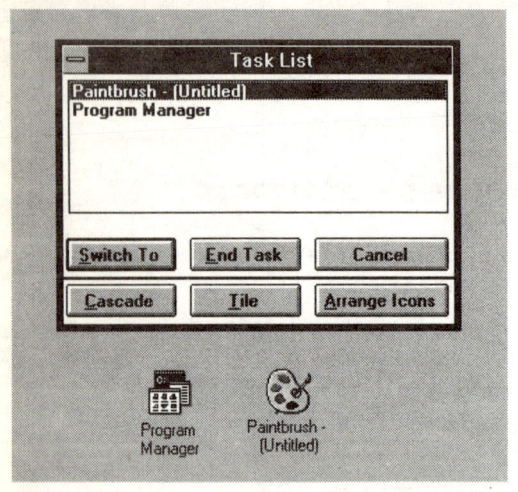

Figure 3.5

- *The Windows Task List contains a list of the programs which are currently active and has six buttons which perform various tasks with the currently open applications. The six buttons allow you to restore the window back to its normal size, close the application and arrange the windows and icons.*
- *The Task List window, like all windows, can be moved to another part of the screen. Move the pointer to the title bar of the Task List box. Click and hold down the left-hand mouse button on the title bar and move the mouse, still holding down the mouse button. As the mouse moves, an outline of the Task List box will be dragged around the screen.*
- *Drag the box to the bottom left of the screen, so that this area of your screen looks like figure 3.5. Release the mouse button. The Task List window should look the same as before, but will now be in a different place.*
- *Choose the application that you opened (not Program Manager) by clicking once with the left mouse button on the name of the application. This selects or highlights the application.*

FUN WITH A MOUSE

- *Close this application by clicking on the End Task button in the Task List window. The application may ask for confirmation before closing.*
- *Double click on the background as before to display the Task List again. This time, the program will not be listed as an active application. Click once on Cancel to remove the Task List box.*
- *Your screen should now only show Program Manager minimised as an icon. Move to this icon and double click on it to restore Program Manager.*
- *Move the pointer to the FILE menu and click the left mouse button. This will pull down the File menu shown in figure 3.6.*

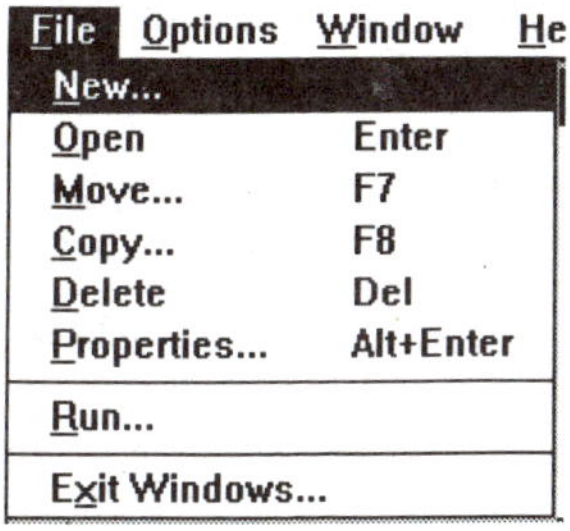

```
File  Options  Window  He
 New...
 Open          Enter
 Move...       F7
 Copy...       F8
 Delete        Del
 Properties... Alt+Enter
 Run...
 Exit Windows...
```

Figure 3.6

- *Move the pointer to the EXIT option and click once to select the option.*
- *This displays the Exit Windows box. Click on the OK button to exit Windows, as in chapter 2. This will remove Windows and return you to DOS or DOS shell.*

Windows tutorial

3.1 only

Windows version 3.1 includes a tutorial which introduces the use of the mouse and demonstrates the basic features of the Windows environment. The tutorial is accessed by pulling down the HELP menu then selecting WINDOWS TUTORIAL. Press M to work through the lesson on using the mouse, or W for the lesson on Windows features. The tutorial can be ended at any time by pressing the Escape key.

Restart Windows. If Program Manager is minimised, use one of the methods you have already learnt to maximise Program Manager. Click on HELP to display the Help menu shown in figure 3.7.

WINDOWS

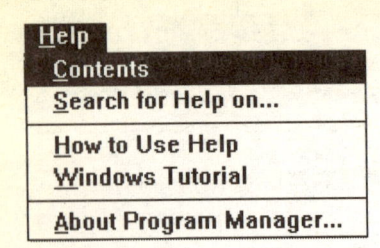

Figure 3.7

Click on WINDOWS TUTORIAL. Press M to start the Mouse lesson.

Mouse lesson

The mouse lesson introduces the basic mouse techniques of clicking, double clicking and dragging, and enables new users to practise these techniques using the basic elements of the Windows screen. The start of the mouse lesson is shown in figure 3.8.

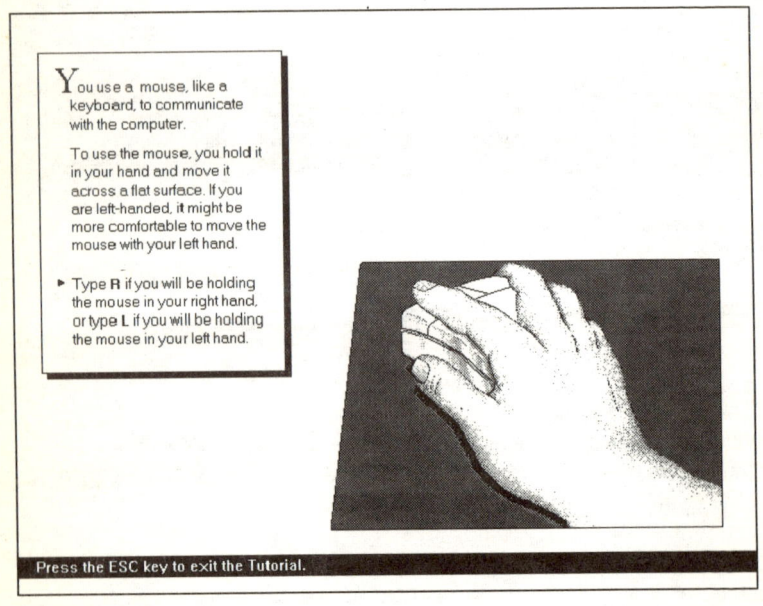

Figure 3.8

Follow the lesson through to the end until the screen shown in figure 3.9 is displayed.

FUN WITH A MOUSE

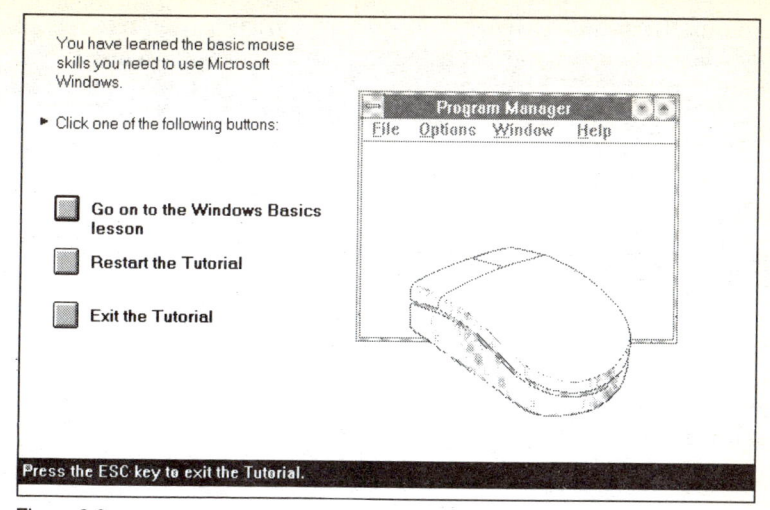

Figure 3.9

Windows lesson

The Windows lesson introduces the basic elements of the Windows desktop and allows you to practise the various techniques. A sample screen demonstrating opening the Accessories group is shown in figure 3.10.

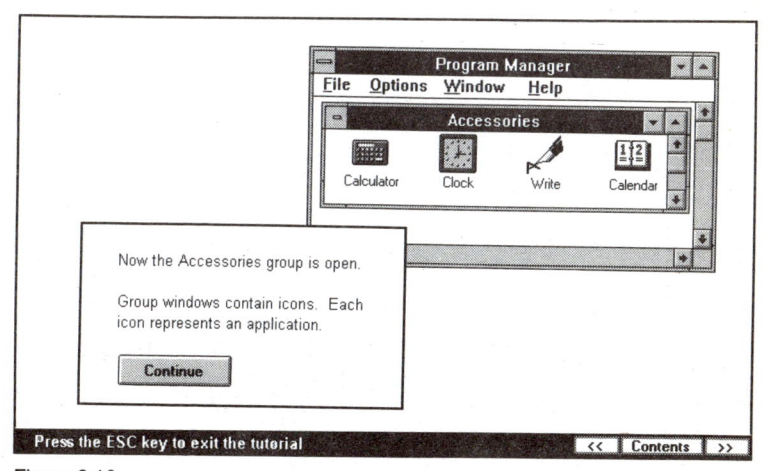

Figure 3.10

— 27 —

The lesson can be followed through from start to finish, or at any time you can click on Contents at the bottom right of the screen to display the Contents list, as shown in figure 3.11. From this, you can continue with the lesson, select another lesson, repeat a particular technique or exit from the tutorial.

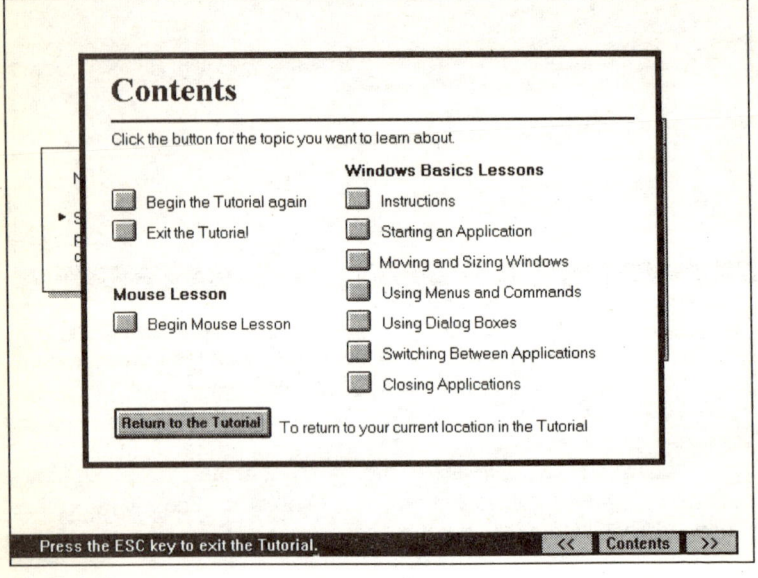

Figure 3.11

Summary

In this chapter you have

- learnt and practised the various mouse techniques;
- worked through the Mouse lesson in the Windows tutorial;
- used the Windows Basics tutorial.

These basic techniques will be used throughout the rest of the book. Life will be considerably easier if you master the mouse techniques early in your Windows career.

4
— FUN WITH GAMES —

This chapter looks at the games supplied with the Microsoft Windows package. These are Minesweeper and Solitaire with Windows version 3.1 and Solitaire and Reversi with Windows 3.0. Windows 3.11 has an additional game, Hearts, which can be played with other users on the network. There are many other Windows games now available from various sources. You will find some Windows games on the companion disk to this book. This chapter should carry a health warning – games can get in the way of real work and can be frustrating, annoying and addictive!

The starting point for loading games is the Program Manager window. You will have a program group called Games. If you do not have this group visible on your desktop, check the area at the bottom of the screen to see if the Games group appears there as a group icon. If it does, double click on the icon to open the Games window. Your screen will probably only have two of the three icons shown in figure 4.1.

Figure 4.1

WINDOWS

Solitaire

The Solitaire game is supplied with both Windows 3.0, 3.1 and 3.11. It is a card game which you can play on your own. The basic idea behind the game is to move all the cards up to the top of the screen in the four chequered boxes. Each box must contain cards of the same suit starting with the Ace and working upwards to the King. Double click on the Solitaire icon to load the game.

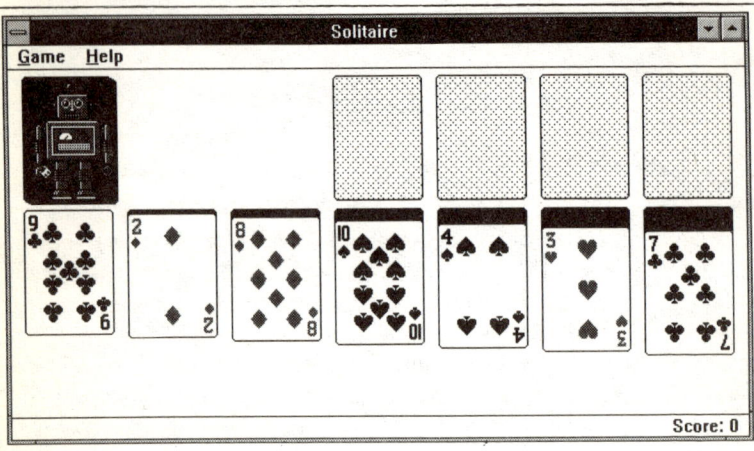

Figure 4.2

Figure 4.2 shows the start of the game. The cards are laid out in seven piles. Each pile has a card face up on the top with an increasing number of cards face down underneath it. The first pile has no cards face down, there is one card face down in the second pile, two in the third pile and so on, so that the last pile on the right has six cards face downwards. The rest of the pack is placed face down at the top left of the screen. The robot is the chosen design for the back of the playing cards. There are a number of different designs available. Changing the design is described later in the chapter.

As the game progresses, the cards are built into stacks in descending sequence and with alternate red and black suits. When all the face-up cards are removed from a stack, the face-down card can be turned over.

For example, in figure 4.2:

- the black seven of Clubs could move onto the red eight of Diamonds,

F U N   W I T H   G A M E S

- the red eight of Diamonds, with the seven of Clubs on top of it, could then move onto the black nine of Clubs,
- the red three of Hearts could move onto the black four of Spades.
- the black nine of Clubs **cannot** move onto the black ten of Spades.

To move a card, click on it with the mouse. Hold down the left mouse button and drag the card onto the other card. Release the left mouse button, and the card will be positioned on the other card so that both are visible.

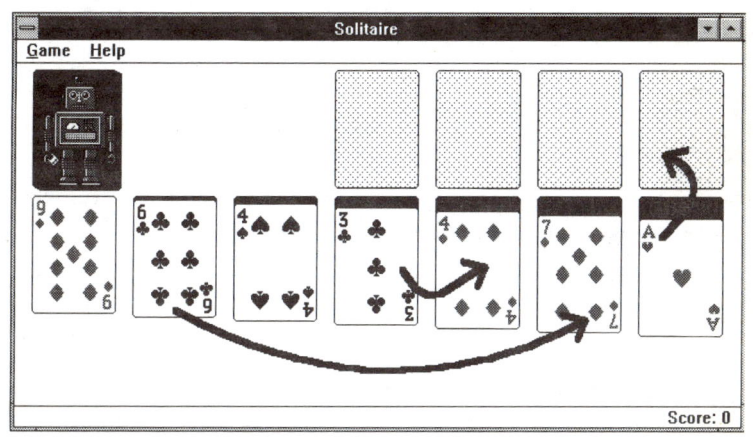

Figure 4.3

In the game shown in figure 4.3, the first thing to do would be to move the six of Clubs onto the red seven of Diamonds. The three of Clubs can also be moved onto the four of Diamonds. The ace of Hearts can be dragged up to one of the chequered boxes at the top of the screen because it is the first card in the sequence. Double clicking on the ace has the same effect. After these moves, the screen would be as shown in figure 4.4.

The face down cards which have been exposed can now be turned over. Click on the card back to turn the card over. If you make a mistake or wish to take a move back, click on GAME and then on UNDO. This will take the last move back.

Continue moving and turning over face down cards in this way. Eventually you will get to a stage where you have no cards which can be placed on the boxes at the top, and you cannot move any cards onto other cards. This stage could easily be at the start of the game. If there is a King

WINDOWS

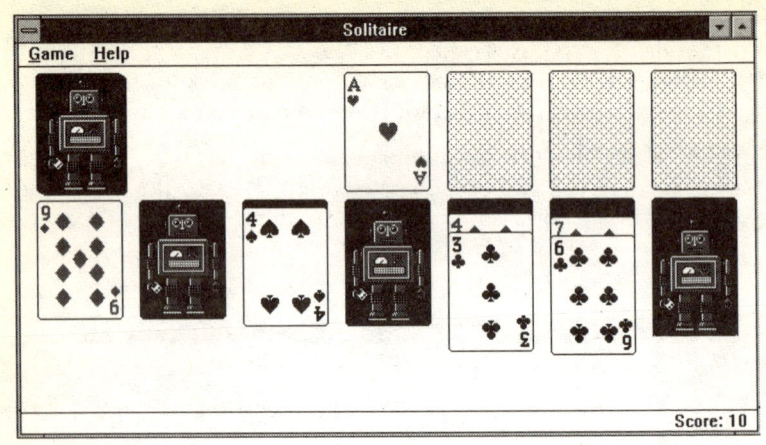

Figure 4.4

showing and you have an empty space the King can be moved into this space. The face down card can then be turned over.

When no further moves can be made, it is time to start working through the cards in the pack at the top left of the screen. These cards can either be turned over individually or in threes, depending on the options set. Changing options is described later in the chapter. In figure 4.5, the first set of three cards from the pack has been turned over. The top card in the set can be played as any other card, either onto another card or up to the top as the next in the same suit. If the card cannot go, as in this case, then the pack is clicked again to reveal the next card.

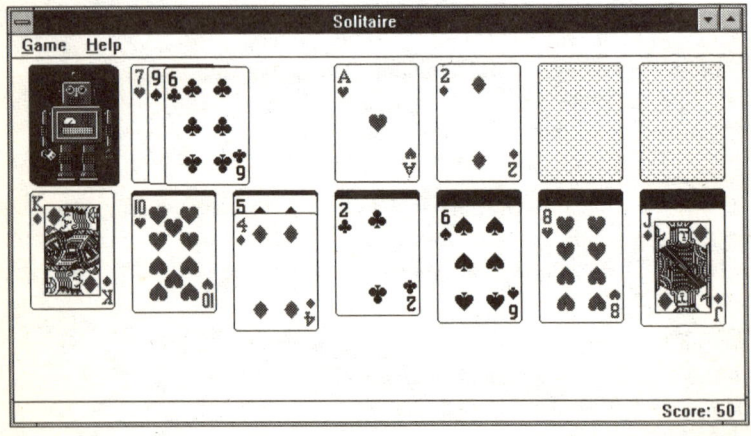

Figure 4.5

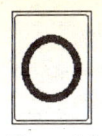

Figure 4.6

If a circle, as shown in figure 4.6, appears in the place of the pack this means that all the cards in the pack have been turned over. Click on the circle to turn the pack over and start again.

Figure 4.7

If a red cross, as shown in figure 4.7, appears in place of the pack then this means that you cannot turn the pack over again. This indicates that your system is set to the Vegas scoring system, which only allows you to flick through the pack three times if the cards are being drawn in sets of three, or once if the cards are being drawn singly. Scoring systems are described in more detail later in the chapter.

If at any point you cannot move any cards, place any cards up to the top or play from the pack, then the game is over. Solitaire does not automatically indicate that the game is over. To start a new game click on GAME then on DEAL.

You can also start a new game by pressing F2.

The game is over when all the cards are in ascending order in four piles in the chequered boxes at the top of the screen. When this happens, Solitaire displays an attractive sequence in which all the cards fall down from the top of the screen. Part of this display is shown in figure 4.8.

Eventually, a dialog box will come up asking you whether you would like another game or whether you want to quit. Choose Yes to play again, No to exit the game.

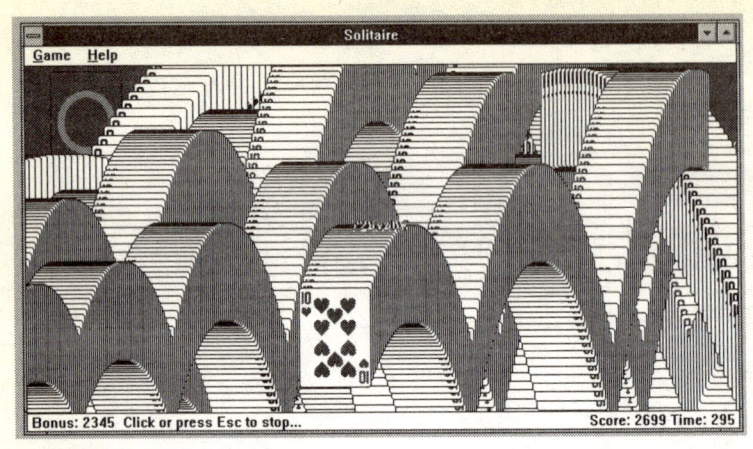

Figure 4.8

Changing the card back

To change the design of the playing cards, click on GAME and then on DECK. Figure 4.9 shows the card backs available.

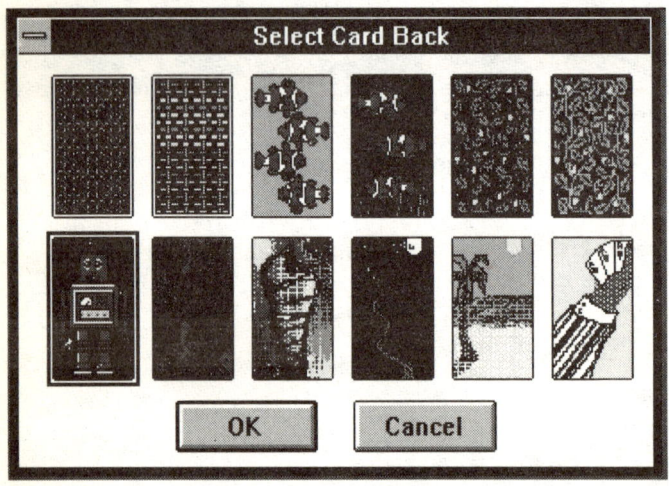

Figure 4.9

Double click on the required card back, or click once and click on OK. Some of the deck backs are animated. These are the robot, the hand holding the cards and the desert island.

Options

Click on OPTIONS to display the Options box, shown in figure 4.10.

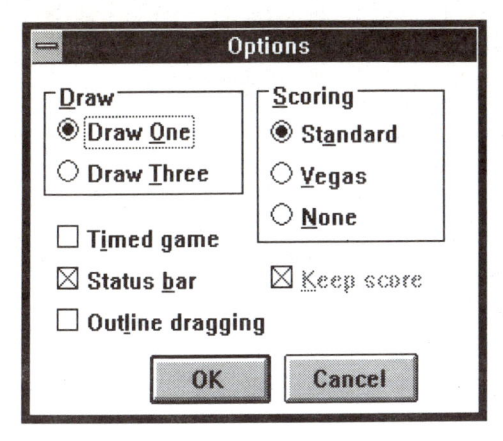

Figure 4.10

Option	Effect
Timed Game	Displays a timer on screen. Click on the check box to turn the timer off.
Status Bar	Displays a Status Bar on screen. Click on the check box to turn this off. If you do so, no timer or score will be displayed.
Outline Dragging	Reduces the jerkiness of the card movement. Click on the check box if the game is running too slowly.
Draw	Sets the number of cards turned over at a time.
Scoring	Standard gives points for playing cards, deducts points for turning over the pack or playing too slowly.
	Vegas starts with you owing money to the casino. Every card you place on the top pile reduces the amount of money owed until you show a profit. This system only allows the pack to be turned over once so you hardly ever win!

Aim for over 5000 points on standard scoring!

Using Help

If you require assistance at any point while working in Windows, you can use the excellent built-in Help facilities. Help can be accessed by clicking on HELP on the menu bar to pull down the Help menu. The built-in Help menus are different in Windows 3.1 and 3.0. Windows Help is described in more detail in Chapter 16.

The 'About' dialog box

Nearly every Windows program has an About option on the Help menu which gives basic information about the program.

Windows Help contents

In version 3.1, click on HELP then on CONTENTS to display the Solitaire Help contents as shown in figure 4.11. In version 3.0 the Help menu is different but the Index option is quite similar to that shown in the figure.

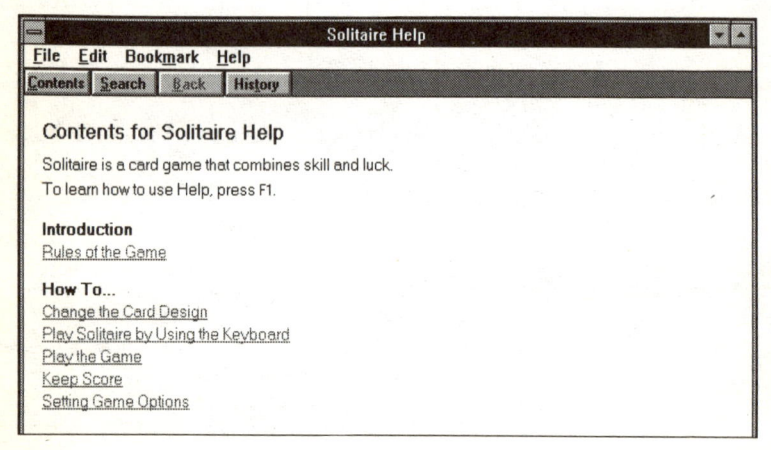

Figure 4.11

Topics which are underlined are **hot links** and can be clicked on to display the related Help topic. There may be several layers of hot links taking you through related topics to the required Help screen which contains the information.

Searching in Help

Often you will require help on a particular topic. Windows Help offers a Search facility as a quick way of doing this. Search can be accessed from the button bar on the line at the top of the window or directly from the Help menu. Both methods will display the Search box shown in figure 4.12.

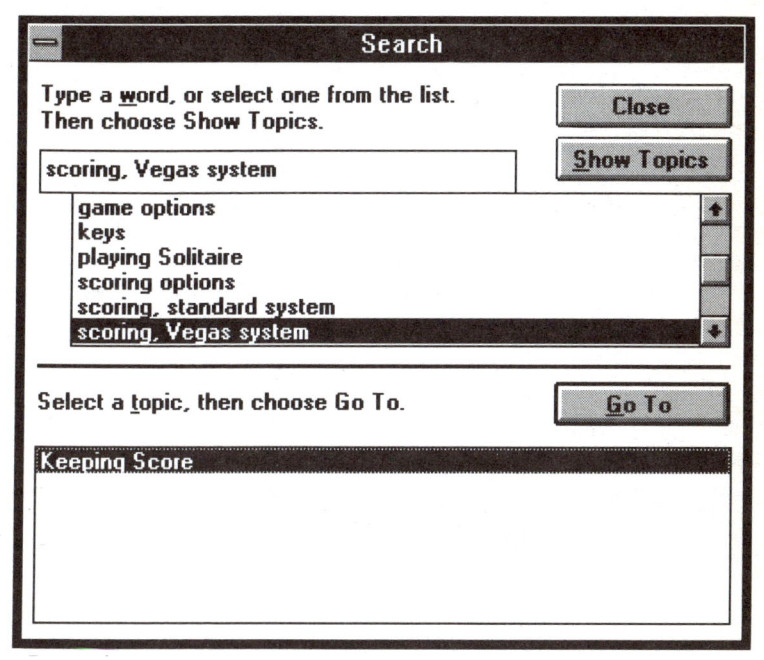

Figure 4.12

Type the required topic in the box. As soon as you start to type, Windows Help will display the topics which match what you have typed. If the topic is not in the list you can re-enter the required topic phrased in a different way or browse the list using the scroll bars. When the topic you require is shown in the list click on it to highlight it then click on Show Topics. This will display the names of the related screens. Hopefully one of these will be the one you want! Click on it and then on GO TO to display the Help screen. This sounds a very long complicated process but with a little practice, particular help screens can be accessed very quickly using Search. The Back button will take you back to the previous screen, usually back to the Contents list.

WINDOWS

3.1 only

The History button displays a History box which keeps a record of your use of the Help facilities.

———————— Minesweeper ————————

3.1 only

Minesweeper is a game which is supplied with Windows 3.1 only. The idea of the game is to locate all the mines in a grid without uncovering any of them. If you uncover a mine, the game is over and you have lost. If you manage to mark all the mines and uncover all the other squares, the game is over and you have won! Once you have mastered the game, the object is to reduce your playing time. Like Solitaire, Minesweeper has good built in Help facilities. Click on the HELP menu to use the Help features at any time while you are playing the game. Minesweeper can be a frustrating game to play as games can be ended very quickly if you are unlucky and uncover a mine in the first few moves.

Double click on the Minesweeper icon to load the game and display the playing grid.

Mine-sweeper

Number of mines left to mark

Number of seconds since start of game

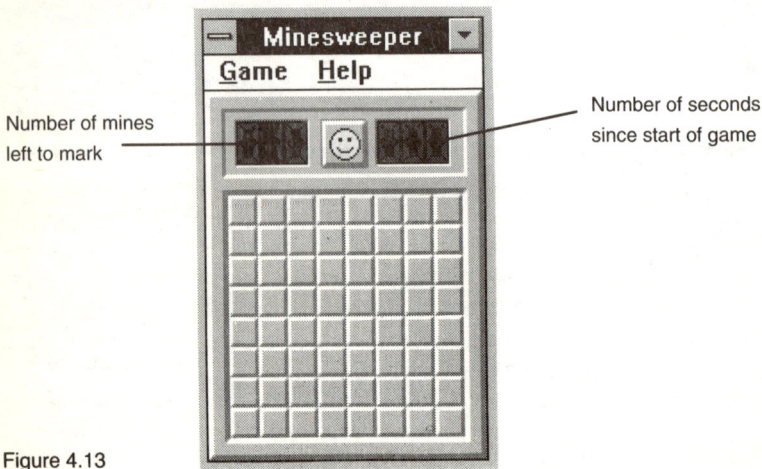

Figure 4.13

Figure 4.13 shows the main grid for Minesweeper when played at beginner level. The number of squares on the grid varies with the level of

FUN WITH GAMES

difficulty, (beginner, intermediate and expert). It is also possible to design your own grid. These options are found in the Game menu.

Playing the Game

Action   **Method**
Uncover square   Click left mouse button in square.
Mark a mine   Click right mouse button in square.
Start a new game   Click on the smiling face
                    or click on GAME then on NEW
                    or press F2

Choose a square on the grid and click with the left mouse button. One of three things will happen. A number may appear in the square, some numbers around a blank square may be displayed or you will have hit a mine, in which case the game is over! If a number appears in a square, it indicates the number of mines contained in the eight squares surrounding the numbered square. In figure 4.14 the squares which have been uncovered do not contain mines.

Figure 4.14

Figure 4.15

Figure 4.15 shows that this time a blank square was uncovered. This means there are no mines around the square, and all the squares around can be opened up. Some of these squares were also blank so more squares were opened up.

So far, so good! We have made a good start. The square which is highlighted in figure 4.15 has one mine surrounding it. The only possible square where this mine can be is the square up and to the left. The mine can therefore be marked in the square using the right mouse button.

If you accidentally mark a mine, pointing to the square and pressing the right mouse button will either remove it or change it to a question mark (?). The ? can be used where you are not sure of a mine but you think there might be one. To remove a ?, click with the right mouse button again.

Figure 4.16

Figure 4.16 shows a **flag**. The flag appears when you mark a mine with the right hand button. If you have marked all the mines in the squares adjacent to a numbered square, then positioning the pointer on the square and pressing **both** mouse buttons (or the middle button on a three buttoned mouse) will uncover all the other squares surrounding the numbered square.

This process of logical deduction can be repeated until the whole puzzle is complete or you uncover a mine and end your game!

Hall of Fame

The figure in the top right of the window is your time. If you manage to better the lowest time in the Hall of Fame, then you can enter your name. To view the Hall of Fame, click on GAME and then select BEST TIMES.

FUN WITH GAMES

Our best scores are:

Beginner   7 seconds
Intermediate 64 seconds
Expert   253 seconds

See if you can beat these!!

Good Minesweeping!

Reversi

3.0 only

The Reversi game is supplied only with Windows 3.0. Figure 4.17 shows the start of the game.

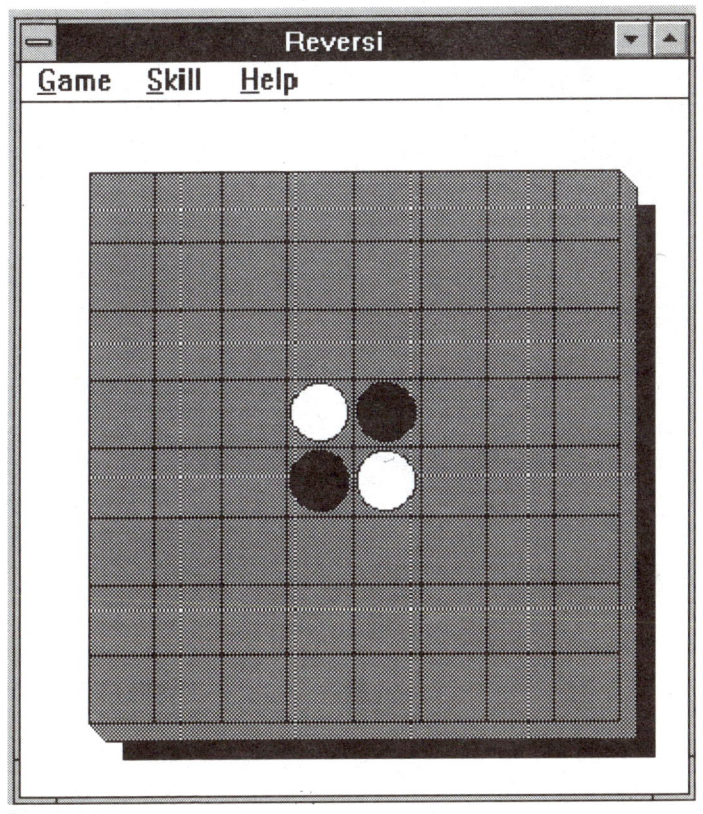

Figure 4.17

WINDOWS

The game starts with two pieces of each colour on the board. You use the red playing pieces (shown in black in the figures) and the computer plays the blue pieces (shown in white in the figures). The idea of the game is to get more pieces of your colour on the board than the computer. A piece may be played in any square which would enclose any number of the computer's pieces between two of your pieces. To play a piece on a square, move the pointer to that square. If the pointer becomes a cross then you may play in that square. Click the left mouse button to play the piece.

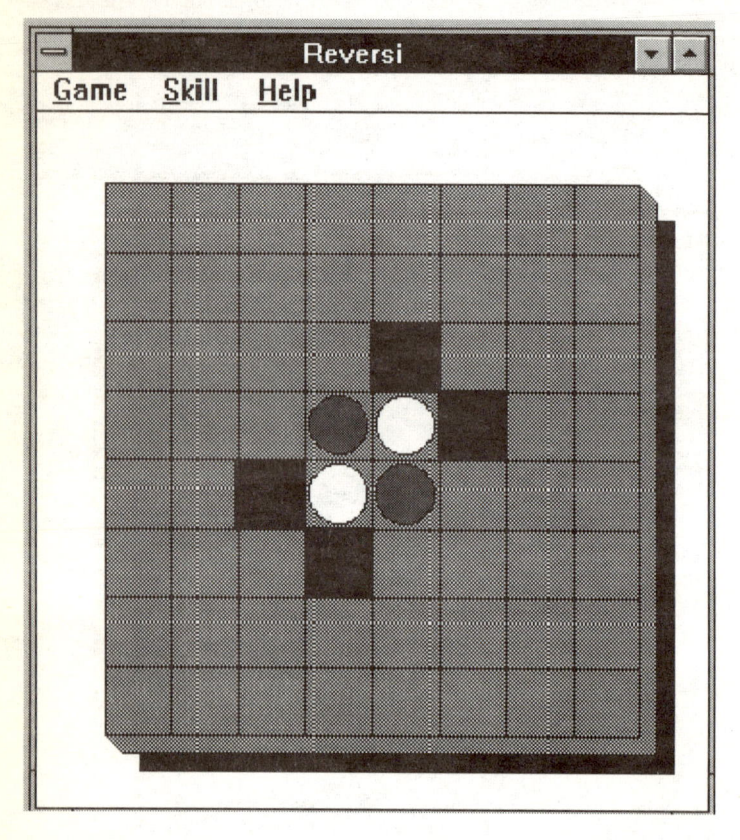

Figure 4.18

In figure 4.18, you can play in any of the highlighted squares. When you play, all of the opponent's pieces between your played piece and the closest piece in each direction will be changed to your colour. If you are completely stuck for a move then you can alwys ask for a hint. Click on GAME and select HINT. If at any point during the game you find that you can make no legal move, then you have to pass that go. To pass a go, click on GAME and then PASS.

At the end of the game, the computer will say who has won and by how many pieces. Not surprisingly, this is usually the computer! To play again, go to the GAME menu and click on NEW.

There are four levels of play; beginner, novice, expert and master. The computer plays a very solid game of Reversi, even at beginner level, so you have to be careful. We have never won on Master level. Our best score is lost by four!

Summary

This chapter has introduced the standard Windows games and shown you how easy they are to play. Hopefully this hasn't put too great a strain on your time and temper! The games on the companion disk are just as easy and fun to play. Built-in Help means that instructions are often to be found in the games themselves – look for Help or About screens. Good luck!

5
FUN WITH THE DESKTOP

The desktop is the working area on the Windows screen. The standard desktop is fairly plain. This chapter will show you some of the more interesting things that can be done to change the appearance of the Windows desktop. This includes moving and sizing windows, arranging icons, changing colours and choosing wallpapers and screen savers.

— Customising Program Manager —

When installed, the Program Manager display is similar to that shown in figure 5.1. The windows are said to be **cascaded**. With this arrangement, there is plenty of space in each window for the icons but only the icons in the active window are visible.

If your screen is like that shown in figure 5.1, you will probably find it easier to work with the desktop **tiled** so that all windows and icons can be seen. An example of a tiled desktop is shown in figure 5.2.

Click on WINDOW then on TILE to rearrange your desktop.

FUN WITH THE DESKTOP

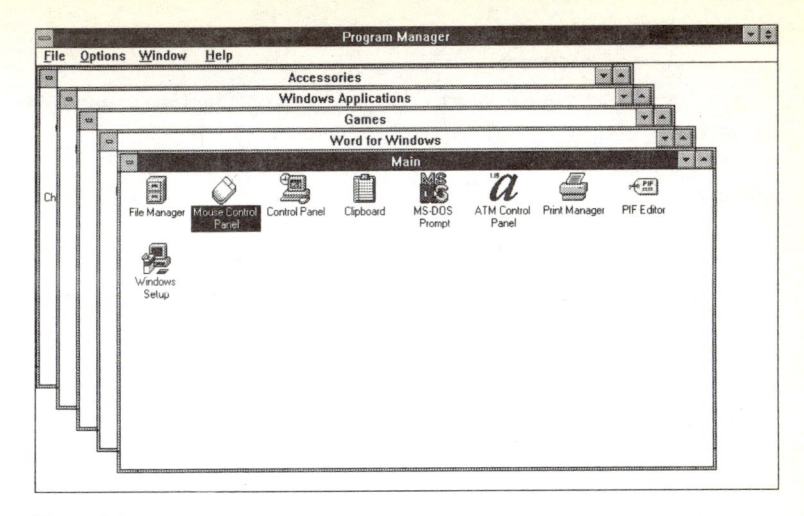

Figure 5.1

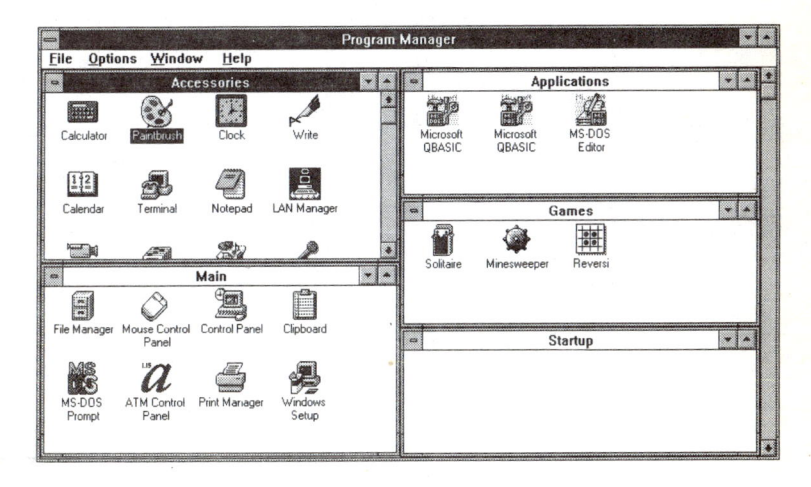

Figure 5.2

Moving windows

Windows can be moved around the screen. Click on the title bar and hold down the left mouse button. Move the mouse to drag the window to the required position. Windows can be moved so that they overlap each other.

Sizing windows

Each of the smaller windows or groups can be sized individually, as well as the main Program Manager window. You may wish to size windows so that you can fit more windows onto your screen, or to size the windows according to the number of icons in the group.

To size a window, move the mouse pointer to the edge of the window. It will become a double headed arrow. Click on the edge of the frame and drag the frame. As the frame, moves an outline of the window will indicate the new size and shape. Figure 5.3 shows you what each of the edges does. Release the mouse button and the window will remain at the new size.

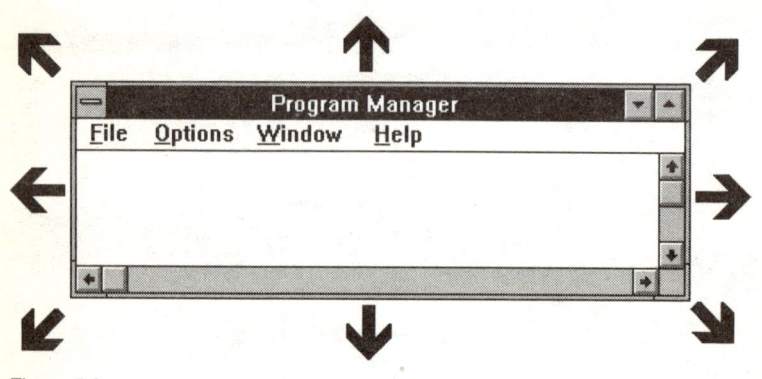

Figure 5.3

Try sizing and moving each of your group windows in Program Manager so that the windows fit together, and windows with many icons occupy more space than windows with fewer icons. An example of this is shown in figure 5.4.

FUN WITH THE DESKTOP

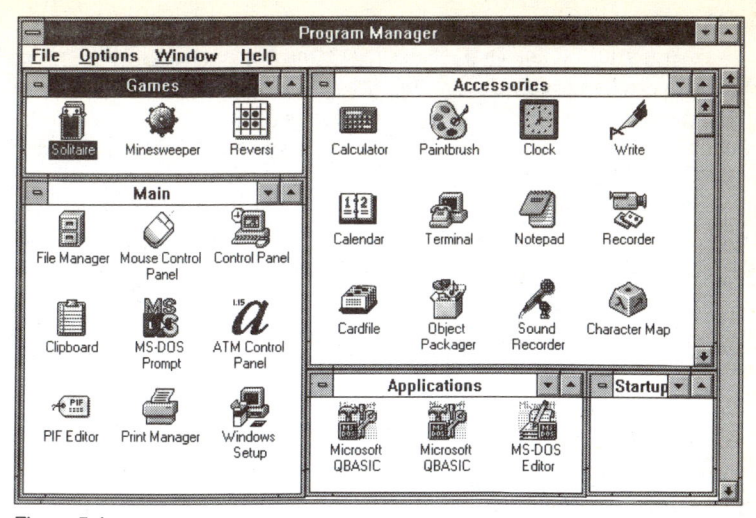

Figure 5.4

Saving changes

Before you exit from Windows, the changes you have made to the Program Manager window should be saved. If you do not save the changes you have made to the group windows, then next time you load Windows, all of your groups will be as they were before the changes. Saving changes is done in different ways in Windows 3.0 and Windows 3.1.

3.0 only

Under Windows 3.0, when you choose EXIT from the FILE menu to leave Windows you get the Exit Windows box, shown in figure 5.5.

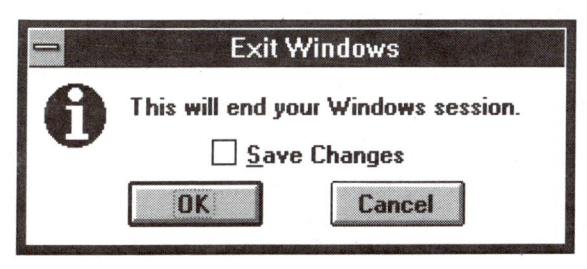

Figure 5.5

— 47 —

WINDOWS

To save the changes you have made, the Save Changes check box should have a cross in it. If it does not, then click on the box to check it. When the box is checked, you can click on OK to exit and save any changes you have made.

3.1 only

In Windows 3.1, the Exit Windows box does not have a Save Changes check box. Changes are saved from the Save Changes setting on the Options menu. Click on OPTIONS and check whether there is a tick next to the Save Changes on Exit option. If there is no tick click on the option to select SAVE CHANGES. When you exit from Windows the changes you have made to the Program Manager window will be saved.

Customising the desktop

The standard colours and defaults of the Windows desktop are shades of grey with blue title bars. Many users are happy to work with these colours. However, hidden behind this muted façade is a whole world of bright colours and interesting effects. Here is an opportunity for you to express your individuality!

The desktop in configured from the Windows Control Panel. Control Panel can be found in the Main group. Double click on the Control Panel icon to display the Windows Control Panel as shown in figure 5.6. This screen will be different if you have Windows version 3.0. This chapter will only deal with the more visually exciting options such as colour and patterns. The other options are explained in chapter 18 in the Reference section.

Changing colours

Double click on the Colour icon in the Control Panel window to display the screen shown in figure 5.7.

This option box allows you to change the colours used on the desktop. Windows provides a number of predefined colour schemes. The available colour schemes can be displayed by clicking on the arrow at the right of the Color Schemes drop down list box. Selecting different schemes displays a sample of the colours in the central portion of the window. For

FUN WITH THE DESKTOP

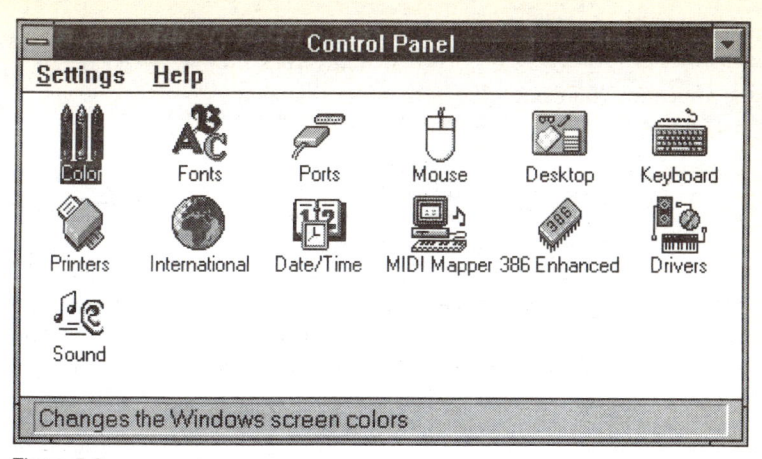

Figure 5.6

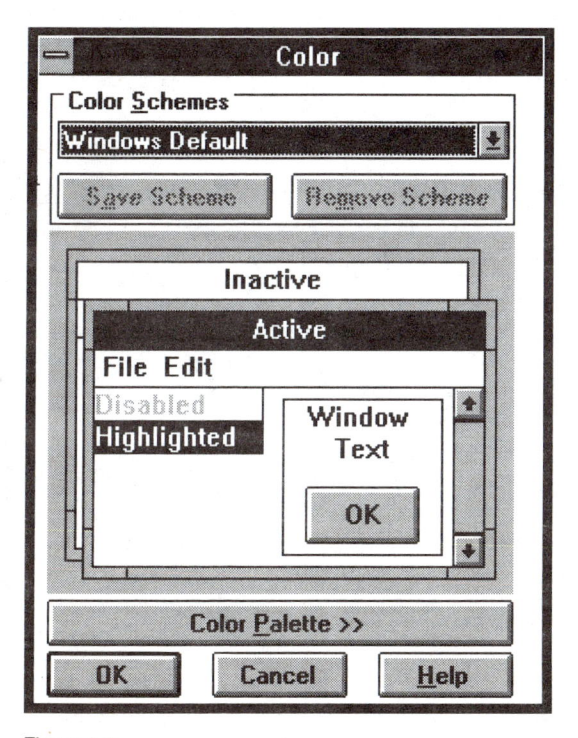

Figure 5.7

W I N D O W S

example, the Hotdog Stand colour scheme supplied with Windows 3.1 has red windows and menus with black title bars and a yellow border! Not all of the colour schemes are this bright, there are some peaceful colour schemes available. The Mahogany colour scheme is our favourite.

Highlight a number of different colour schemes and view the effects. If you find one you would like to use click on OK. Close the Control Panel and your desktop will be in the new colour scheme.

When colours are referred to in this book it is assumed you are using the standard Windows colour settings. If you have chosen your own, then the colours referred to in the book will not be the same as the colours on your screen. You are advised to leave the colours unchanged until you are a bit more familiar with Windows.

Repeat the same process to return the desktop to the Windows default colour scheme.

It is also possible to create your own colour scheme. Details of how to do this and further information on colours can be found in chapter 18 in the Reference section of this book.

Wallpapers and screen savers

There are other aspects of Windows which can be changed to suit your preferences. For example, you can set wallpapers and screen savers. Both of these options are accessed from the Desktop option in Control Panel.

Double click on the Desktop icon to display the Desktop window, as shown in figure 5.8.

Wallpapers

Wallpapers are designs or pictures which are displayed as a background while you are working. They add a touch of colour and individuality to your desktop. Wallpapers are graphic files called **bit-map** files. There are a number of suitable wallpaper files supplied with Windows. Figure 5.9 shows the MARBLE.BMP wallpaper supplied with version 3.1. Bit-mapped files can also be created in Paintbrush. Using Paintbrush is described in chapter 6.

The wallpaper settings are changed from the Wallpaper area of the Desktop box, shown in figure 5.10. The Center and Tile buttons below

— 50 —

FUN WITH THE DESKTOP

Figure 5.8

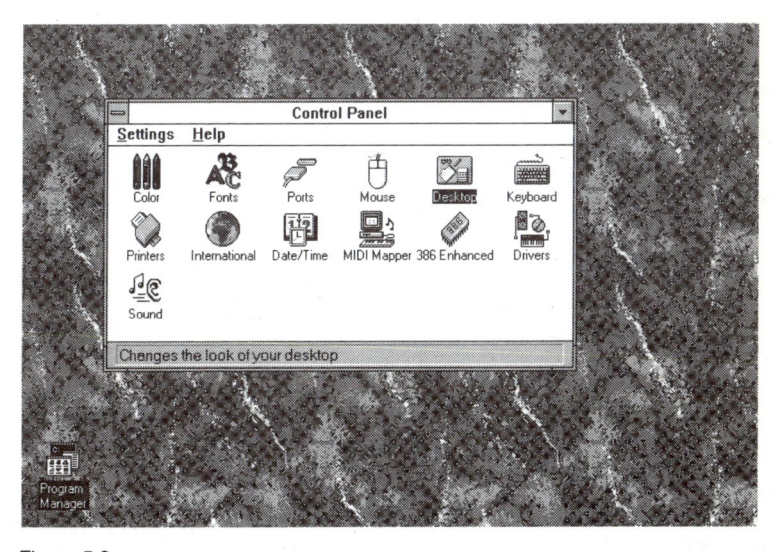

Figure 5.9

the list box allow you to choose whether the wallpaper is displayed just once in the centre of the screen or many times to cover the screen. It is usually better to have the wallpaper design covering the screen by using the Tile option.

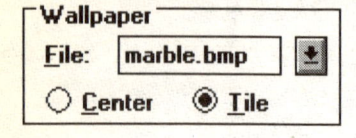

Figure 5.10

Click on the drop down list box and try a few of the available wallpaper designs.

Screen savers

3.1 only

Screen savers are only available in Windows version 3.1. A screen saver is a moving design which comes into action when the mouse has not been moved and no keys have been pressed for a preset period of time. Screen savers are designed to stop your screen being 'burnt' by constantly displaying the same image at the same position on the screen. However, with modern monitors there is very little burn at all, and there is really no need for a screen saver. They are just another excuse for pretty pictures! Screen savers do serve some purpose though as passwords can be specified to prevent other users returning to the main Windows desktop without entering the password. This is of little use in the home, but in the office this can be very useful to prevent unauthorised eyes seeing important documents. Details of screen saver passwords can be found in chapter 18 in the Reference section.

Figure 5.11

The area of the Desktop window which deals with screen savers is shown in figure 5.11. The available screen savers are listed opposite.

FUN WITH THE DESKTOP

Blank Screen	blank screen
Flying Windows	Windows 3.1 icons in different colours
Marquee	text banner moving across screen
Mystify	lines flowing around screen, changing shape as they move
Starfield Simulation	many coloured points of light, like stars

The Flying Windows screen saver is shown in figure 5.12.

Figure 5.12

The number in the Delay box is the number of minutes of inactivity before the screen saver will appear. This should be about 3–5 minutes.

Click on the drop down list box and select a screen saver.
Check the effect by clicking upon the Test button. This gives you an example of how it will work.
Repeat with a different screen saver.

Customising the screen saver

Each screen saver has different options that can be set. Click on the Setup button to access the options screen. The options for the Flying Windows screen saver are shown in figure 5.13. In this case, the speed and number of icons can be altered. Some other screen savers allow you to change colours and text. Screen saver setup is described in more detail in chapter 18.

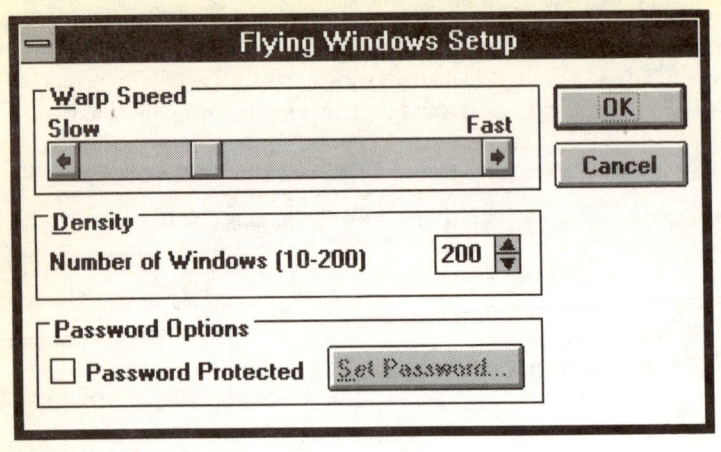

Figure 5.13

Try out the effects of some of the settings on the screen saver you have chosen. In the same way, you might like to try using the Marquee screen saver, and changing the text and colour of the message.

Summary

This chapter has introduced

- tiling and cascading windows;
- moving and sizing windows on the desktop;
- changing the window color schemes;
- using wallpaper;
- using screen savers.

6
FUN WITH PAINTBRUSH

This chapter looks at Paintbrush, the graphics program supplied with Microsoft Windows. You will very quickly learn to create simple designs and pictures to add interest to your work. Paintbrush is a powerful painting program which will enable you to create many different pictures and graphics which can be printed and saved. Paintbrush can read graphic files in a variety of formats offering you the facility of using clip art files which are supplied with many graphic packages and can also be purchased on disk. Pictures created in Paintbrush can be imported into other Windows programs.

Paintbrush is in the Accessories group of Program Manager. To start Paintbrush double click on the Paintbrush icon. When Paintbrush has loaded the screen will be as shown in figure 6.1.

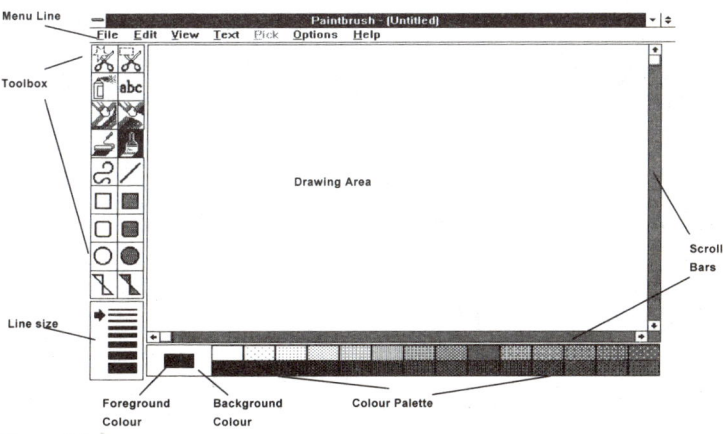

Figure 6.1

WINDOWS

This is the Paintbrush drawing surface. If your Paintbrush window is too small you can maximise it by clicking on the up arrow in the top right corner, or enlarge it by dragging the sides and corners as you learnt in chapter 5. The visible drawing area is the top-left hand corner of a picture which can fill a sheet of A4 paper. If your drawing is larger than the displayed drawing area, the drawing window can be moved around the picture using the scroll bars.

Moving the mouse on the drawing area causes a cursor to move around the screen. The appearance of the cursor changes according to the tool selected. For example, when drawing lines the cursor is a crosshair, when entering text the cursor is an I bar.

The left hand side of the screen contains the Paintbrush **toolbox**. The toolbox contains a number of different icons to produce particular shapes or effects. Figure 6.2 shows the functions of the various tools. The required tool is selected by clicking on the relevant icon in the toolbox.

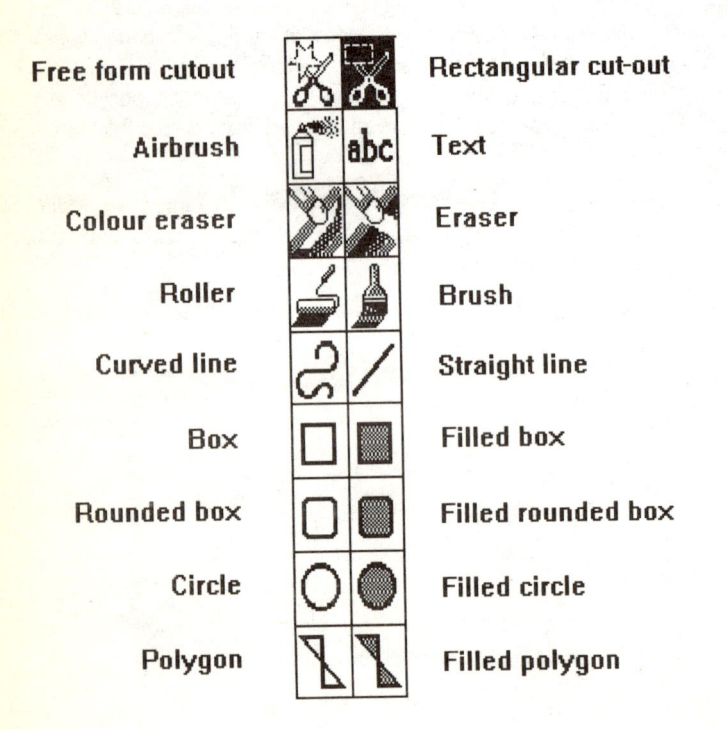

Left tool		Right tool
Free form cutout		**Rectangular cut-out**
Airbrush		**Text**
Colour eraser		**Eraser**
Roller		**Brush**
Curved line		**Straight line**
Box		**Filled box**
Rounded box		**Filled rounded box**
Circle		**Filled circle**
Polygon		**Filled polygon**

Figure 6.2

FUN WITH PAINTBRUSH

Drawing lines

The line tool

To draw a line, click on the line tool. Move the cursor onto the drawing area. The cursor will be a crosshair. Move the crosshair to the point where the line is to start. Click the left hand mouse button and drag the crosshair to the point where the line is to end, then release the mouse.

Changing line thickness

Figure 6.3

Figure 6.3 shows the line thickness box. The arrow in this box points to the thickness of line which is currently selected. To change this click on the required line thickness.

Practise using the line tool by drawing some lines of different thicknesses on the drawing area.

Selecting colours

The lower area of the Paintbrush window contains the colour palette. On a colour screen, each of the boxes shows a different colour. The box at the left shows the currently selected foreground and background colours. These are normally black on white when you start Paintbrush. The selected foreground colour is used for the colour of any lines, the colour of any filled boxes, the brush and roller colours and the colour for the colour eraser. One part of the painting can be in one colour and then you can switch colours without changing the colour of what you have already done.

- To select foreground colour click on the colour you require with the **left** mouse button.
- To select a background colour click on the colour you require with the **right** mouse button.

Practise changing colours and drawing some different coloured lines. Notice that lines are always drawn in the foreground colour. Changing the background colour has no effect on the lines.

After this your screen will probably be something like the one shown in figure 6.4.

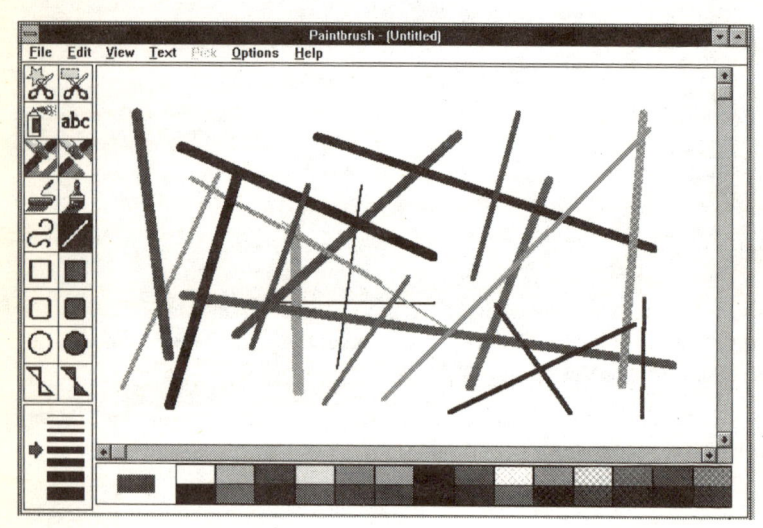

Figure 6.4

The eraser tools

The **normal eraser** is the one on the right. Click on the tool. The eraser appears as a square on the drawing surface. Its size depends on the setting in the line thickness box. When the eraser is dragged across the screen, all the areas it covers will be changed to the current background colour so making them disappear.

The **colour eraser** is the one on the left, without the white trail. The colour eraser turns all occurrences of the foreground colour to the background colour when the eraser tool is dragged across it. You can use this to change the colour of lines on your drawing.

Try erasing and changing the colours of some of the lines on your picture.

Clearing the drawing

By now, your drawing may be cluttered with lines and look rather messy. There are several ways of removing elements from a drawing which you will meet later in the chapter. The quickest way to clear the complete drawing and start again is to click on FILE to display the File menu then on NEW. This brings up the dialog box shown in figure 6.5. This dialog box appears whenever you have made changes to a picture and not saved the changes. It enables you to save any required pictures. As we do not wish to save the picture, click on No. This will clear the screen ready for you to start again. You will learn how to save a picture later in the chapter.

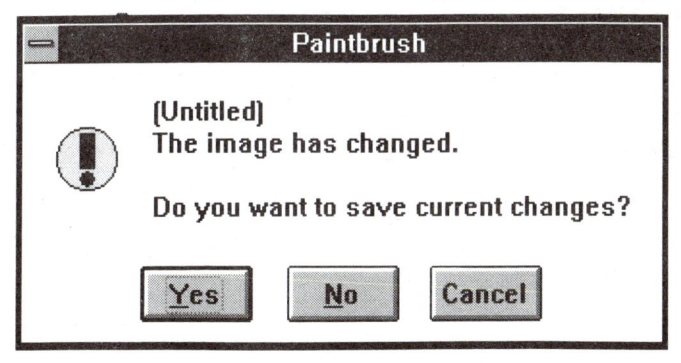

Figure 6.5

WINDOWS

Drawing shapes

The box and filled box tools

These two tools are used to draw squares and rectangles in the drawing area. To use them, first click on a colour in the colour box at the bottom, then select the required tool. Move the mouse into the drawing area, to the point where the top left-hand corner of the box is to be. Click the left mouse button and hold it down. Move the mouse across and down the screen. As it moves a rectangle will move around the screen attached to the mouse pointer. When the shape is as you require it, release the left mouse button. This should have drawn a rectangle, as shown in figure 6.6.

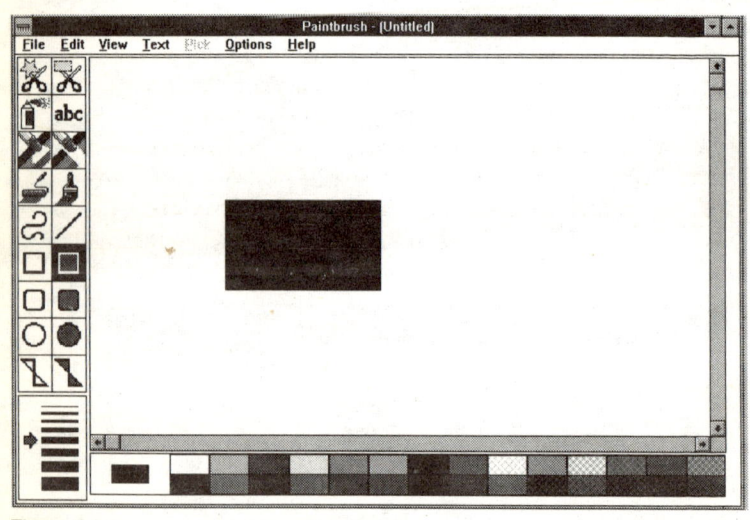

Figure 6.6

If you want to draw a perfect square rather than a rectangle, hold down the Shift key while dragging the mouse. All the sides of the shape will be the same length.

Try drawing a few rectangles, some in outline and some filled in a number of different colours. Draw two squares, one outline and one filled in.

FUN WITH PAINTBRUSH

The circle and filled circle tools

These two tools are used for drawing circles and ellipses in the drawing area. First, select a colour, then, as for the rectangle, drag the mouse across the area where you want the circle to be. To draw a perfect circle, hold down the Shift key while dragging the mouse. Figure 6.7 shows some circles added to the picture.

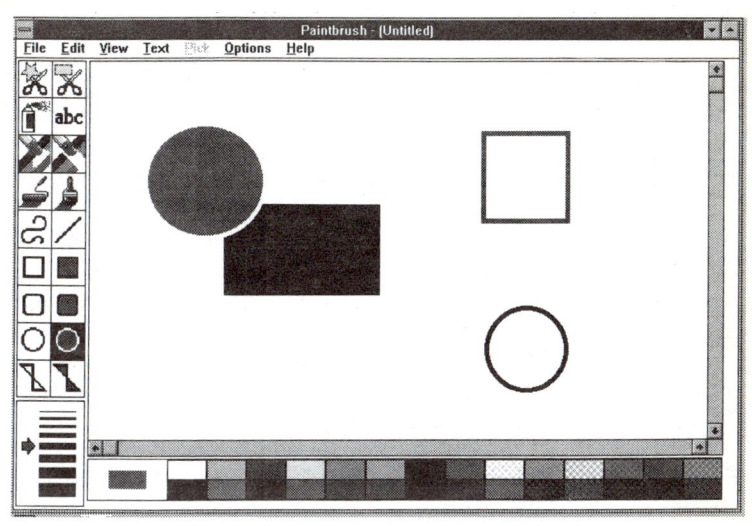

Figure 6.7

Try adding some circles and ellipses to your rectangles and squares which are already there.

The rounded corner box tools

These two tools draw rounded cornered boxes. These are drawn and placed in exactly the same way as rectangles and circles. Hold down the Shift key to draw a square.

Try adding some rounded corner boxes to your drawing.

The polygon tools

A polygon is a closed shape with any number of sides. These tools are used for drawing shapes which are not necessarily regular but still involve

— 61 —

WINDOWS

straight lines. Click on the required colour and tool. Move into the drawing area and draw a line. Release the mouse button at the end of the line and draw a second line, starting from the end of the first line. Release the mouse button again. Repeat this process until all the lines are in place. Then double click to finish off the shape, join up the last side and fill it.

Try placing some polygons on your picture.

The curved line tool

This tool allows you to draw curved lines. It is not a freehand line tool. There is no freehand line tool in Paintbrush. Using the curved line tool requires more practice than most tools in Paintbrush.

Select the curved line tool and the required colour. Draw a line. This puts a thin line on the screen. The line can now be bent in two ways. If you want a curved line with only one curve in it, drag the line until the curve is correct. If you don't like the curve you have drawn, click on the right mouse button to clear the line and start again. Click on the second end point to fix the curve. If you want a line with two curves in it, drag the line again to form the second curve. Release the mouse button to fix the curve. When the line is complete it will change to the correct colour and thickness. Figure 6.8 shows some curved lines added to the picture.

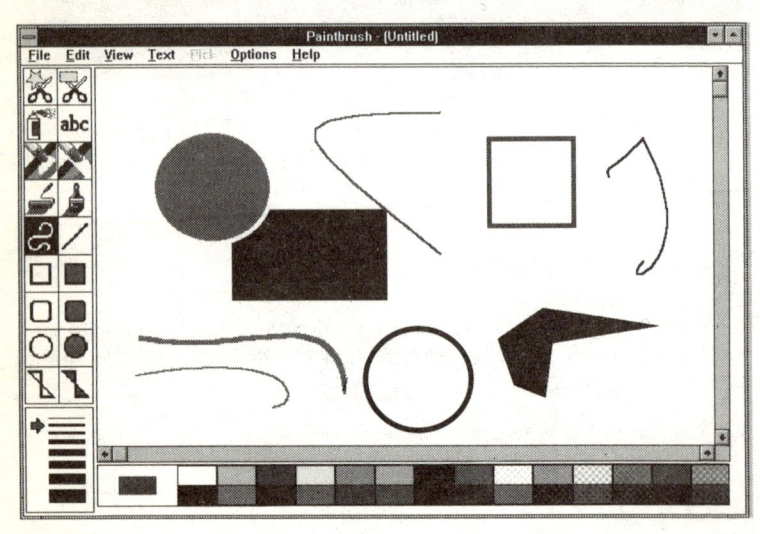

Figure 6.8

Try putting some curved and straight lines onto the picture.

Saving

Saving is the process of storing the picture on disk for future use. The picture can be saved at any time.

Click on FILE then on SAVE.

As the picture has not been saved before, the Save As box will be displayed, as shown in figure 6.9, so that you can specify a file name for the picture. File names can be up to eight characters with no spaces. By default, the file will be saved in the WINDOWS directory of the hard disk. Paintbrush files are saved with an extension of BMP which stands for bit-mapped. A bit-mapped graphic is stored as a large number of dots or pixels. It can be read by any Windows application. Bit-mapped files are very large. Paintbrush offers an alternative format (PCX) which is a far more compact graphics format and can be used in non-Windows packages. The graphics files on the companion disk are in PCX format to reduce the amount of disk space required.

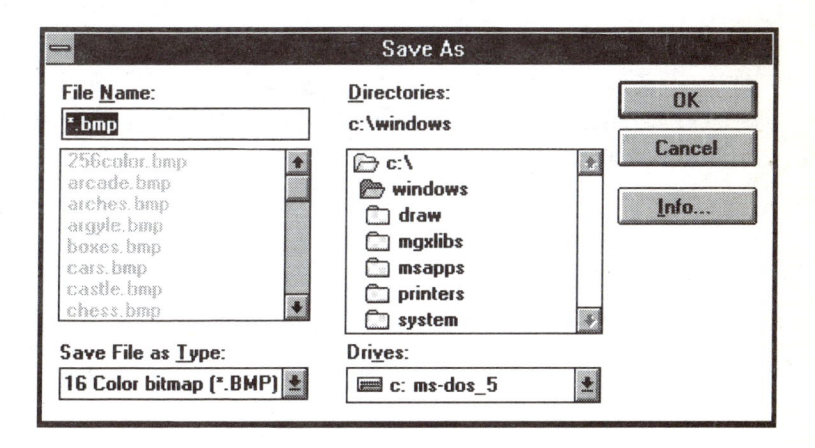

Figure 6.9

Type a file name. You could use the file name SHAPES.
Click on OK to save your picture.

Printing

To print your picture, click on FILE then on PRINT.

This displays the Print box shown in figure 6.10.

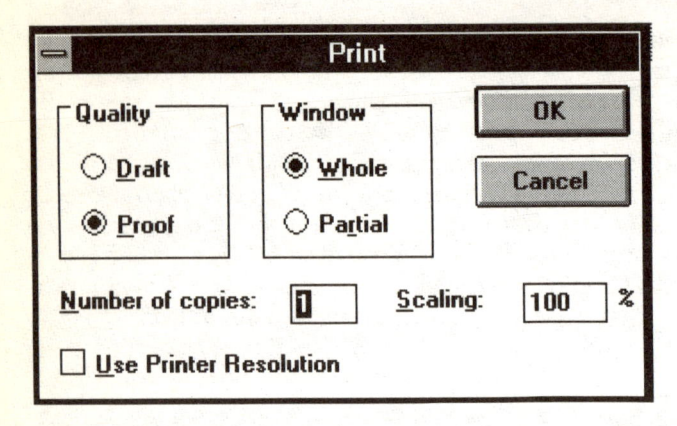

```
┌─────────────────────── Print ───────────────────────┐
│  ┌─ Quality ──┐  ┌─ Window ──┐   ┌──────────────┐   │
│  │ ○ Draft    │  │ ● Whole   │   │      OK      │   │
│  │ ● Proof    │  │ ○ Partial │   └──────────────┘   │
│  └────────────┘  └───────────┘   ┌──────────────┐   │
│                                  │    Cancel    │   │
│                                  └──────────────┘   │
│  Number of copies:  [1]   Scaling:  [100] %         │
│  ☐ Use Printer Resolution                           │
└─────────────────────────────────────────────────────┘
```

Figure 6.10

The default settings are correct for most users. Standard Paintbrush drawings using the visible drawing area occupy approximately the top half of a sheet of A4 paper. Change any required settings and click on OK. The picture will be sent to Windows Print Manager and queued along with any other print jobs. Print Manager is described in chapter 19 in the Reference section.

After all this your picture will probably be cluttered again. Start a new picture to be used for the next tools.

The brush tool

The brush tool is used for drawing solid blocks of colour freehand. It draws in the selected foreground colour. The size of the brush tool depends on the line size selected.

FUN WITH PAINTBRUSH

Changing brush shape

The brush can be a line, or a round or square headed brush. Click on OPTIONS on the menu bar then on BRUSH SHAPES. This displays the Brush Shapes box shown in figure 6.11.

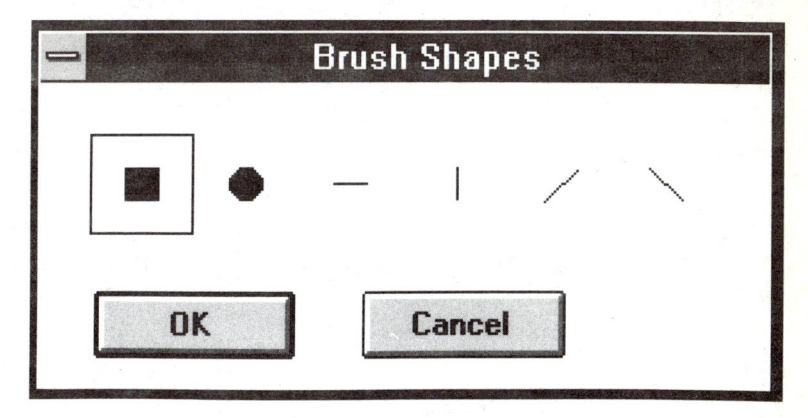

Figure 6.11

Select the required shape. Click on OK.

Try putting some freehand lines and shapes on your picture using the brush tool and different brush shapes. Try freehand drawing or writing – it's not as easy as it looks!

The airbrush tool

The airbrush tool is like a spray can. It puts dots of the foreground colour on the picture in the area where it is dragged. The longer it is left in one place, the higher the density of the colour. The airbrush can be used to good effect when used quickly to give a mottled effect.

Try spraying some colour on the picture with the airbrush tool.

The picture in figure 6.12 was drawn using only the brush and airbrush tools.

— 65 —

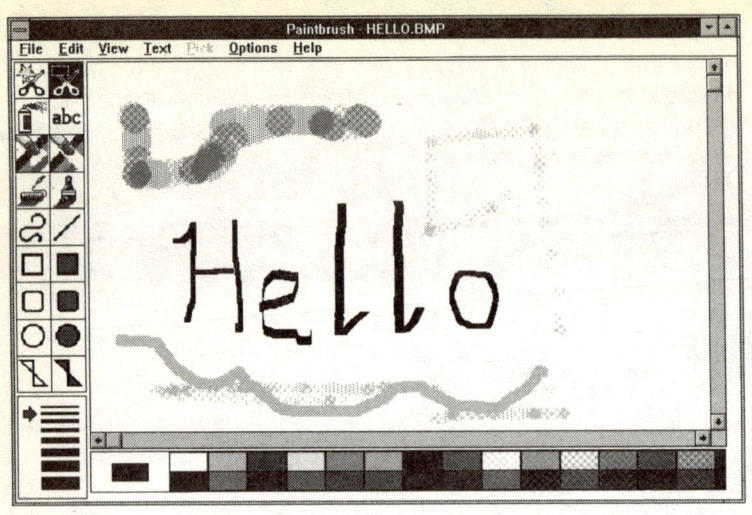

Figure 6.12

The roller tool

The roller tool is used to fill areas of the picture with the foreground colour. The area will be filled until it meets a different coloured edge. This is a useful technique for colouring the background, or changing the colour of shapes already on the drawing. It is not always possible to change the colour because some of the colours which Paintbrush uses are made up of one dot of one colour and one dot of another colour, so the roller would only fill in a dot at a time. These colours are usually the ones in the right half of the palette.

Use the roller to colour the background of your picture in a tasteful pastel colour. Fill in any smaller enclosed areas on your drawing, such as the o of Hello in figure 6.12.

The text tool

abc This tool allows you to add text to a picture in different sizes and styles. Select the required colour for the text and click at the position where the text is to start. This makes a text insertion point and displays a flashing I bar cursor. Click again if the insertion point is not in the correct place. Be careful when entering text, as Paintbrush does not provide facilities for changing text once it has been added. While typing you can use the Backspace key to remove incorrect characters. Once the text has been fixed, mistakes can only be corrected by deleting the text and retyping it. This can be difficult if the text is close to other parts of the picture.

There are a number of properties of the text which can be changed. This is done in different ways in Windows 3.0 and 3.1. Version 3.0 uses three separate menus to control the appearance of the text. The Font menu selects the font. The Style menu selects styles such as bold or italic text. The Size menu selects the size of the text. In version 3.1 the text features are all found on one menu, the Text menu, shown in figure 6.13.

Figure 6.13

The different options can be on or off, shown by a tick at the side. Click on the required option to select it, click again to deselect. The available text styles are shown in figure 6.14. There can be any combination of these, such as bold, italic and outline text.

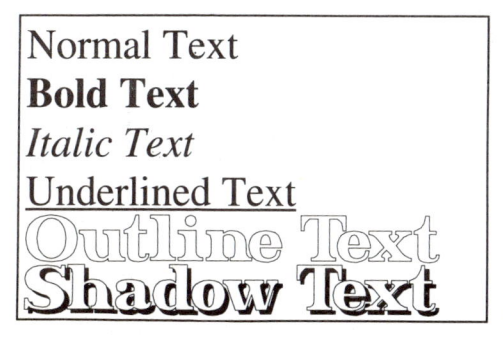

Figure 6.14

— 67 —

Try adding some text in different styles to your picture. If you are happy with your picture, save and print it.

If you wish to change any of the elements of the picture, the following section describes how to edit the picture.

Correcting mistakes

You have already used the eraser tools. These are very useful for removing lines or shapes drawn incorrectly. However, other mistakes such as placing a shape in the wrong place, roller filling the wrong part, slipping with the eraser, etc. are harder to rub out, especially when the picture contains overlapping shapes and colours. There are several ways to correct such mistakes. The first thing to try is Undo. Click on EDIT and then on UNDO. This takes back the last change to the picture.

Selecting parts of a picture

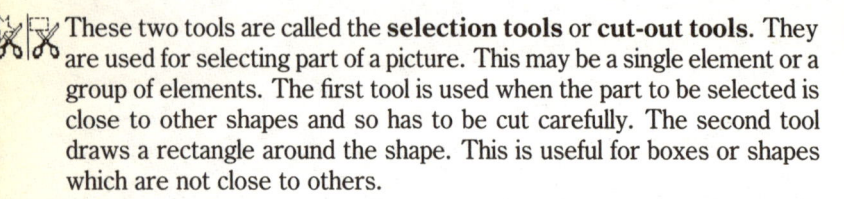

These two tools are called the **selection tools** or **cut-out tools**. They are used for selecting part of a picture. This may be a single element or a group of elements. The first tool is used when the part to be selected is close to other shapes and so has to be cut carefully. The second tool draws a rectangle around the shape. This is useful for boxes or shapes which are not close to others.

To use the free-form tool, drag the pointer all the way around the shape to be highlighted. A line will be drawn as you go. If you make a mistake, release the mouse and click away from the selected area to remove the line and try again.

To use the box tool, drag the pointer so it forms a rectangle which completely encloses the shape. A dotted line will be drawn as you go.

Both of these methods will then create a dotted line around the shapes. This indicates the areas are **selected**. The selected area can now be moved, copied or deleted.

Moving

To move a selected shape, click in the centre of the shape, hold down the left mouse button and drag the shape to its new position. This can be used to move elements within the picture and can also be used to move the whole picture so that you can add a title or place text or graphics around the outside.

Copying

To copy a selected picture element, click on EDIT then on COPY. The copied shape or shapes are placed in the Clipboard. To paste from the Clipboard, click on EDIT then on PASTE. This will place a copy of the element in the top left-hand corner of the picture. The element is selected and can be dragged to its required position. The element in the Clipboard is also available to all other Windows programs. More details on using the Clipboard can be found in chapter 19.

Deleting

To remove part of the picture, click on EDIT then on CUT. This places the deleted element in the Clipboard.

Exiting from Paintbrush

Click on FILE then on EXIT. You will be prompted if any pictures have not been saved. Click on Yes to save the changes, No to exit without saving, or Cancel to carry on working in Paintbrush.

Opening a picture

Click on FILE then on OPEN. Paintbrush will close any existing picture before allowing you to open a new one. You will be prompted to save any

WINDOWS

changes as above. By default, the open box displays all BMP files in the Windows directory as shown in figure 6.15. This can be changed to display other file types.

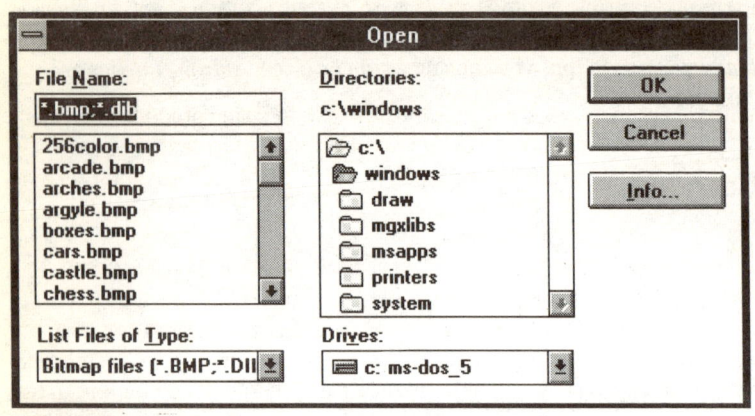

Figure 6.15

Use the scroll bars to locate the required file then double click to open it, or click once to highlight then click on OK.

See if you can open the file named CHESS.BMP.

This is one of a number of Paintbrush files which are supplied with Windows. CHESS.BMP is shown in figure 6.16.

Figure 6.16

— 70 —

FUN WITH PAINTBRUSH

Use Open to look at some of the other standard Paintbrush pictures.

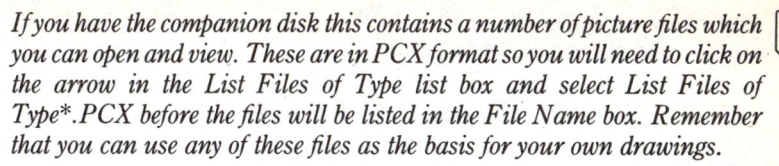

If you have the companion disk this contains a number of picture files which you can open and view. These are in PCX format so you will need to click on the arrow in the List Files of Type list box and select List Files of Type.PCX before the files will be listed in the File Name box. Remember that you can use any of these files as the basis for your own drawings.*

With this range of techniques and a little patience and practice you will be able to create graphics to add interest to your text based work. Paintbrush offers excellent scope for all those artists out there to experiment with computer drawing.

Practice Tasks

Task 1 *Home Sweet Home*

Start a new picture. Using all the tools and methods which you have learnt, draw a house. Try to include windows, door, house number, chimney, sky, grass, flower beds, path, garage, smoke, seagulls, etc. If you think you can, make it 3D, otherwise stick to 2D. Our efforts are shown in figure 6.17!

Figure 6.17

WINDOWS

Task 2 *From MENUS to Menus!*

You are holding a Chinese dinner party and you want to produce some menus for the guests. The menu should contain the date of your party, your name and address and the dishes for each of the courses. Try to have about four or five courses. Give the picture a nice border and use some effective fonts. Try to give the whole menu a Chinese effect.

There is a suitable font on the companion disk. Using this will give a result similar to that shown in figure 6.18.

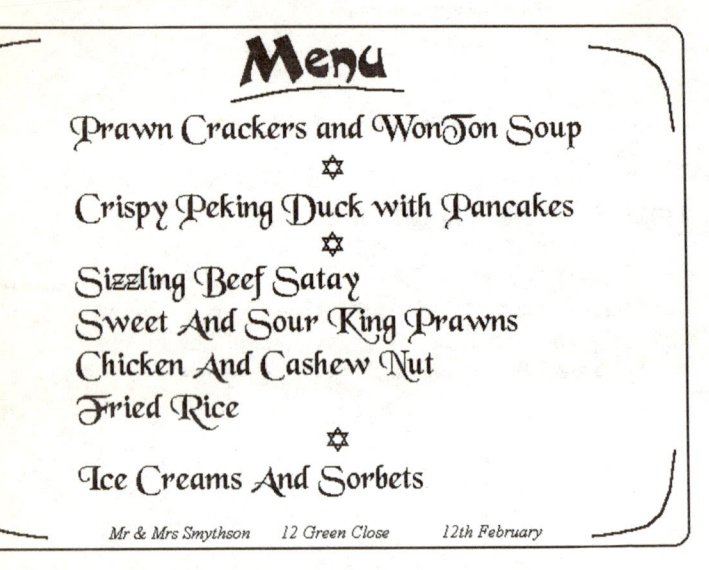

```
Menu

Prawn Crackers and WonTon Soup
              ✿
Crispy Peking Duck with Pancakes
              ✿
Sizzling Beef Satay
Sweet And Sour King Prawns
Chicken And Cashew Nut
Fried Rice
              ✿
Ice Creams And Sorbets

   Mr & Mrs Smythson    12 Green Close    12th February
```

Figure 6.18

Summary

In this chapter you have learnt how to

- draw lines and shapes on the picture;
- change colour;
- to fill shapes with colour;
- use the brush, roller and airbrush;

- add text to pictures;
- undo mistakes;
- move, copy and delete parts of drawings;
- save and print;
- open existing drawing files;
- exit from Paintbrush.

7
USING WRITE

Write is a word processor which can be used to write letters, produce mailshots, etc. This chapter looks at the main features of the program. Chapter 21 contains more details of the Write program.

Double click on the Write icon in the Accessories group of Program Manager. After Write has loaded, the screen shown in figure 7.1 will be displayed. The important parts of the window are labelled in figure 7.1.

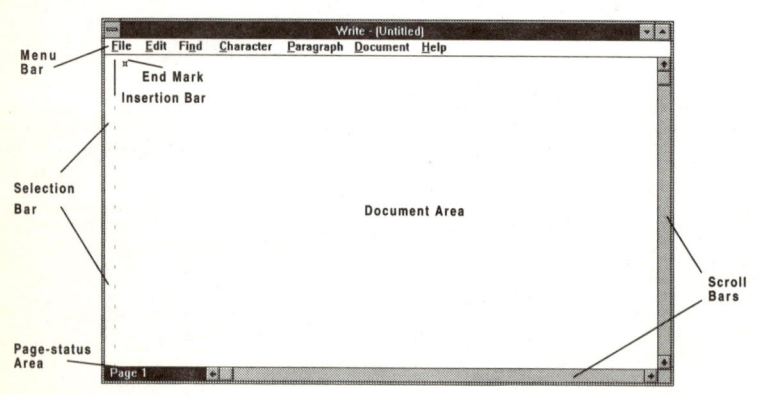

Figure 7.1

USING WRITE

Entering text

The text is entered in the document area, simply by typing on the keyboard. As the text is typed, the insertion bar or **cursor** will move along the lines. The small blob displayed after the cursor is the **end mark**.

When typing using a word processor, you should not press a carriage return at the end of each line. When you reach the end of the line, Write will automatically start a new line. This is called **word wrap** because the text is wrapped around from one line to the next.

Capital letters are obtained by holding down either of the Shift keys while pressing the letter key. If you want a lot of text in capitals, press the Caps Lock key and then type the text. After the text has been typed, press the Caps Lock key again to return to lower case. You can see if the Caps Lock switch is on or off by an indicator on the keyboard.

If you make any mistakes as you are typing they can be removed by using the BackSpace key. The BackSpace key removes the character to the left of the cursor and moves the cursor one space left. Do not worry if you overlook some errors, as a word processor makes it very easy to correct them later.

Type the following text into a blank Write document.

```
CITY OF MANCHESTER RECREATIONAL SERVICES DEPARTMENT

ASHVALE HORTICULTURAL CENTRE

The Horticultural Centre is located in Woodside Park and is open each weekend
throughout the year. If you are interested in gardening then a regular visit
to the Centre is essential.

Staff from the centre are responsible for floral decorations at major events
ranging from Royal visits to exhibitions and shows. Over 750 hanging baskets
are made up and planted in the spring. These are used to decorate roads and
parks throughout the city. Civic buildings are also decorated to provide
colour throughout the year.

A good selection of quality plants is usually available for visitors to buy.
Special visits and guided tours can be arranged by contacting the Centre
Manager.

Mr H S Plant
Centre Manager
Ashvale Horticultural Centre
```

Proof read the text and correct any errors you may have made.

Saving your document

Saving is very important to avoid losing all your hard work. You should save regularly and frequently, about every ten minutes. When you save, Write stores your text on disk for future use.

To save a document, click on FILE and then on either the SAVE or SAVE AS option. The Save As option prompts you for a name, whereas the Save option uses the current name, if it has one. Figure 7.2 shows the Save As box.

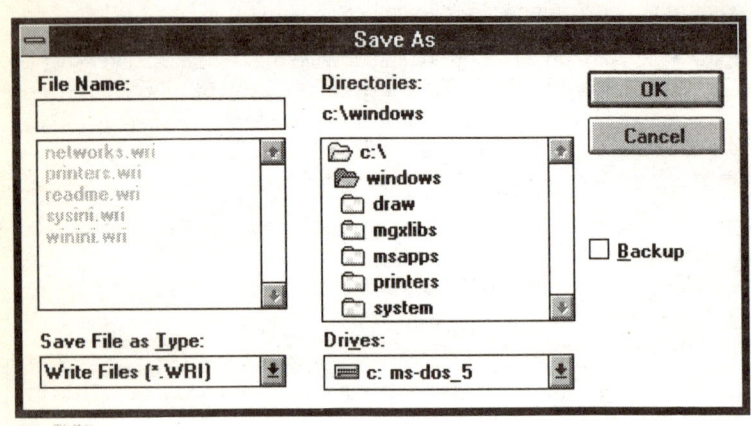

Figure 7.2

Type the name of the file to be saved in the File Name box. Click on the OK button. A Write file is saved with the WRI extension in the WINDOWS directory.

Use Save As to save the current text with the file name HORT. Write will add the extension WRI to the file name.

Ensure that you save regularly as you modify the document.

Correcting the text

Incorrect characters can be removed using the editing keys. Click in the text to make an insertion point or use the arrow keys to move the cursor to the required location.

BackSpace   deletes character left of cursor
Delete   deletes character right of cursor

Selecting sections of text

Before any modifications can be made to particular sections of text, the section has to be **selected**. When a piece of text is selected, it is colour reversed so it appears as white on black instead of black on white, as shown in figure 7.3.

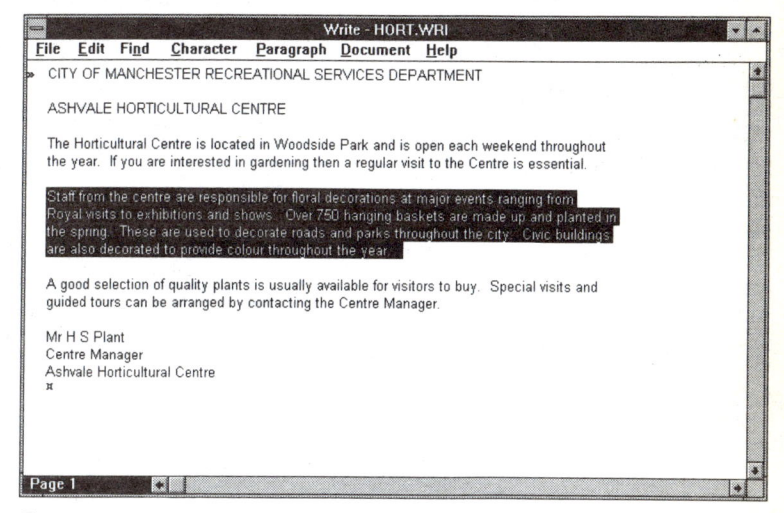

Figure 7.3

The Selection Bar is a vertical column at the left-hand edge of the document. In this area, the mouse cursor changes to a pointer pointing to the right. Clicking in the Selection Bar provides a fast method of highlighting a line or block of text, or the complete document.

Mouse methods

Text to be highlighted	**Method**
Line of text	Click on the required line in the Selection Bar.
Section of text	Move the mouse pointer to the left of the text

into the Selection Bar where it will turn into a reverse image of the normal pointer. Drag the mouse down the left side of the text from the start of the selected region and release the button at the end.

Characters or words left or right — Move the mouse pointer to the start of the section of text, click to make an insertion point, then drag the pointer left or right to the end of the required section.

Lines up or down — Move the mouse pointer to the start of the section of text, click to make an insertion point, then drag the pointer up or down to the end of the required section.

Keyboard methods

Keyboard command	Result
Ctrl + click in selection bar	highlights all text
Ctrl + click in text	highlights current sentence
Shift + left or right arrow	highlights characters left or right
Shift + up or down arrow	highlights lines above or below
Shift + Ctrl + left or right arrow keys	highlights words left or right

Changing styles

At the moment, the document consists of plain text. The headings look the same as the rest of the text. Write provides facilities for changing the appearance of sections of text, by using effects such as bold, italic or underlined. Figure 7.4 shows examples of the available print styles.

Before the styles can be changed, the required section of text has to be selected, using one of the methods above. Click on CHARACTER to pull down the Character menu and then select the required style or styles from the menu.

Using the HORT document, embolden the first heading line and underline the second.

Another way of making headings look good is to centre them. To do this

USING WRITE

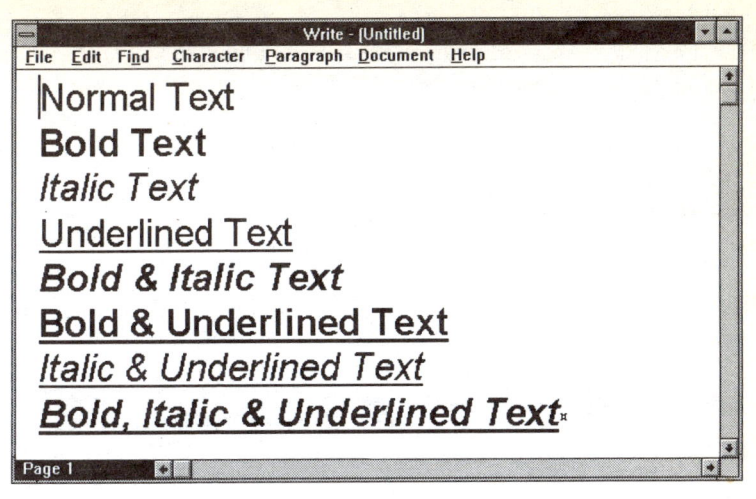

Figure 7.4

highlight the text of the heading and then click on PARAGRAPH and then on CENTRED. This moves the selected text to the centre of the lines.

Using the HORT document, centre both heading lines. Your document should now be similar to that shown in figure 7.5.

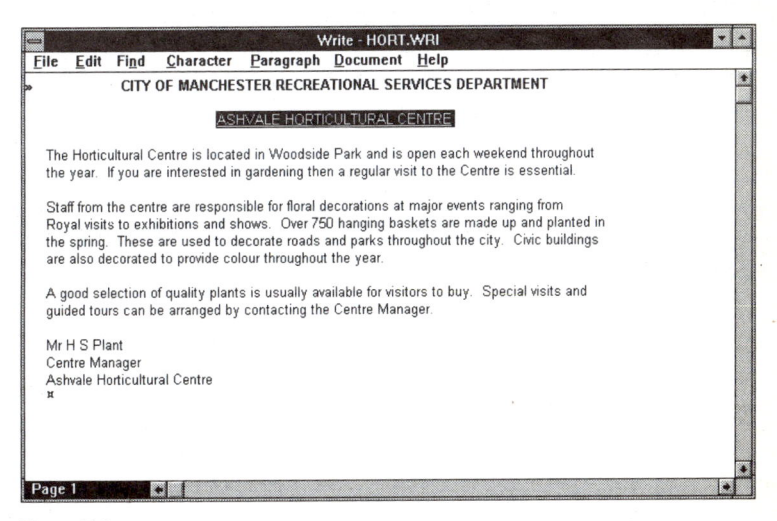

Figure 7.5

There is one other main way of changing the style, and that is to use fonts. Fonts are explained in the next chapter, Fun with fonts.

Save the document again. Click on FILE then on SAVE.

Printing

Click on FILE and then on PRINT to display the Print box, as shown in figure 7.6.

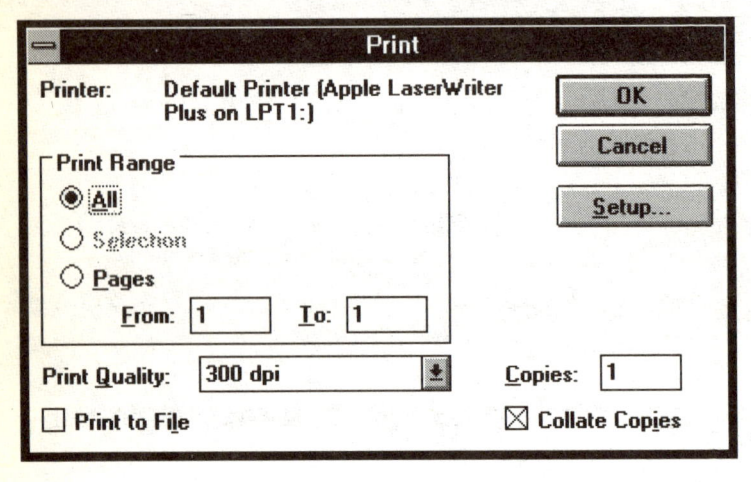

Figure 7.6

By default, the whole document is printed. In Windows 3.1, there are options to print the current page only or to print a range of pages. Select the required option and the number of copies, then click on OK to start the print. Write sends the output to the Windows Print Manager program. Printing is discussed in more detail in chapters 18 and 19.

If you have a printer, produce a printed or hard copy of your work.

USING WRITE

Tabs

Tabs are a very useful way of typing tables of data into your document. Tabs are predefined points across the page. When you press the Tab key, the cursor moves to the next predefined point. This is a lot better than using the SpaceBar which makes it difficult to line the text up properly. Write has pre-set tab stops every half inch across the page. If you insert too many tabs, they can be removed by pressing BackSpace.

Type the following text after the last paragraph but before the name. Use the pre-set tab stops to align the columns.

```
Here are some examples of our very reasonable discount prices for
customers:
            Flower          Number      Price
            Geranium        5           4.80
            Daffodil        10          1.00
            Busy Lizzie     5           1.65
            Crocus          20          0.60
            Snowdrop        20          0.80
            Hyacinth        5           1.40
            Rose bush       1           4.50
```

Embolden the Flower, Number and Price headings. Italicise the complete table. Remember to save your document after making these changes. Your document should now look like that shown in figure 7.7.

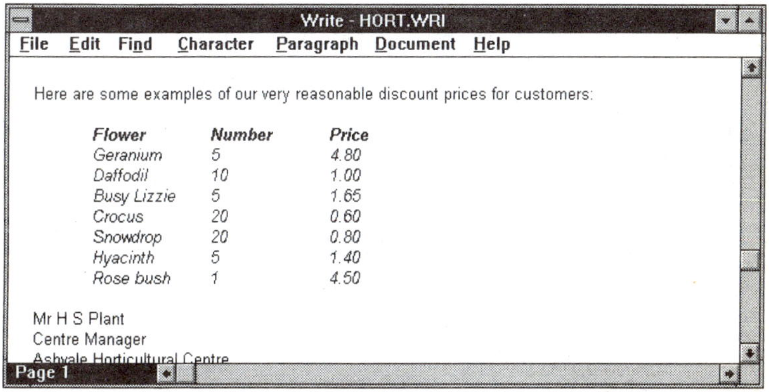

Figure 7.7

— 81 —

WINDOWS

— Inserting pictures into documents —

Write has the facility to add pictures to your document. The Paintbrush program which is supplied with Windows allows you to create very good pictures. The picture must first be created. You can draw a new picture or open an existing picture file.

Minimise Write. Open Paintbrush and try and draw some pictures of plants and flowers.

The companion disk contains three horticultural picture files called PLANT1.PCX, PLANT2.PCX and PLANT3.PCX. Click on FILE then on OPEN. Double click on the required file to open the picture within Paintbrush.

Click on EDIT then on COPY to copy the picture to the Clipboard. Paintbrush can then be closed or minimised if required for future use.

Restore the Write window which will still contain your document. Move the cursor to the position where the picture is to be inserted. A suitable place in this text would be just after the heading lines.

Click on EDIT then on PASTE to insert the Paintbrush picture from the Clipboard.

Check the document for errors. Save and print your finished document. Figure 7.8 shows an example of the document.

Exiting from Write

To leave the Write program, click on FILE then on EXIT. If you have any unsaved files, you will be asked whether you want to save them.

Summary

In this chapter you have learnt how to:
- load Write;
- enter text into a document;

USING WRITE

CITY OF MANCHESTER RECREATIONAL SERVICES DEPARTMENT

ASHVALE HORTICULTURAL CENTRE

The Horticultural Centre is located in Woodside Park and is open each weekend throughout the year. If you are interested in gardening then a regular visit to the Centre is essential.

Staff from the centre are responsible for floral decorations at major events ranging from Royal visits to exhibitions and shows. Over 750 hanging baskets are made up and planted in the spring. These are used to decorate roads and parks throughout the city. Civic buildings are also decorated to provide colour throughout the year.

A good selection of quality plants is usually available for visitors to buy. Special visits and guided tours can be arranged by contacting the Centre Manager.

Here are some examples of our very reasonable discount prices for customers:

Flower	*Number*	*Price*
Geranium	5	4.80
Daffodil	10	1.00
Busy Lizzie	5	1.65
Crocus	20	0.60
Snowdrop	20	0.80
Hyacinth	5	1.40
Rose bush	1	4.50

Mr H S Plant
Centre Manager
Ashvale Horticultural Centre

Figure 7.8

- save documents;
- select sections of text;
- embolden, italicise and underline text;
- change the text alignment;
- print documents;
- use tabs to create tables;
- add pictures to documents;
- exit from Write.

8

— FUN WITH FONTS —

This chapter describes the typefaces, print styles, effects and sizes which you can apply to text in Windows. Much of this chapter is aimed at users of Windows 3.1 because of its extra font capabilities. There is a limited range of fonts available in Windows 3.0. The major differences between the versions are indicated at the appropriate points in the chapter.

What is a font?

A font is a collection of numbers, letters and symbols which have certain design characteristics. Fonts are in everyday use in most written material. A newspaper may use one type style for the main text, and one or more different styles for headlines. This book uses several different fonts. Figure 8.1 shows two very different forms. As you can see, the way the letters are formed is completely different.

This is text in the Optima font.
This is text in the Goudy font.

Figure 8.1

FUN WITH FONTS

— Why should I use different fonts? —

As you have already discovered in the previous chapter on Windows Write, you can make headings stand out by centring them, or emboldening or underlining the text. Using different fonts makes it possible to make these headings larger and more striking. On a mailshot, newsletter, or even just a letter, a variety of fonts makes the whole appearance of the document more eye-catching and professional.

– Where can I use fonts in Windows? –

One of the main advantages of Windows is that all the available fonts can be used in many different applications. Any application or program which allows you to enter text will give you access to all the Windows fonts. For example, fonts can be used in Windows Write and Paintbrush.

Using fonts in Paintbrush

Load Paintbrush in the normal way (see chapter 6) and draw some basic shapes onto the drawing area.

Click on the text tool in the toolbar. This will give you a text insertion point as shown in figure 8.2.

Text is typed at the insertion point. The standard font is **System**. In Windows 3.0, fonts are accessed from the Font menu shown in figure 8.3. In version 3.1, fonts are accessed from the Text menu. To change the font, click on the TEXT menu and then on the FONTS option. This will display the Font box as shown in figure 8.4.

The Font list shows you the available fonts and allows you to select the font you want to use. Don't worry that in figure 8.4 there seem to be more fonts than are on your system; it just depends on what type of printer you are using and how many extra fonts you have installed. The Font Style list box allows you to select Bold or Bold Italic. The Size list box allows you to choose the point size of the font. In version 3.0, the style and size are selected from their own separate menus.

WINDOWS

Insertion Point

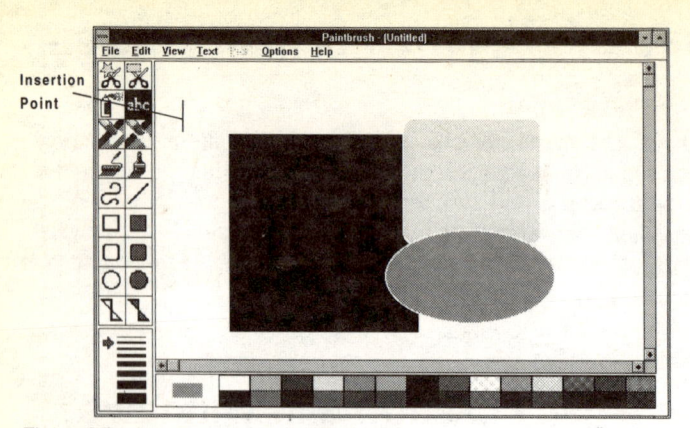

Figure 8.2

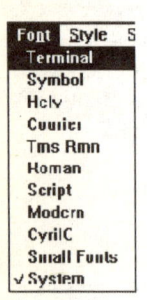

Figure 8.3

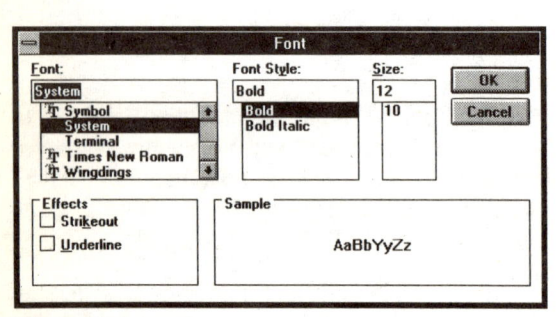

Figure 8.4

Add some text and then change the fonts and sizes of this text to see the effects.

Figure 8.5 shows a Paintbrush screen with samples of some different fonts.

— 86 —

FUN WITH FONTS

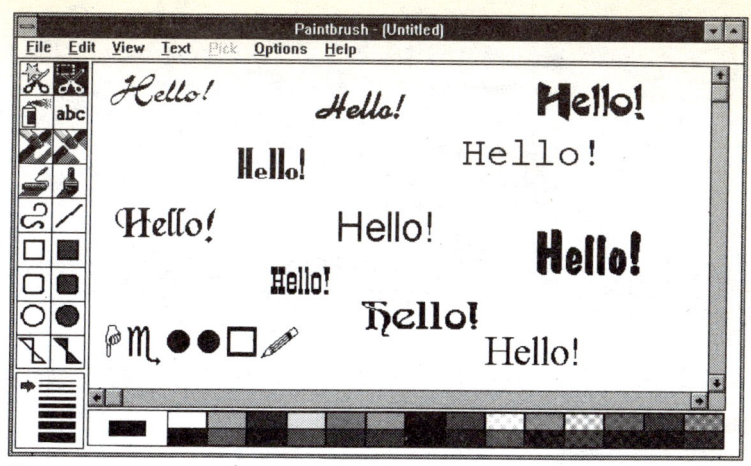

Figure 8.5

Using fonts in Write

Fonts work in much the same way in every application. In Write they are accessed by clicking on CHARACTER then on FONTS. Text which is already typed can be changed by selecting the text and then selecting a different font for the text.

──────── TrueType fonts ────────
3.1 only

There are some standard fonts which are supplied with Windows. Version 3.1 has some fonts called **TrueType** which look exactly the same on the screen as they do when printed out. In the Font list TrueType fonts are shown with a ₸ symbol.

TrueType fonts give you the advantage of allowing a dot matrix printer to use fonts usually only available to laser printer users.

──────── Installing a new font ────────
3.1 only

The companion disk contains two extra fonts which you can install and use.

The availability of TrueType fonts within Windows 3.1 has led to many extra fonts being produced by software developers for use within Windows. These can be purchased from a variety of sources. Extra fonts need to be installed in your system before you can use them. This is done from the Windows Control panel. To load the Control Panel program, double click on its icon in the Main window of Program Manager. This will display a screen as shown in figure 8.6.

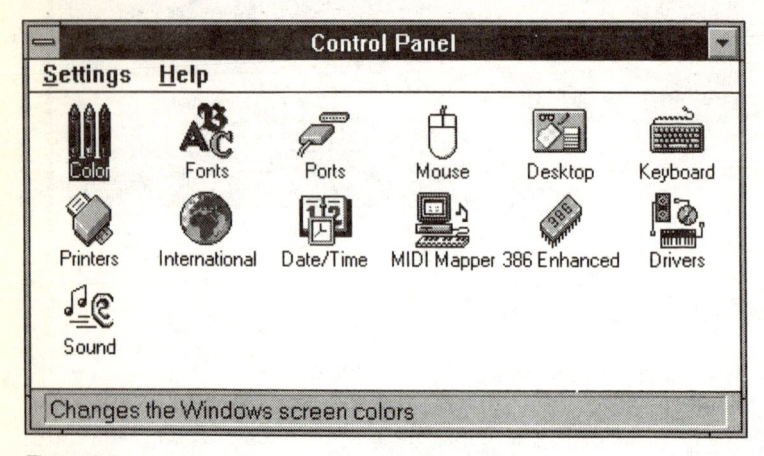

Figure 8.6

Double click on the Fonts icon to display the Fonts window as shown in figure 8.7.

The Installed Fonts list box shows the fonts already installed on the system and allows you to view or remove them. The Sample box shows a sample of the currently selected font. Click on the Add button in this window to display the Add Fonts window, as in figure 8.8.

The fonts which are found in the current directory are shown in the List of Fonts box at the top of the window.

Use the Directories and Drives list boxes to choose the drive and directory containing the font file. In the case of the fonts on the companion disk this will either be A: or B:.

When the drive is changed to that containing the companion disk there should be three names in the List of Fonts box as shown in figure 8.8.

To install the fonts on your system permanently, ensure that the Copy Fonts to Windows Directory box is checked. If this is not switched on,

FUN WITH FONTS

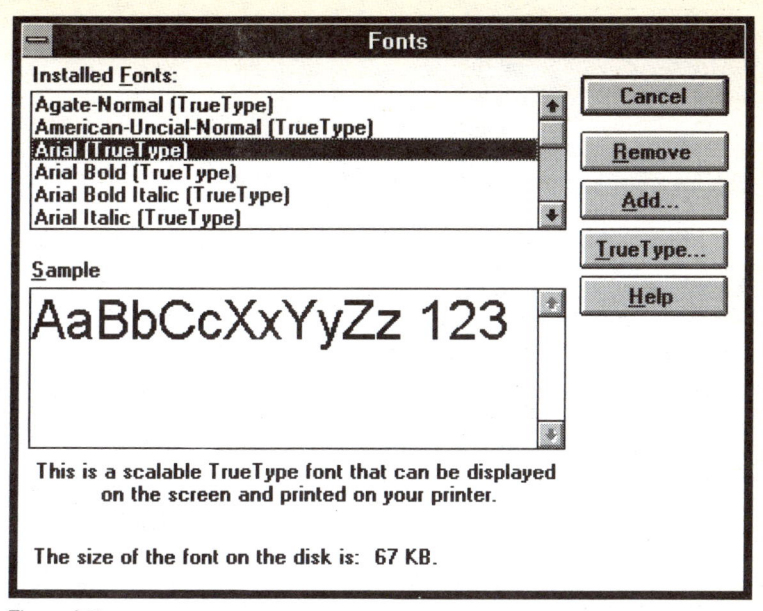

Figure 8.7

Figure 8.8

the fonts are not copied to the hard disk and you would need to insert the disk every time you used the font.

Summary

In this chapter you have learnt
- what a font is;
- the different types and styles of fonts;
- how to change the font and size;
- how to use fonts in Paintbrush;
- how to use fonts in Write;
- how to add new fonts to your system.

9
— USING CARDFILE —

This chapter will show you how to use Cardfile. Cardfile is one of the accessories supplied with Windows. It is a simple database used for storing sets of information such as might be stored on index cards. Each card can contain free-form text and graphics, and can have a summary entry used as an index.

Double click on the Cardfile icon in the Accessories group. After Cardfile has loaded, the screen shown in figure 9.1 will be displayed. The box near the bottom of the window is the first card, ready for text to be entered. Cardfile

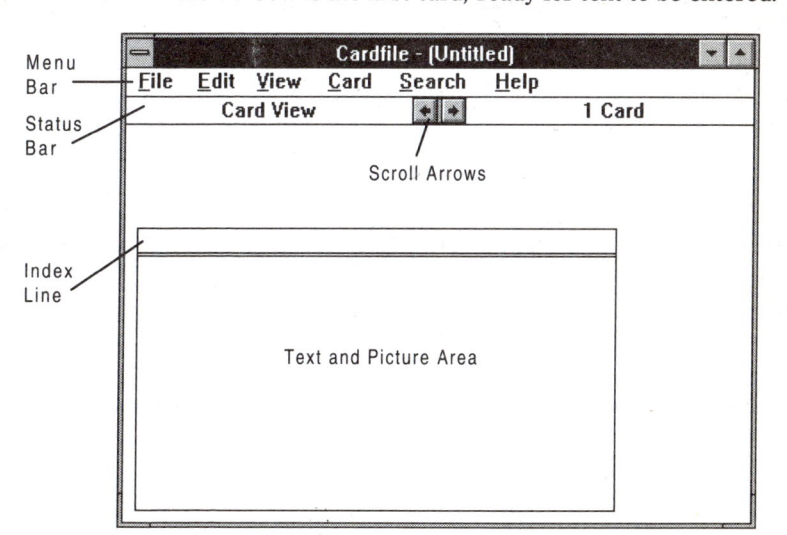

Figure 9.1

WINDOWS

The bar across the top of the box is the **Index Line**. The Index Line contains a name or key words which will be used for locating particular cards. The **scroll arrows** near the top of the screen allow you to move through the cards in the file.

Entering information

To enter text onto a card, click on the card and then type the text. The text will appear in the body of the card.

Load Cardfile and create a card with the following information.

Mr & Mrs R Smith
72 Kings Road
Little Park Estate
Sixoaks
Kent SX7 9GH

Entering the Index Line

Each card has an Index Line which is used for arranging the cards in order and for searching. Cardfile automatically maintains the cards in alphabetical order of Index Lines. Double click on the line at the top of the card to display the Index dialog box, as shown in figure 9.2.

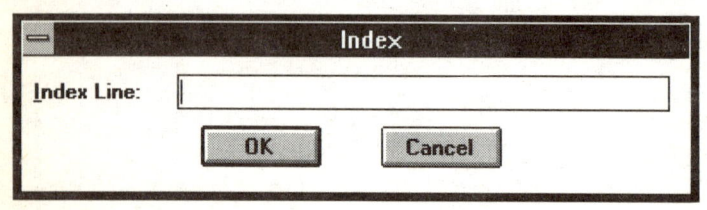

Figure 9.2

Type the Index Line for the card. The Index Line is likely to contain a surname or reference number. Figure 9.3 shows one card in a file completed.

USING CARDFILE

```
┌─────────────────────────────────────────────┐
│ ═       Cardfile - (Untitled)         ▼ ▲  │
│  File  Edit  View  Card  Search  Help       │
│         Card View      ← →        1 Card    │
│                                             │
│                                             │
│  ┌─────────────────────────────────────┐   │
│  │Smith R                              │   │
│  │Mr & Mrs R Smith                     │   │
│  │72 Kings Road                        │   │
│  │Little Park Estate                   │   │
│  │Sixoaks                              │   │
│  │Kent SX7 9GH|                        │   │
│  │                                     │   │
│  │                                     │   │
│  │                                     │   │
│  └─────────────────────────────────────┘   │
└─────────────────────────────────────────────┘
```

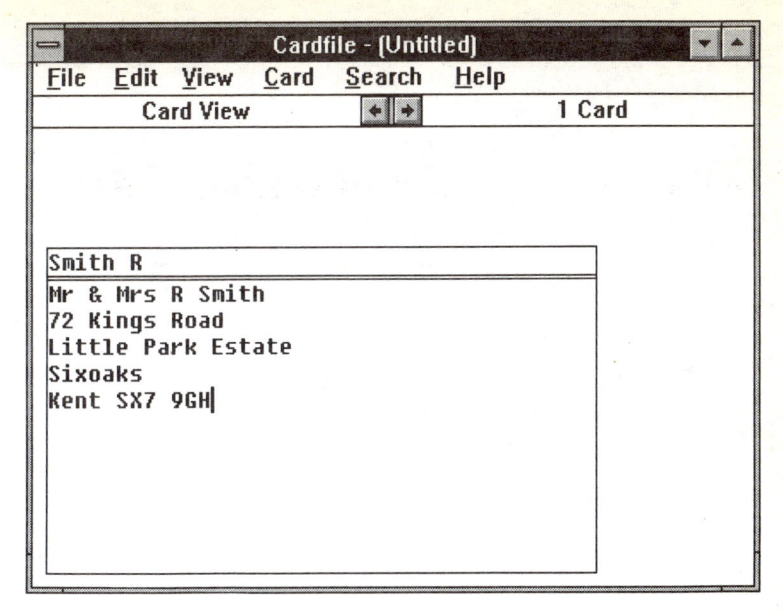

Figure 9.3

Add an index line to your card for Smith R.

─────────── Adding cards ───────────

Of course you would not only have one card in a file, you would want many more cards. Cards can be added to the Cardfile by clicking on CARD and then on ADD. The Add entry box is very similar to the Index box as shown in figure 9.2. Type the required Index Line entry for the new card.

The key shortcut for adding a new card to the Cardfile is to press F2.

After the Index Line has been entered, the card is added to the file. The information still needs to be added to the body of the card.

Add another seven cards to your file. Make up some names or add some of your friends and colleagues to the file.

Your card file will now look something like the one shown in figure 9.4. It may not be possible to see all the cards you have entered. The total

— 93 —

number of cards in the file is shown on the Status Bar. The other cards have not been lost, there is just not enough room for them to be displayed in the window. If the size of the window was increased or the window was maximised, then more of the cards would be displayed.

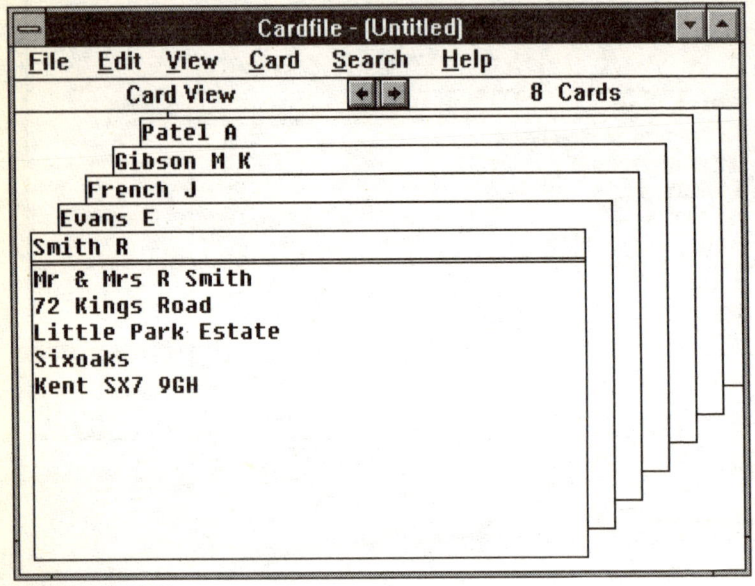

Figure 9.4

Deleting cards

If a card is no longer required or has been entered incorrectly, it can be removed from the file. Click on CARD then on DELETE and confirm that the card is to be removed.

Use this to remove any cards you have entered in error.

Saving a Cardfile

To save a Cardfile click on FILE then on SAVE. If the file does not yet have a name, the Save As box shown in figure 9.5 will be displayed. If the file has already been named, it will be saved again with the same file name.

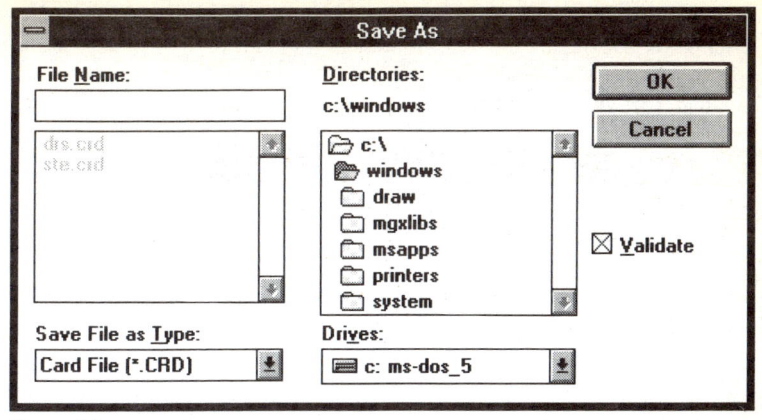

Figure 9.5

Type a file name for your Cardfile in the entry box. By default, Cardfile gives its databases the extension of CRD and saves them in the WINDOWS directory.

Make sure you save your Cardfile so that you don't lose your work. You could use your initials for the file name.

Searching the file

To view or edit a card in the file, the required card needs to be brought to the front. There are four ways of doing this:

- Click on the Index Line of the required card.

or
- Click on the scroll arrows until the required card is displayed.

or
- Switch to List view by clicking on CARD then on LIST VIEW. List view shows only the Index Lines. This means that more cards can be viewed on screen at the same time. Double click on the required Index Line to view the card.

or
- Search for the required card. Click on SEARCH then on GO TO to display the Go To box shown in figure 9.6. Type the index (or part of the index) of the card which you want to locate. Cardfile will then

WINDOWS

search through all the cards for the first card which matches the search text.

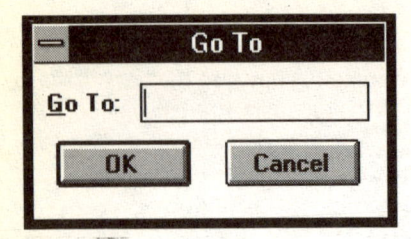

Figure 9.6

Try entering Smith in the Go To box and see if you can locate your first card.

It is also possible to search for text contained in the actual card. Click on SEARCH then on FIND to display the Find box shown in figure 9.7.

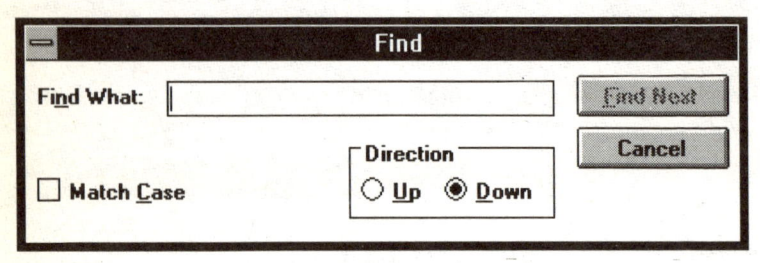

Figure 9.7

Enter the characters which are to be found. The Direction box allows you to choose whether the computer should give you the first match up or down the file. Click on the Find Next button. Cardfile automatically moves to the next card which contains the desired text.

Try searching for part of an address or a telephone number and see if Cardfile finds the correct card.

Adding pictures to a Cardfile

It is also possible to add pictures to the cards in the file. The pictures have to be created before they can be added to the cards. Paintbrush can be used to create your own picture files.

USING CARDFILE

The companion disk contains a number of clip art files which you can use as practice files. These are in PCX format, ready for loading into Paintbrush.

Minimise Cardfile and open Paintbrush. Open a clip art file or create your own drawing. When the picture is complete, copy it to the Clipboard. In Paintbrush this is done by selecting the picture using the cut-out tools and then clicking on EDIT and on COPY. Minimise Paintbrush and restore Cardfile ready to paste the picture.

To insert the picture, Cardfile has to be switched into **Picture mode**.

Click on EDIT then on EDIT PICTURE. Now you are in picture editing mode you can paste your picture onto the card. Select EDIT then PASTE. You will probably find that the picture has been pasted on top of the text. This is because pictures are always pasted in at the top left. The picture can be moved around on the card to the required position. Click and drag the picture to the required position. Pictures usually look best at the right of the card, with the text on the left, as shown in figure 9.8. Windows 3.1 adjusts the size of the picture to fit on the card. This does not happen with Windows 3.0, which has limited picture capabilities in Cardfile.

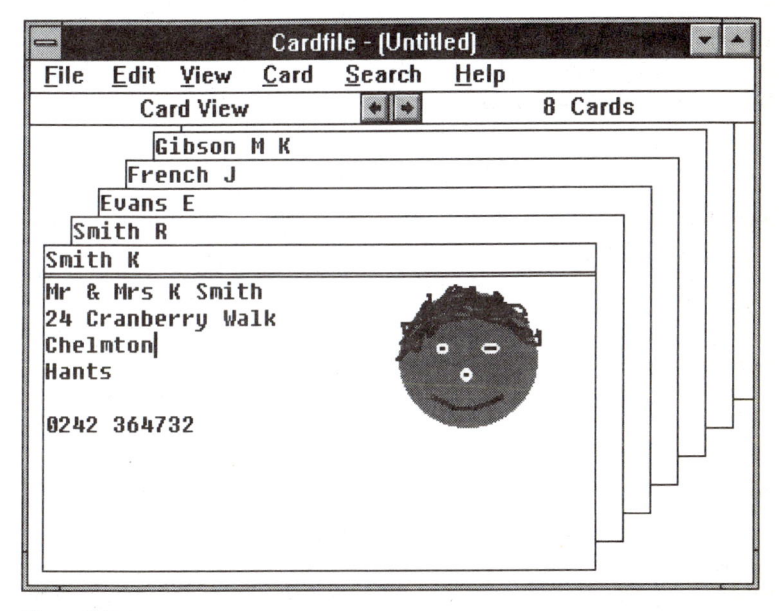

Figure 9.8

WINDOWS

3.1 only

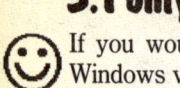

If you would like to edit your picture, one of the big advantages of Windows version 3.1 is that you can double click on the picture to open the picture file in the application in which it was created. For example, if you created the picture in Paintbrush, Windows will automatically open Paintbrush with your picture in it.

Try to draw a picture of one of your friends (as I have done in figure 9.8!) and insert it into the correct card. If you have access to a scanner you could try scanning a photograph.

Printing a Cardfile

Click on FILE then on PRINT to print the current card. Click on FILE then on PRINT ALL to print all the cards. The printed output shows the card and Index Line, as you would see it on the screen. A sample printout is shown in figure 9.9.

Printing Index Lines

If Cardfile is in list view, only the Index Lines will be printed.

Use PRINT to print the current card.
Use PRINT ALL to print out the complete file.
Switch to list view and print the list of people on your file.

Practice task

Animal corner!

You are a ranger in the local park and you want to keep a record of all the animals. There are about ten different animals and they all need looking after. You have decided to create a Cardfile of all the different animals and

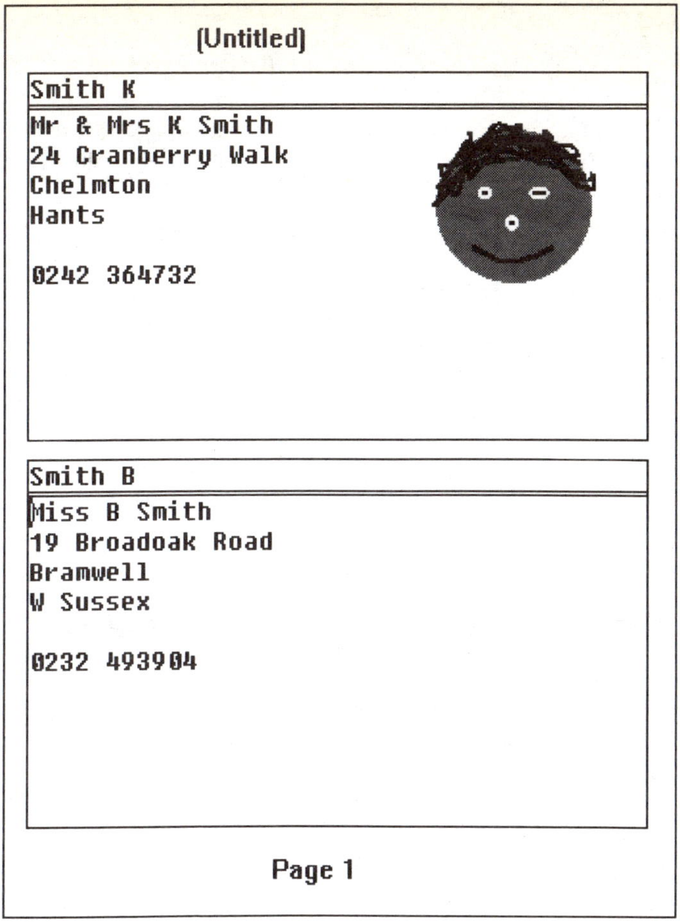

Figure 9.9

information about them. If you are feeling artistic, you could try creating drawings of the animals to include on the cards!

The companion disk contains some animal clip art files in PCX format which can be opened in Paintbrush.

Create a Cardfile to store information about the following animals.

The companion disk contains some animal clip art files in PCX format which can be opened in Paintbrush.

Animal	Pen number	Feeding instructions	Name	Companion disk clip art file
Badger	4	Worms, 2 times a day.	Bettie	BADGER.PCX
Hare	7	Vegetables.	Harry	HARE.PCX
Owl	Aviary	Small rodents, once a day.	Ollie	OWL.PCX
Rabbit	8	Carrots.	Peter	RABBIT.PCX
Robin	Aviary	Nuts, scraps.	Robin	ROBIN.PCX
Skylark	Aviary	Seeds, insects.	Susan	SKYLARK.PCX
Snail	1	Leaves, vegetables.	Sammy	SNAIL.PCX
Squirrel	3	Nuts.	Frisky	SQUIRREL.PCX
Tawny Owl	Aviary	Small rodents. Once a day.	Trish	TAWNY.PCX
Mouse	2	Insects.	Michael	MOUSE.PCX

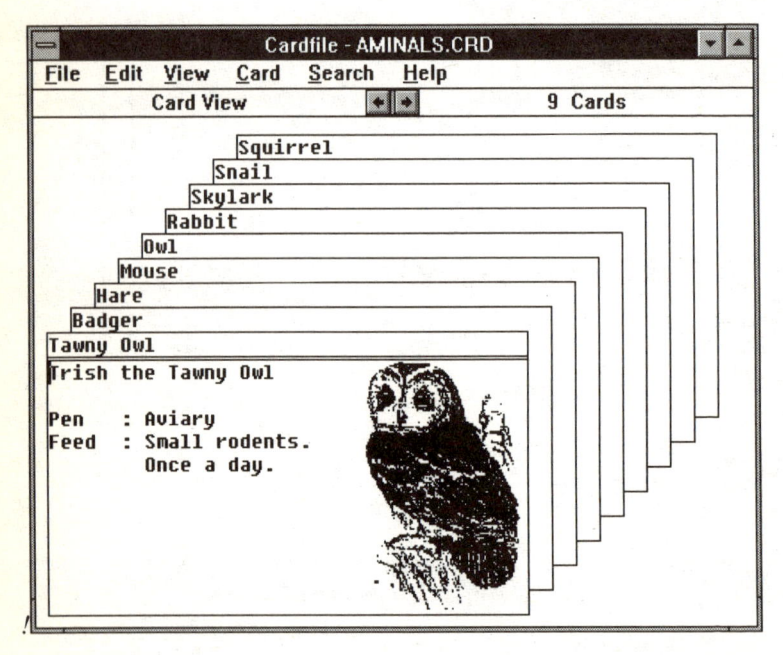

Figure 9.10

Summary

In this chapter you have learnt how to:

- create a Cardfile;
- use index lines;
- add cards to the file;
- remove cards from the file;
- search for cards;
- save a Cardfile;
- print a Cardfile;
- add pictures to the cards.

10
WINDOWS CALENDAR

All desktops have a calendar. The Windows desktop is no exception. This chapter looks at Windows Calendar, which is one of the accessories supplied with Windows. Version 3.11 contains Schedule+ instead of Calendar. This has many of the same features but is more sophisticated. You can use Calendar to maintain your daily schedule for each day of the year. It allows you to specify where you should be at certain times during the day and features an alarm to ensure that you are never late for an appointment!

Double click on the Calendar icon in the Accessories group of Program Manager. This will load the default Calendar screen shown in figure 10.1. The standard display shows the current day divided into hourly intervals from 7 am to 8 pm. The screen can be scrolled up and down to view the rest of the hours in the day. The lower area of the screen is a space for making reminders and general notes.

Using Calendar effectively will clearly be difficult if your computer clock is not correct! Calendar could show appointments for the wrong day and you could have the alarm sounding at the wrong times! Check the date and time shown near the top of the screen. If these are not correct, the date and time can be set from Windows Control Panel. You can find out how to do this in chapter 18.

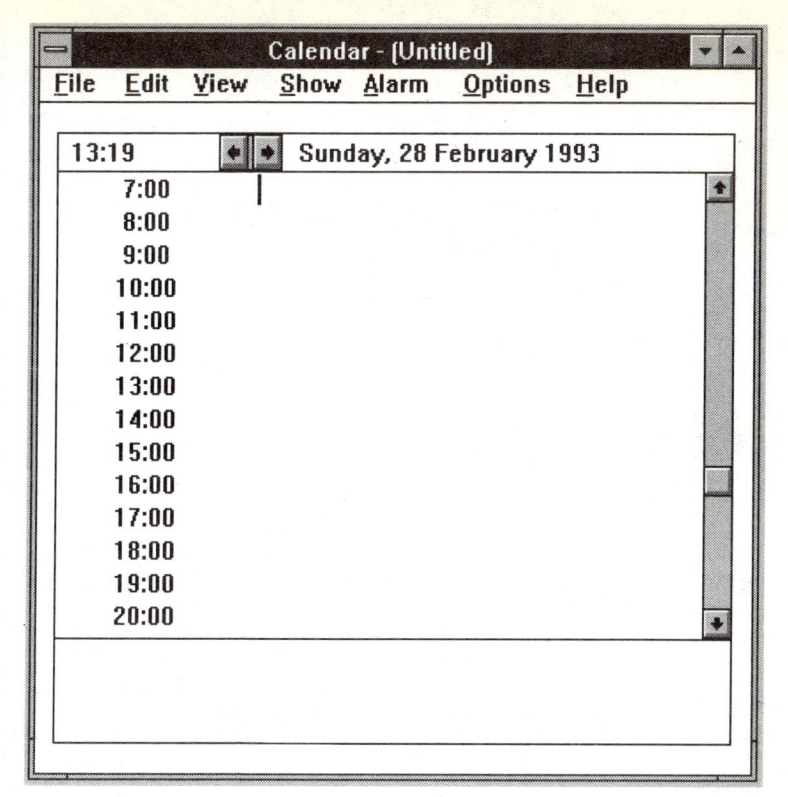

Figure 10.1

− Entering details for the current day −

To enter an item for the current day, click on the line containing the required time or use the up and down arrow keys to move the cursor. The required text can then be typed. Text longer than the space available on the line will cause the line to scroll to the right. Eventually you will reach the limit of text allowed and any further text will be lost. In practice, this is not a problem as the vast majority of entries will be short.

Enter the following activities for the current day:

7.00	Get up
8.00	Go to work
9.00	Start work
10.00	Meeting
13.00	Lunch with Sam
17.00	Go home

– Entering details for a different date –

Calendar displays a single day at a time. To change to a previous day or more usefully to a future date, click on the arrow buttons next to the date, as shown in figure 10.2.

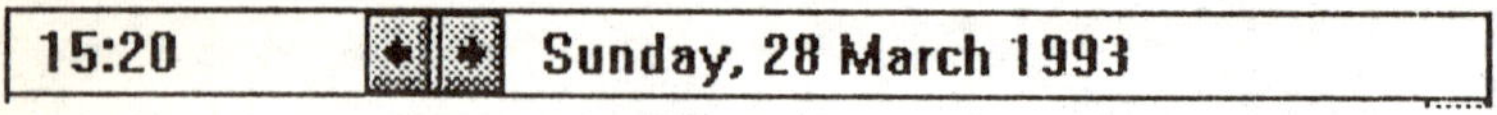

```
15:20              Sunday, 28 March 1993
```

Figure 10.2

You can also navigate around Calendar using the keyboard.

Ctrl Page Down   moves to next date
Ctrl Page Up   moves to previous date

A further method is using the Show menu. Click on SHOW to display the menu. Select the required option from TODAY, PREVIOUS, NEXT or DATE which allows you to move to any specified day. The date should be entered in DD/MM/YYYY format.

Display the Calendar for tomorrow.
Enter the following appointments.

10.00	Hair cut
13.00	Phone Mum

Viewing a complete month

To view a complete month, click on VIEW to display the View menu, then choose MONTH to display a calendar of the month, as shown in figure 10.3. The month displayed will be the month containing the date shown on the date line. The current date, if visible, is marked with > < symbols on either side. The date which was last opened is highlighted. Double click on any required date to display the calendar for that day.

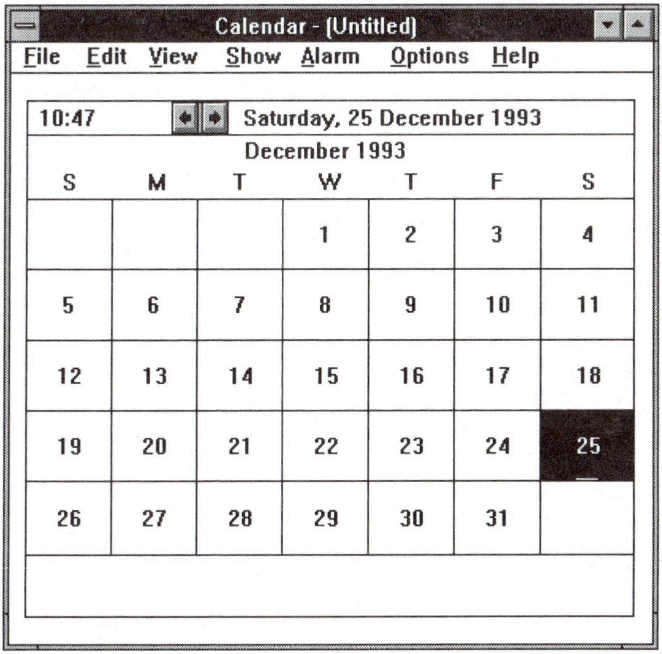

Figure 10.3

Double click on the first day for which you entered appointments. Return to the monthly calendar. Double click on the second day for which you entered appointments.

Use SHOW then DATE to find out the day on which your birthday falls in the year 2000. Remember to use the correct date format of DD/MM/YYYY. Use SHOW then TODAY to return to the current date.

Saving the Calendar file

Your Calendar file can be saved for future use. If you do not save your Calendar file, all your appointments will be lost when you exit the program. Calendar saves all dates in one file. The range of valid dates is from 1980 to 2099. Click on FILE then select SAVE. As the file has not yet been given a file name, Calendar will display the Save As box, shown in figure 10.4.

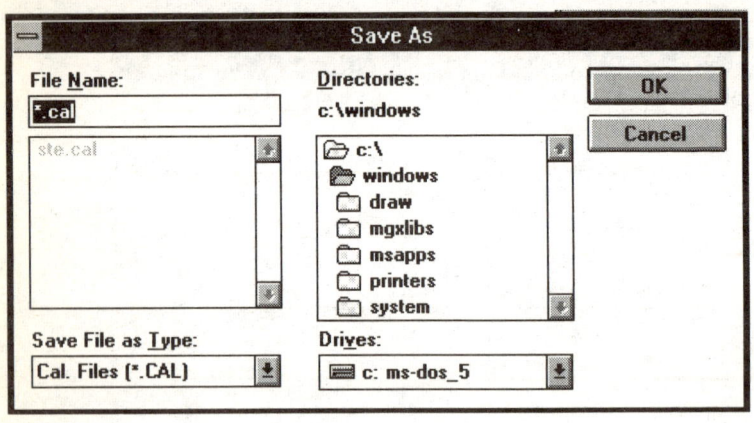

Figure 10.4

Calendar files are normally saved in the WINDOWS directory. Type a suitable file name and click on OK. Any subsequent saves will use this file name. Calendar adds the extension CAL to its files.

Save your Calendar file using your name or initials for the file name. Calendar will save the file with the extension CAL. This avoids any confusion with a file saved with the same file name in another program. For example, Cardfile will save the file with the extension CRD.

Special times

Appointments can be also entered at times which do not coincide with the normal time intervals. Click on OPTIONS then select SPECIAL TIME to display the dialog box shown in figure 10.5.

Figure 10.5

Enter the time required in the format HH:MM and click on AM or PM.

*Add the following appointment to the **second** day of your schedule:*

13:35   Dental appointment

──────── Setting the alarm ────────

The alarm is useful to remind you of important appointments. To set the alarm for a particular appointment, select the required appointment and click on ALARM then on SET. This will place an alarm bell symbol by the side of the appointment. At the appointed time Calendar will sound a number of beeps. If you are working in Calendar at the time, the box shown in figure 10.6 will be displayed as a reminder of where you are supposed to be! If Calendar is minimised at the time, the beeps still sound and the Calendar icon at the bottom of the screen will start to flash. Click on the flashing icon to display the Please remember dialog box. Chapter 22 contains more information on the alarm feature.

Figure 10.6

Practise using the alarm by setting the alarm for the dental appointment. To hear and see the alarm in action, enter a special time in the near future, say in five minutes' time. Set the alarm for this appointment. Sit back and watch! You might like to try this with Calendar open and then set the alarm for another appointment and try again with Calendar minimised.

Opening a Calendar file

Click on FILE then on OPEN to display the Open box. Select the required file or type the file name. The Calendar file will be recalled from the disk. You can then modify and edit the Calendar file to include extra days, more appointments, etc.

Your Calendar file has already been saved. Try recalling it from the disk.

Printing the Calendar file

If you need a written daily schedule, or you don't have access to the computer during the day you may need a printed copy of the Calendar page. Click on FILE then on PRINT to display the Print dialog box shown in figure 10.7. The From date defaults to the current date.

Figure 10.7

Enter the From (start) and To (end) dates to be printed and click on OK. If you only require a single day, you only need to enter the start date. A sample daily Calendar is shown in figure 10.8.

		STE.CAL
	Friday, 19 November 1993	
	8:00	Meeting with John & Paul
	9:30	Phone Fred in Saudi Arabia
	10:30	IT committee meeting
*	14:00	Teach BTEC computing
	17:00	Finish work

Figure 10.8

An asterisk next to an appointment indicates that the alarm has been set for this appointment. The printed version can have a header and footer if required. Chapter 22 contains more details of the Calendar print.

Print out the pages for the dates you have been entering.

Exiting from Calendar

To exit from Calendar, click on FILE then on EXIT. If the current file is not saved, you will be prompted to save it before it is closed.

Try using Calendar to set up your appointments and activities for the coming week. Save the file as each day is entered. When your schedule is complete, print out the pages. You may well find Calendar indispensable!

Summary

This chapter has described the facilities provided by Windows Calendar, including:

- entering details;
- changing dates;
- viewing daily and monthly schedules;
- saving and loading Calendar files;
- setting alarms;
- printing schedules.

11
WINDOWS CALCULATOR

This chapter looks at the Calculator accessory supplied with Windows. The Windows Calculator can be operated in two modes; as a simple calculator or as a sophisticated scientific calculator. The results of calculations can be transferred to other Windows applications using the Clipboard. You can have Calculator running all the time, either in a window or as an icon. Then, at any time when you wish to do a calculation, you only need to restore Calculator.

To load Calculator, double click on the Calculator icon in the Accessories group of Program Manager. Calculator loads in the same mode as it was last used. If Calculator has not been previously used, it will load in the **standard mode** as shown in figure 11.1. The standard calculator mode has the basic functions of a manual calculator, including a memory.

If Calculator displays as shown in figure 11.2 on page 113 then it is in **scientific mode**. To change the mode of the calculator, click on the VIEW menu then on either SCIENTIFIC or STANDARD.

WINDOWS CALCULATOR

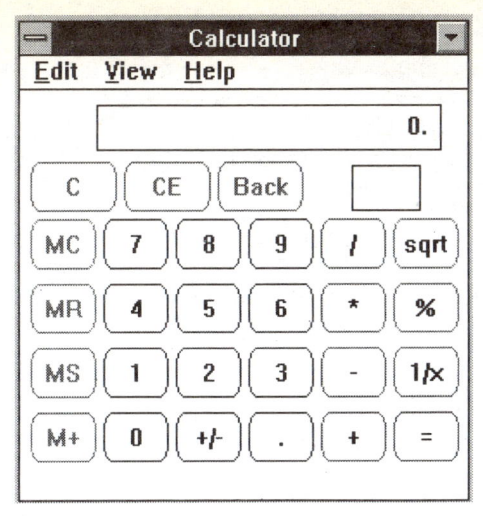

Figure 11.1

Standard calculator

The standard mode calculator shown in figure 11.1 contains all the features of a basic calculator. To enter numbers or use functions, click upon the correct box using the mouse.

Button   Function
0–9   adds this number to the display
+/−   changes the number in the display from positive to negative
.   adds a decimal place to the number at the end
/   divides the current number by the next number
*   multiplies the current number by the next number
−   subtracts the next number from the current number
+   adds the current number to the next number
sqrt   calculates the square root of the number
%   calculates percentages
1/x   calculates the reciprocal of the number i.e. divides the number into 1
=   displays the answer to the current sum
MC   clears the memory

WINDOWS

MR   recalls the number in memory
MS   stores the current number in memory
M+   adds the current number to the number in memory
C   completely clears the display
CE   removes only the current number from the display
Back   removes only the last number keyed in

When working in standard mode, Calculator acts as a left to right calculator. This means that it does not follow the normal rules of arithmetic precedence, where multiplication and division are done before addition and subtraction. This is illustrated in the example below.

On a left to right calculator   20 − 4 * 3   gives 48
Using arithmetical precedence   20 − 4 * 3   gives 8

To get the correct answer to this sum on a left to right calculator is quite difficult. You would have to multiply 4 by 3 and store the answer in the memory. Then clear the current display, enter the number 12 press the minus key then recall the number stored in memory using the MR key, then – at last! – press the = key to give the answer of 8.

Try some of these calculations using the standard calculator. Check your answers against those given. <u>If you do not get these answers, try the sums again and click on the buttons carefully.</u>

Sum	Answer
73 + 23 =	96
107 − 16 =	91
5*3 =	15
64/4 =	16
6 + 7*73 =	949
√144 = (√ means square root)	12
684*63 − 625 =	42467
74*74/−1 =	−5476
−9*−9 =	81
10% of 40 (of is*)	4
£150 + VAT at 17.5%	176.25

The quickest way to do this is to work out 117.5% of £150.

WINDOWS CALCULATOR

Scientific calculator

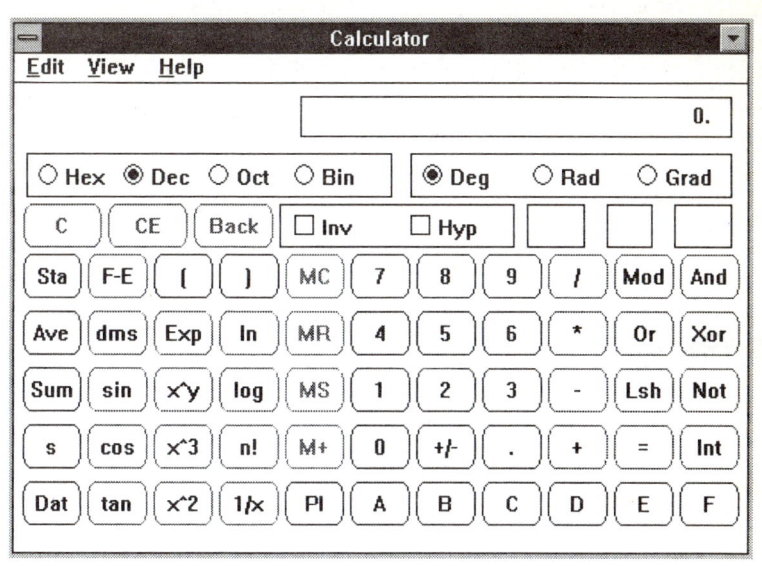

Figure 11.2

The scientific calculator has a number of different modes and will load in the mode in which it was last used. The calculator in figure 11.2 is in the default mode of **Dec** which means it will use the decimal (base 10) numbering system and **Deg** which means that degrees will be used for trigonometric input.

The scientific calculator has many more functions than the standard calculator, including trigonometric functions, logarithms, powers and statistical functions. In addition, the scientific calculator has a number of features used in computer programming, such as the ability to calculate in binary (base 2), hexadecimal (base 16) and octal (base 8), and the use of logical functions AND, OR, NOT, etc. In arithmetic calculations, the scientific calculator follows the rules of arithmetic precedence and also allows the use of up to 25 levels of brackets. Chapter 22 gives more details on the advanced functions of the scientific calculator.

Try some of these calculations using the scientific calculator. The calculations are concentrated on the more commonly used functions and do not require great mathematical ability. Hints are given as to which buttons to use. Check your answers against those given.

— 113 —

WINDOWS

Sum	Hint	Answer
(234 + 892)/23		48.95652173913
45^2		2025
Cube root of 5940	Switch to **Inv** mode then use **cubed** button	18.11043221039
12 factorial	! button	479001600
Convert 400 to binary		110010000
Convert 1563 to hexadecimal		61B
2 to the power 15	Use **x^y** button	32768
278.546*.4618 as a whole number	Do the calculation then use the **Int** button to give the integer part of the answer.	128
Remainder when 36105 is divided by 13	Type the first number, press the **Mod** button then type the second number.	4
Sine of 45°		0.7071067811865
$(31 + 121)^3/(15^2-99)$		27871.49206349

Using the Clipboard

Whenever you use Calculator to perform a calculation, the answer can be copied to the Clipboard. The result can then be pasted into any other Windows application. This saves you having to remember or write down the answer. To place the answer in the Clipboard, click on EDIT then on COPY.

Summary

In this chapter you have

- loaded and used the Windows Calculator;
- seen the limitations of the standard calculator;
- used the scientific calculator;
- explored some of the more advanced functions of the scientific calculator;
- exported results of calculations to the Clipboard.

12
— FUN WITH SOUND —

3.1 only

With Windows 3.1, your computer gains an added dimension. Windows 3.1 offers a range of features for **multimedia** use. Multimedia encompasses the use of CD ROM drives, videos, sound, etc. to add variety and interest to computer output. This chapter shows you how to use Windows Sound Recorder to play sounds, edit them and even record your own. Chapter 24 in the Reference section contains more detailed information on using Sound Recorder.

NB **The facilities described in this chapter are only available in Windows 3.1. Windows 3.0 does not support sound cards. The chapter also requires a sound card which is supported by Windows.**

A sound card is a printed circuit board which can be installed in your computer. Sound cards often come with speakers so that you can hear what you produce in stereo sound, rather than through the feeble internal speaker in the computer.

Choosing a sound card

Which sound card you should buy depends on three main factors:

- your budget;
- what you want to use it for;
- the sound quality you require.

The price of sound cards varies from about £50 to £200, so you have to make sure that you are buying one which is suitable for your needs. If you require good quality stereo sound, then buying some speakers would be a wise option. Many sound deals come with speakers included, and these are often cheaper than buying them separately. You should look for speakers similar to those used for personal stereos or portable CD players. These are of sufficient quality and are of a reasonable price. Larger speaker units generally produce a higher quality of sound because they have more speakers inside them, one for each frequency range. When buying speakers, make sure they can be connected to your sound card. All sound cards use speakers which are connected by a single 3.5 mm jack plug.

One of the most popular sound cards is the SoundBlaster card produced by Westpoint Creative Labs Inc. The SoundBlaster card is supported by almost every program which supports a sound card including Windows. The AdLib card from AdLib Inc. was one of the first sound cards and is still the most widely supported. Nearly all other sound cards can emulate the AdLib card.

If you only want to use your sound card for games or playing the occasional tune, you don't want to record your own sounds and are not particularly bothered about quality, you should be looking at one of the cheaper cards. You can fit external speakers or head-phones if you wish.

If you want to use your card more frequently with a high quality of sound output and wish to record your own sounds, you should invest in a sound card in the middle price range and some speakers. One of the most popular of this kind is the SoundBlaster 2 card which, at the time of going to press, costs about £70.

If you wish to record your own sounds, sample and play them back, you need a card which allows for sound input from external sources. At the time of going to press, these cards can cost anything from £80 upwards.

To get the best out of one of these sound cards, stereo speakers are essential. The SoundBlaster Pro card or the Maestro Pro from Computer Peripherals Inc. are currently about £100 and will allow you to record your own sounds.

Microsoft offer the Microsoft Sound System, which is designed to operate within Windows. The pack includes a microphone and headphones, and software which will enable you to 'talk' to the computer.

Sound in Windows

The Windows 3.1 sound program is called Sound Recorder. Sound Recorder can be found in the Accessories group of Program Manager.

Double click on the Sound Recorder icon. When Sound Recorder has loaded, the screen shown in figure 12.1 will be displayed.

Figure 12.1

The horizontal line in the display in figure 12.1 shows the pattern of the sound sample currently in memory. This line is shown in green on your screen. The buttons at the bottom of the window perform the same functions as on a tape recorder. These are shown in figure 12.2.

Rewind   Forward   Play   Stop   Record

Figure 12.2

FUN WITH SOUND

Loading a sound file

To load a sound file, click on FILE then on OPEN to display the Open box. This shows a list of the standard sound files which are supplied with Windows. The standard files are mainly dings, chimes and chords. The Windows format for sound files is the WAV format. All files of this format will be displayed in the File Name box. Select the file to be opened. The screen after a WAV file has been loaded is as in figure 12.3. The horizontal green line has changed to a pattern of different thicknesses which represents the volume and frequency of the sounds in the sample.

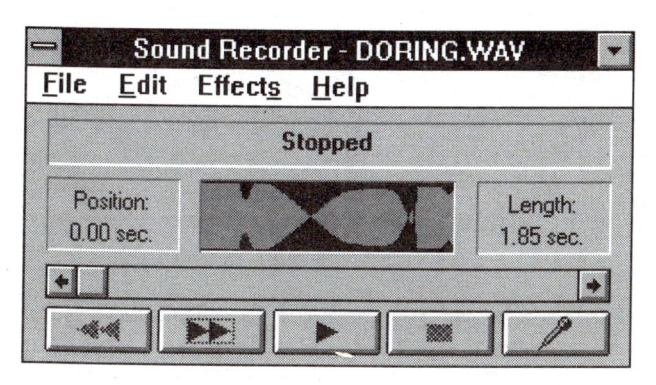

Figure 12.3

Load the TADA.WAV file from the WINDOWS directory. Click on Play to hear the sound and view the frequency pattern.

Special effects

Sound Recorder allows you to change the sound in a number of different ways. Click on EFFECTS to display the Effects menu shown in figure 12.4.

WINDOWS

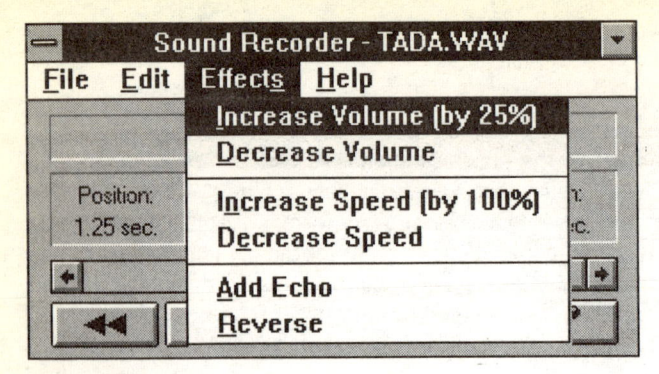

Figure 12.4

The available effects enable you to change the volume, change the speed, add an echo and reverse the sample. These are explained in more detail in chapter 24.

─────── Mixing sounds ───────

You can also change the sample from the Edit menu. This allows you to delete parts of the sample and insert and mix the sample with other files. Click on EDIT to display the Edit menu as shown in figure 12.5.

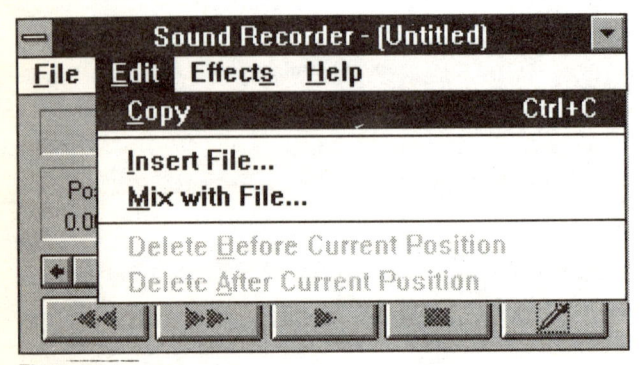

Figure 12.5

When you mix the current sample with another sample, both of the samples are played together. Mixing is effective when the tune and lyrics

— 120 —

FUN WITH SOUND

are recorded in separate files. To mix the samples, click on MIX WITH FILE to display the box as shown in figure 12.6.

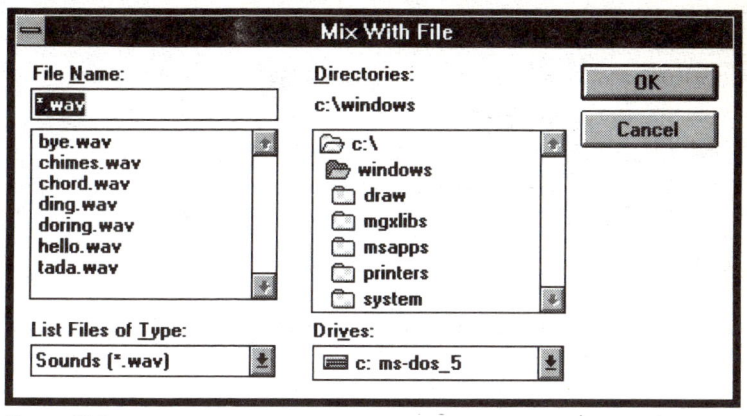

Figure 12.6

Highlight and select the file to be mixed. The selected file will then be mixed with the current sample. Mixing starts from the current point in the first file. If the sample which is being mixed is longer than the current sample, the length of the sample will be increased to match.

- *Load TADA.WAV as the current sample.*
- *Add an echo to TADA.WAV.*
- *Now insert the DING.WAV file at the beginning.*
- *Speed up the sample by 100%.*
- *Mix the CHIMES.WAV file with the whole sample.*
- *Decrease the speed by 100%.*

You should now have a sample which has slow chimes mixed with a beep and a fanfare.

The next task can only be done if you have purchased the disk pack version of the book.

- *Mix the file WORDS.WAV (from the companion disk) with TADA.WAV file from the Windows directory.*
- *Click on Play to hear the sound.*
- *Try changing the volume and speed.*
- *Add an echo.*

Saving the sound file

To save the sound file, click on FILE then on SAVE or SAVE AS. If you choose Save, the file will be saved with the current file name. Save As requests you to enter a file name. Enter a file name for the sample and click on OK. Windows sound files are saved with a WAV extension. The default directory is the WINDOWS directory.

When you are happy with the effects, save your mixed file with a suitable file name.

Embedding a sound

Sounds can be placed into the Clipboard. This makes them available to other applications. For example, you can embed sound files into a Write document. Then, when looking through your document, you can double click on the embedded sound icon to play the sound. A Write document with an embedded sound is shown in figure 12.7.

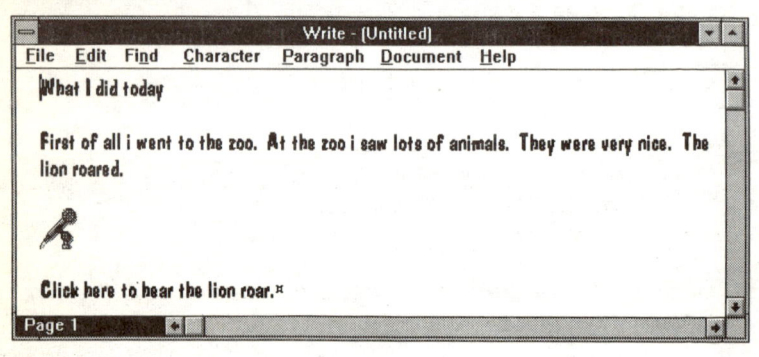

Figure 12.7

To embed a sound, first copy the sound to the Clipboard. To do this, click on EDIT then on COPY. Then go into Write and click on EDIT then on PASTE. This will insert the embedded sound icon into the document. The sound can then be played by double clicking on the icon.

FUN WITH SOUND

Recording sound samples

More sophisticated sound cards will have a socket on the card for a microphone. If your sound card has this facility, you can plug a suitable microphone with a 3.5 mm jack plug into the socket. You can then record your own voice into Sound Recorder, add an echo to it, or change the sound in other ways using the Effects menu. To record from a microphone, click on the microphone button to put Sound Recorder into record mode. Recording sound samples requires large amounts of memory, so it is better to record short sound samples.

It is also possible to buy a lead which has a 3.5 mm jack plug on one end and two plugs (usually one red and one white) on the other end. A suitable lead may well be supplied with your sound card kit, particularly the more sophisticated cards. With this lead, the sound card can be connected to some hi-fi systems and some electronic keyboards as well. The 3.5 mm end of the wire is plugged into the sound card and the two plugs on the other end into the hi-fi keyboard sockets. To record the output from the hi-fi or keyboard, click on the record button and play on the keyboard or start the music playing.

If you have a sound card with recording facilities, experiment with different sounds, recording them into the computer and playing them back. Some activities are suggested below:

Record an appropriate message for starting or exiting from Windows. To replace the existing sound (TADA) with your own version requires a change to the Windows sound settings. This is done through Control Panel and is described on page 212 in chapter 18.

Record the sound of a lion roaring (or any other animal noise), and try out the sound embedding techniques by creating the document shown in figure 12.7.

Summary

In this chapter you have
- opened Windows sound files;
- added effects to sound files;

- inserted and mixed sound files;
- saved sound files;
- embedded sound files in documents;
- recorded your own sound files.

13

PROJECTS

This chapter aims to put together the skills you have learnt in previous chapters and use them in a number of small projects to create something useful. Extension tasks are suggested for most tasks, and the ideas can be expanded or adapted to meet your own personal interests. By now, you will be pretty good at finding your way around Windows. This chapter expects you to be able to do the basic things. The few new methods which are needed are explained. If you need help, you will either have to look back at your previous work, use Windows Help or look at the Reference section of the book.

Remember to save your work frequently when working in Windows, or any other computer program. You are advised to save every ten minutes or so, and also every time you achieve a target. If you are creating a complicated drawing with lots of picture elements, it would be a good idea to save each time an element was finished. Then, if you make a mess of the next stage, you can always re-open the previously saved version on the disk and start again. This is often quicker than undoing the mistakes you have made.

— Project 1   Design a business card —

This is a simple project for you to start with. You can design a card to either advertise yourself or your business, or you could invent a fictitious company.

WINDOWS

Paintbrush is the best program for producing a business card. The first thing that needs to be done is to draw a frame for your business card. Aim for a card about 10 cm by 6 cm, as shown in figure 13.1. Add the text for the card – probably the company name, your name, your position and the address and telephone number(s). Use different fonts for the different parts of the text.

You can give the card more impact and make it look more visually attractive by adding graphics. You could draw a logo for your company and place this onto the card as a finishing touch, as shown in figure 13.1.

The brain logo is an element of the file PSYLOGO.PCX on the companion disk and can be extracted from the picture in Paintbrush, copied to the Clipboard and then used in your design.

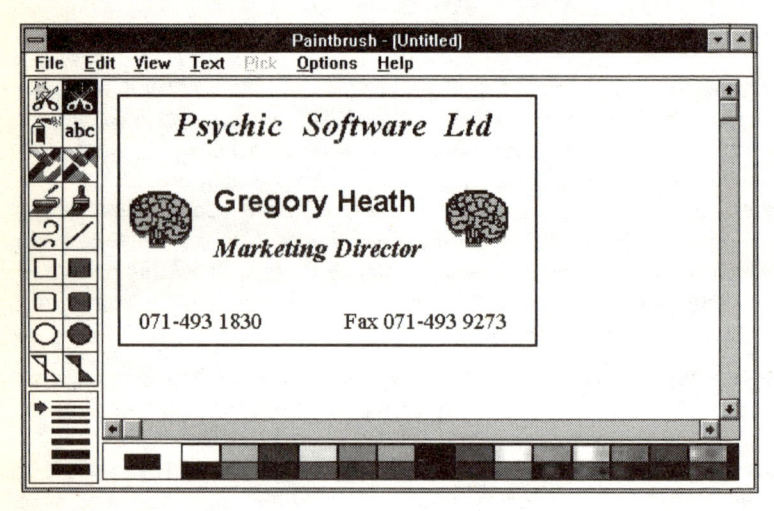

Figure 13.1

The business card is now finished. Remember to save your work frequently, and, if possible, print the card to see what it looks like.

Some further ideas for you to try

- Duplicate this business card several time on a page and then print it on coloured card. You can then cut the cards up and use them!
- Create some cards for your friends and colleagues.
- Similar cards could be used as invitation cards.

PROJECTS

– Project 2 Christmas card mailing list –

Don't you hate having to write out the same names and addresses year after year on your Christmas card envelopes? Not to mention forgetting to send a card to some people. Wouldn't it be a lot easier if you had all the names and addresses stored on a database? Using a database has the advantage of making it easy to keep the list up to date by adding new cards, changing addresses when required, and removing cards that are no longer required.

The best Windows program to do this job is Cardfile. Load Cardfile and enter the name and address of one of your friends. It might be a good idea to use the Index Line to hold their surname followed by their initials or first name. You will want more than one card on your Cardfile of names and addresses, so add some more of your colleagues and friends to the file. The finished Cardfile will look something like the one in figure 13.2. You will probably want to create the file gradually rather than all at once. Remember to save your work at regular intervals.

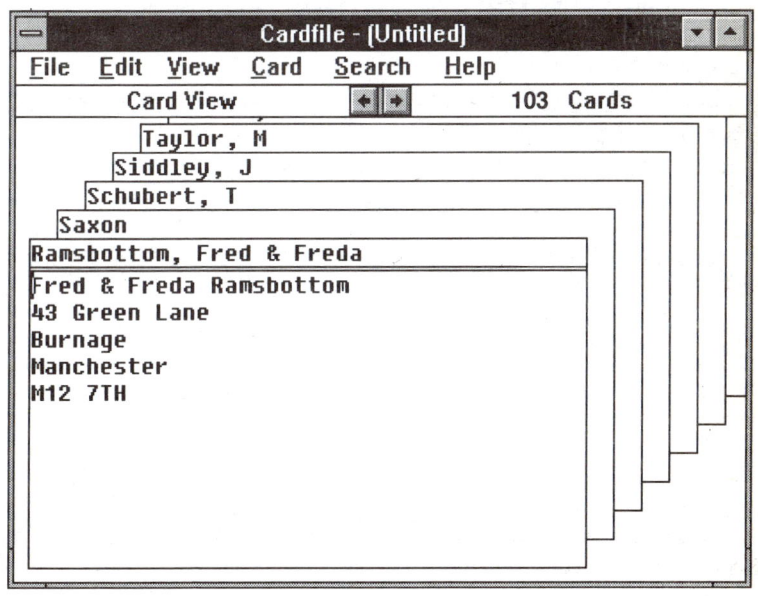

Figure 13.2

Once the Cardfile has a reasonable number of cards, you can begin to use it. Printing from List view will produce a printed list for you to use when writing the cards. Printing the cards themselves will produce an address list which will save you having to look up all the addresses as you write the cards.

Some further ideas for you to try

- Create a file of people to whom you send birthday cards. Include their date of birth so you know when to send the card. You could then enter and mark these dates in Calendar so that you will be reminded in the correct month.
- Print out the information on the Cardfile for your diary or address book.

Project 3 SuperTex 3

A company called Psychic Software has written a software package called SuperTex 3 which it now plans to market. The Managing Director has decided to stage a nationwide launch, and it is your job to get the publicity information out to as many people as possible. You have decided to hold the launches at prestigious hotels in major cities, with a champagne presentation of the new package. You need to produce an effective and striking mailshot to be sent out with complimentary tickets to people on a pre-produced database. With only the basic Windows setup, you set about the task.

Writing the main text

To write the main text you have decided to use Microsoft Write. Try to write your own text in Write to advertise this event. If you are completely stuck, you could use the text opposite.

The following text is supplied on the companion disk and is stored with a file name of PSYCHIC.WRI.

PROJECTS

```
SuperTex 3 Launch

Psychic Software is very pleased to announce the release of its latest
computer application for the Windows environment. SuperTex 3 is to be
launched in May at a number of special launches across the country. You have
been invited to these launches and your complimentary ticket is included.

At the launches there will be demonstrations of SuperTex 3, as well as other
Psychic Software applications. For all who attend there will also be a glass
of champagne and informal time to allow you to ask any questions and have
hands on experience of SuperTex 3.

At each venue you will have the opportunity to purchase SuperTex 3 at the
special launch price of £299 as opposed to a retail price of £399. You can
take your copy away with you on the day.

The dates for the launches across the country are:

    10th May     Dorchester Hotel, London
    14th May     Victoria Hotel, Manchester
    17th May     Hotel Greenforth, Birmingham
    22nd May     Edinburgh Hotel, Edinburgh

We hope to see you on one of these dates.


Gregory Heath
Marketing Director
Psychic Software Ltd
```

Now the main text is written, you can improve its appearance. This is a good point to remind you to save your work. You don't want to lose the work you have already done.

Making the document more eye-catching

There are a number of ways in which you can make your documents more exciting. Text can be centred, emboldened, underlined or italicised, sections of text can be tabbed or indented, and different fonts and text sizes can be used. All the fonts installed on your system are available. Beware though, too many fonts can make a document look cluttered and unclear, so stick to two or three different fonts. Remember that fonts can also be bold and italic so use these to add impact. Try using larger and bolder fonts for your headings, as these stand out better.

Figures 13.3 and 13.4 show two copies of the same document, one without fonts and one with fonts. As you can see, using different fonts can make all the difference to a document.

WINDOWS

Before

```
SuperTex 3 Launch

Psychic Software is very pleased to announce the release of its latest computer application for
the Windows environment. SuperTex 3 is to be launched in May at a number of special launches
across the country. You have been invited to these launches and your complimentary ticket is
included.

At the launches there will be demonstrations of SuperTex 3, as well as other Psychic Software
applications. For all who attend there will also be a glass of champagne and informal time to
allow you to ask any questions and have hands on experience of SuperTex 3.

At each venue you will have the opportunity to purchase SuperTex 3 at the special launch price
of £299 as opposed to a retail price of £399. You can take your copy away with you on the day.

The dates for the launches across the country are:

        10th May         Dorchester Hotel, London
        14th May         Victoria Hotel, Manchester
        17th May         Hotel Greenforth, Birmingham
        22nd May         Edinburgh Hotel, Edinburgh

We hope to see you on one of these dates.


Gregory Heath
Marketing Director
Psychic Software Ltd
```

Figure 13.3

After

SuperTex 3 Launch

Psychic Software is very pleased to announce the release of its latest computer application for the Windows environment. SuperTex 3 is to be launched in May at a number of special launches across the country. You have been invited to these launches and your complimentary ticket is included.

At the launches there will be demonstrations of SuperTex 3, as well as other Psychic Software applications. For all who attend there will also be a glass of champagne and informal time to allow you to ask any questions and have hands on experience of SuperTex 3.

At each venue you will have the opportunity to purchase SuperTex 3 at the special launch price of £299 as opposed to a retail price of £399. You can take your copy away with you on the day.

The dates for the launches across the country are:

10th May   *Dorchester Hotel, London*
14th May   *Victoria Hotel, Manchester*
17th May   *Hotel Greenforth, Birmingham*
22nd May   *Edinburgh Hotel, Edinburgh*

We hope to see you on one of these dates.

Gregory Heath
Marketing Director
Psychic Software Ltd

Figure 13.4

PROJECTS

You have shown the document to your Managing Director, and he likes it, but thinks it still lacks the impact to make people really notice it and not throw it away without reading it. He suggests adding some pictures or graphics to the document to make it look more eye-catching. You decide to add Psychic Software's logo to the document. Draw a suitable logo using Paintbrush. You can use any of the tools and colours to produce your logo.

Psychic Software Ltd

Figure 13.5

Figure 13.5 shows the sample brain logo which is supplied on the companion disk. If you wish to use it load the Paintbrush package and open the file called PSYLOGO.PCX.

When you have drawn and saved your logo it needs to be added to the Write document. Copy the Paintbrush logo to the Clipboard. Switch to the Write window and insert the logo at the required place. The best place to add the logo is probably at the top of your document, maybe in the centre, or at the left or at the right. To move the logo to the centre or to the right, use the alignment options. If your logo is too big and overpowers the rest of the document then it can be reduced from the Edit menu.

As the finishing touch to the leaflet, you now decide to add an extra picture to the main body of the text. This will break up the bulk of the text and make it more attractive to the reader. Draw another picture in Paintbrush and insert it in the document in the same way as before. Some ideas may be champagne glasses, disks, software cases, etc.

For those with the disk version of the book, there is a picture file on the companion disk called PSYCHAMP.PCX which is a picture of some champagne glasses.

After adding this picture, you should have a finished mailshot looking something like that shown in figure 13.6.

WINDOWS

> **Psychic Software Ltd**
>
> ### SuperTex 3 Launch
>
> Psychic Software is very pleased to announce the release of its latest computer application for the Windows environment. SuperTex 3 is to be launched in May at a number of special launches across the country. You have been invited to these launches and your complimentary ticket is included.
>
> At the launches there will be demonstrations of SuperTex 3, as well as other Psychic Software applications. For all who attend there will also be a glass of champagne and informal time to allow you to ask any questions and have hands on experience of SuperTex 3.
>
> At each venue you will have the opportunity to purchase SuperTex 3 at the special launch price of SuperTex 3 of £299 as opposed to a retail price of £399. You can take your copy away with you on the day.
>
> The dates for the launches across the country are:
>
> | | |
> |---|---|
> | 10th May | Dorchester Hotel, London |
> | 14th May | Victoria Hotel, Manchester |
> | 17th May | Hotel Greenforth, Birmingham |
> | 22nd May | Edinburgh Hotel, Edinburgh |
>
> We hope to see you on one of these dates.
>
> Gregory Heath
> Marketing Director
> Psychic Software

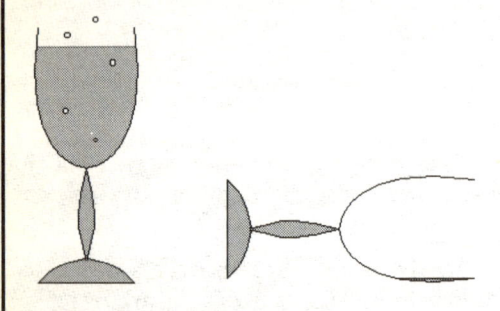

Figure 13.6

Some further ideas for you to try

- Draw a signature in Paintbrush and import it into the space at the bottom of the document.
- Try creating the invitation to the event, with information and pictures.

PROJECTS

- Create an advertising leaflet for an event with which you are involved.

─── Project 4 ID Cards ───

You are a Security Manager at a large film studio. One of your many duties is to ensure that the people who are entering the sets are actually supposed to be there. To do this, you decide to issue them all with cards, showing their photograph, to allow them into the building.

You decide to use Cardfile for the task. The first thing to do is to enter the basic information for each person. Use their name as the Index Line. Some sample data which you might like to use is given below.

Surname	First name	Job	Film	Times
Allen	Woody	Director	Interiors	All day
Chaplin	Charlie	Comedy Actor	Many	All day
Dickens	Charles	Script Writer	Scrooge	10am - 5pm
Hardy	Oliver	Comedy Actor	Many	All day
Garland	Judy	Actress	The Wizard of Oz	All day
Monroe	Marilyn	Actress	Some Like it Hot	9am - 9pm
Mozart	Wolfgang	Composer	Many	10am - 6pm
Niven	David	Actor	Separate Tables	10am - 7pm
Shakespeare	William	Playwright	Hamlet	9am - 8pm
Tolkein	John	Script Writer	The Hobbit	All day
Van Gogh	Vincent	Artist	Many	All day
Wayne	John	Actor	Red River	All day

The data is supplied on the companion disk as a file called ID1.CRD.

When all the data has been entered, you should have a file similar to the one shown in figure 13.7.

Remember to save your Cardfile. Now you can add pictures of each of the stars to the cards. First you will have to draw them! Open Paintbrush and use the tools to draw the faces. With the limited capabilities of Paintbrush, you may not be able to draw very good pictures of the stars, but it doesn't matter!

If you have the companion disk there are clip art files of the stars on this disk. The file names are listed below. The pictures are stored in PCX format and can be opened in Paintbrush.

— 133 —

WINDOWS

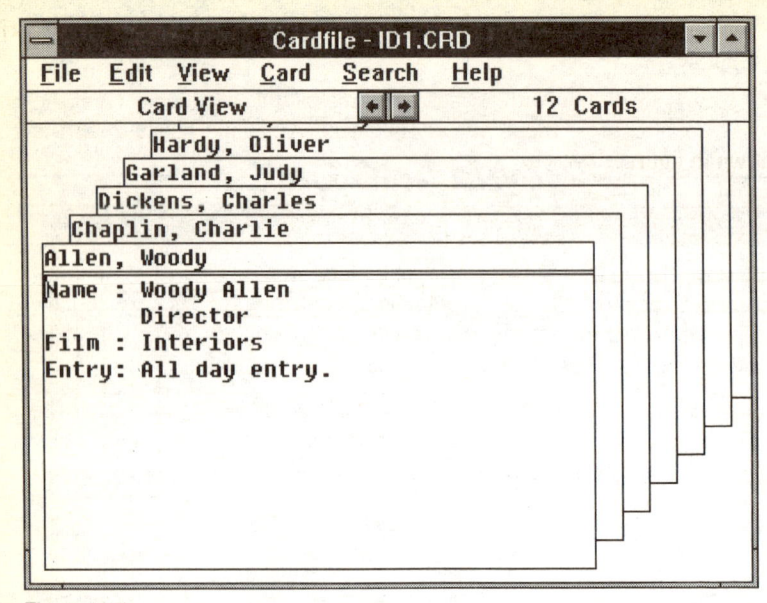

```
┌─────────────────────────────────────────────────┐
│ ─         Cardfile - ID1.CRD              ▼ ▲  │
├─────────────────────────────────────────────────┤
│ File  Edit  View  Card  Search  Help           │
├─────────────────────────────────────────────────┤
│        Card View      ◄ ►        12 Cards      │
│          Hardy, Oliver                          │
│         Garland, Judy                           │
│        Dickens, Charles                         │
│       Chaplin, Charlie                          │
│ Allen, Woody                                    │
│ Name : Woody Allen                              │
│         Director                                │
│ Film : Interiors                                │
│ Entry: All day entry.                           │
│                                                 │
└─────────────────────────────────────────────────┘
```

Figure 13.7

Woody Allen	ALLEN.PCX
Charlie Chaplin	CHAPLIN.PCX
Charles Dickens	DICKENS.PCX
Oliver Hardy	HARDY.PCX
Judy Garland	GARLAND.PCX
Marilyn Monroe	MONROE.PCX
Wolfgang Mozart	MOZART.PCX
David Niven	NIVEN.PCX
William Shakespeare	SHAKSPRE.PCX
John Tolkein	TOLKEIN.PCX
Vincent Van Gogh	VANGOGH.PCX
John Wayne	WAYNE.PCX

The pictures will have to be inserted into Cardfile one by one.

- Create or open the picture in Paintbrush.
- Copy the Paintbrush picture to the Clipboard.
- Switch to Cardfile.
- Paste the picture from the Clipboard onto the card. Make sure you have the correct card at the front of the Cardfile. Remember you will need to be in Edit Picture rather than text.
- Move the picture over to the right hand side of the card.

PROJECTS

Remember that Windows 3.0 is unable to size the picture to fit onto the card.

You will finally end up with a Cardfile with a picture card for each of the stars. You can print these out as ID cards. A sample finished card is shown in figure 13.8.

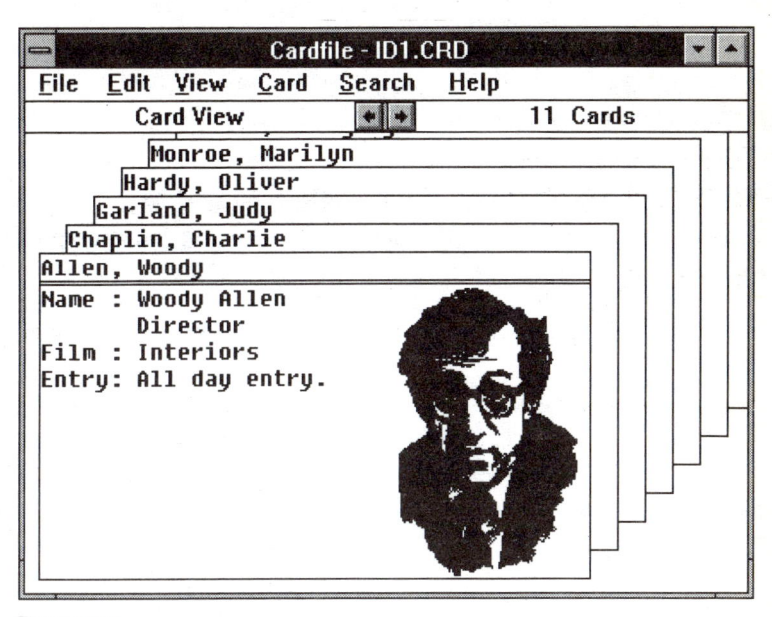

Figure 13.8

Project 5 Deserted!

This project requires you to have the companion disk, because the files which are needed are on the disk. The following files are included on the disk for you to use:

DES.WRI   the basic text
DESCAR.PCX   a picture of a police car
DESDOG.PCX   a picture of the clay dog
DESDOWN.PCX   a plan of the downstairs
DESMAN.PCX   a picture of a man

— 135 —

WINDOWS

DESOUTS.PCX	a plan of the outside
DESSND1.WAV	sound files:
	'Let's make a getaway guys! Easier said than done! Ouch!' sound with a car in the background
DESSND2.WAV	the sound of a person falling over pipes
DESSPEE.PCX	a picture of speech bubbles, 'Let's make a getaway guys!'
	Easier said than done! Ouch!'
DESSTRS.PCX	a picture of pipes by the stairs
DESUPST.PCX	a plan of the upstairs

☺ As well as the files listed above you can use any graphics files and clip art used in previous activities or that you have created yourself.

The idea is that you are a publisher and you have received a story written as a basic Windows Write file. You have commissioned an artist to draw some pictures to go into the book. Your job is to insert all the graphics and the sound files at suitable places in the document to create the finished product.

The artist has forgotten to draw the final THE END! sign to put at the end of the story. It looks like you will have to draw one of these yourself. Use Paintbrush and make it really eye-catching!

🎵

If you do not have a sound card, you will not be able to play the sounds. Leave the two sound files out of your document.

Hard luck, you get no help with this one!

Summary

This chapter has suggested some ideas for using the programs in Windows to produce useful output. You will have thought of many other ideas while working through the chapters in this part of the book. You now have the necessary skills to put your ideas into practice.

14
FUN WITH THE COMPANION DISK

The whole of this chapter requires the use of the companion disk. The games and programs are used from the floppy disk, and do not need to be installed on your hard disk.

In addition to the two basic games and set of accessories which are supplied with Windows, there are many more which can be obtained from various sources; shareware libraries, for example, have a wide selection. Shareware software is available for the cost of the disks on a trial basis. Payment is made to the owner if you decide to use the program. The companion disk to this book contains an accessory and three extra games. This chapter shows you how to use the programs on the companion disk.

IconWorks icon editor

IconWorks is a sample application supplied with Microsoft Visual Basic. As you will know by now, an icon is a small picture used to represent a program. IconWorks allows you to create your own icons and save them in icon files. The icons you produce can then be used instead of the standard icons in Program Manager.

Loading IconWorks

To load the IconWorks program, insert the disk in drive A:, and click on FILE then on RUN to display the Run box shown in figure 14.1. On the Command Line, type A:ICONWRKS and press the Enter key.

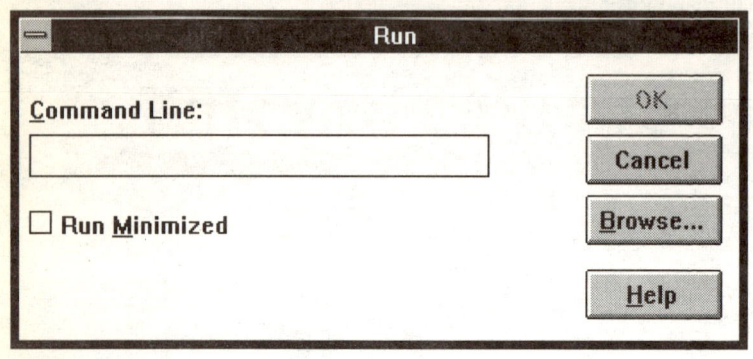

Figure 14.1

3.1 only

Windows 3.1 offers an alternative method using the Browse option. Browse enables you to use the mouse to select the drive, directory and file name of the file to be run. Click on Browse to display the Browse dialog box, as shown in figure 14.2.

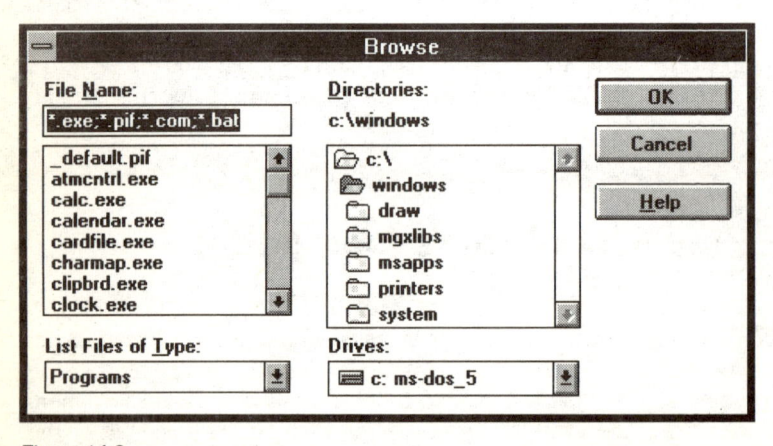

Figure 14.2

FUN WITH THE COMPANION DISK

To load the program, first click on A: from the Drives box. This will display the program files available on drive A. Double click on ICONWRKS.EXE in the File Name list box.

If, when trying to load this program, a message appears, saying that you need to be running in either standard or enhanced mode, please refer to chapter 25 for information on these modes.

IconWorks is quite a large program so it may take a while to load. After the IconWorks program has loaded, the screen shown in figure 14.3 will be displayed. The main parts of the screen are labelled in this diagram.

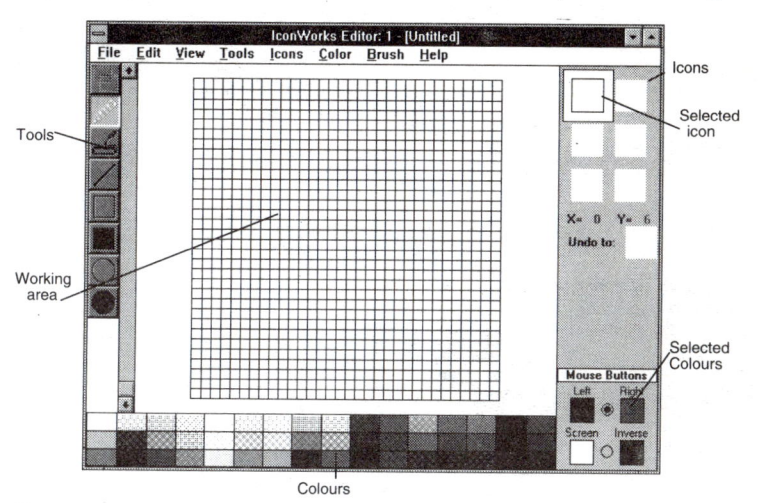

Figure 14.3

Editing an icon

The IconWorks tools are shown in figure 14.4. They are similar to the tools used in Paintbrush.

Try using the different tools to draw a car or a van icon like the one shown in figure 14.5.

This icon is stored with the file name VAN.ICO on the companion disk.

IconWorks allows you to have up to six icons open at once. This is useful when you wish to copy part of one icon into another. The icons are shown

— 139 —

WINDOWS

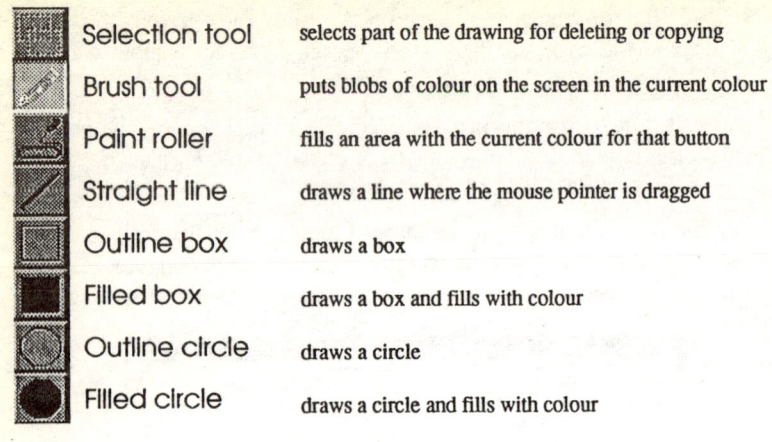

	Selection tool	selects part of the drawing for deleting or copying
	Brush tool	puts blobs of colour on the screen in the current colour
	Paint roller	fills an area with the current colour for that button
	Straight line	draws a line where the mouse pointer is dragged
	Outline box	draws a box
	Filled box	draws a box and fills with colour
	Outline circle	draws a circle
	Filled circle	draws a circle and fills with colour

Figure 14.4

Figure 14.5

in the top right-hand corner. The icon shown with the border around it is the currently selected icon.

IconWorks is a full featured application and has many options, including comprehensive on-line Help. Click on HELP or press the F1 key to call up the Help screens.

Saving an icon

To save an icon, select the icon to be saved. Click on FILE then on SAVE or SAVE AS to display the Save Icon box shown in figure 14.6.

FUN WITH THE COMPANION DISK

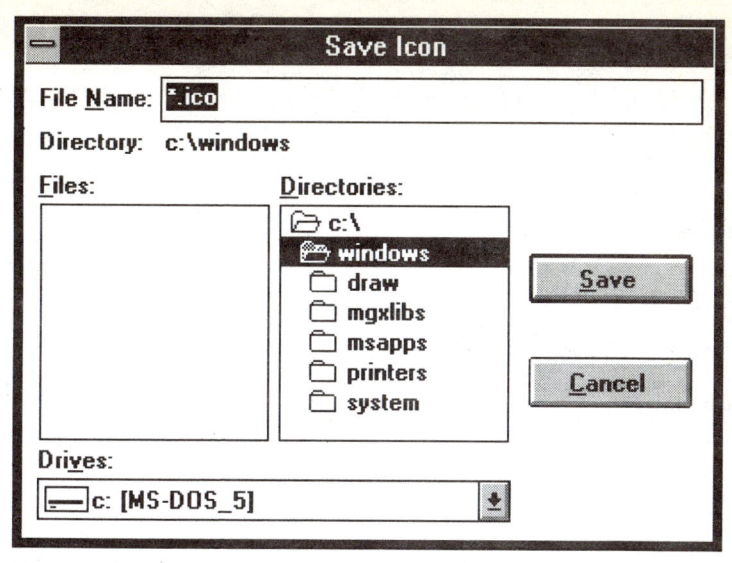

Figure 14.6

Type a file name and click on OK. The file will be given an extension of ICO and saved in the WINDOWS directory by default. Any icons you save can be re-loaded into IconWorks and can also be used in Program Manager groups.

Loading an icon

Remember that up to six icons can be open at the same time. Your van or car icon will be in the first icon space. To open an icon into one of the other icon spaces, click on the icon space to select it, then click on FILE and on OPEN. This will display the IconWorks Viewer window as shown in figure 14.7. Select the file or files to be loaded. The icon will be loaded into the current icon space.

Open any five of the following icon files (shown in figure 14.8) into the spaces on the screen.

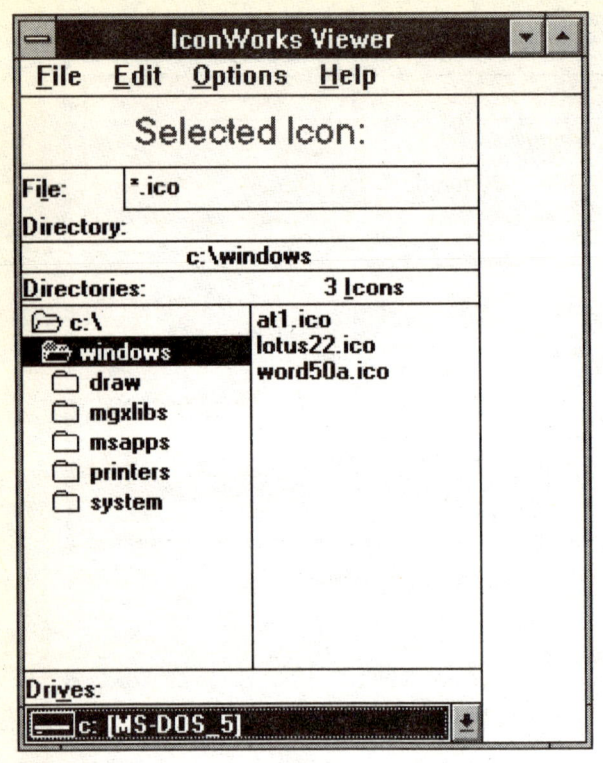

Figure 14.7

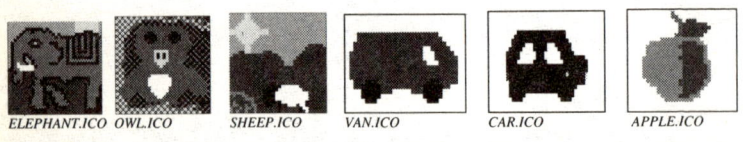

ELEPHANT.ICO OWL.ICO   SHEEP.ICO   VAN.ICO   CAR.ICO   APPLE.ICO

Figure 14.8

Adding an icon to Program Manager

Icons used in Program Manager, particularly for DOS programs, tend to be very much the same. An example of this is shown in figure 14.9. Tools such as IconWorks can be used to replace these with icons which are more representative of the application. The windows could then look like figure 14.10.

FUN WITH THE COMPANION DISK

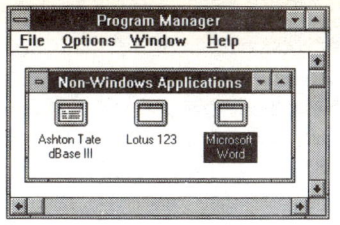

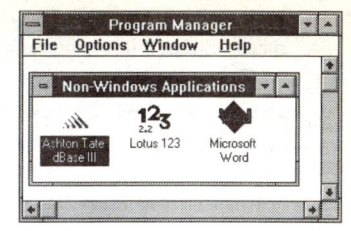

Figure 14.9

Figure 14.10

Click on FILE then on PROPERTIES to display the Program Item Properties box shown in figure 14.11. Select Change Icon and enter the icon name or use the Browse option. The new icon will be displayed in the Properties box. Click on OK and the icon will be changed in the group.

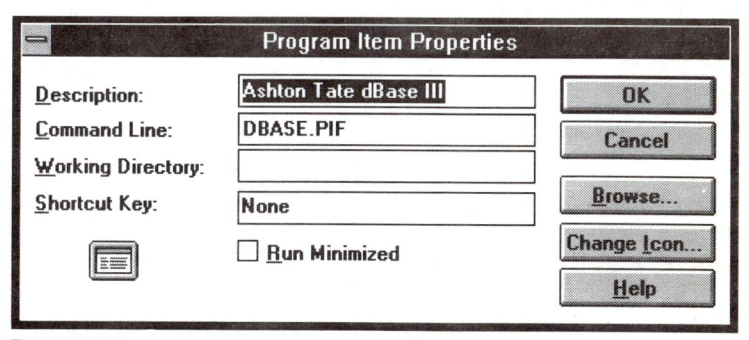

Figure 14.11

Dominoes

This game is a computer version of dominoes in which you play against the computer. The dominoes used in the game range from double blank to double six. If you can play all your dominoes before the computer, you win!

How to play Dominoes

The basic idea of the game is to play all your dominoes before the other player. You can only play a domino if either of its ends are the same as one

— 143 —

of the ends of the dominoes already played. The game is started by the player who holds the highest double. After you have played a domino, you automatically get another from the pile of dominoes still to be picked up. If there are no dominoes left in the pile, you are not given another. If you find that you cannot play any of the dominoes in your rack then you should pick up an extra domino from the pile. Continue picking up until you have a domino that can be played. If there are no dominoes left, you have to pass your turn to the other player. If neither player has any dominoes that will go, the computer counts up the number of dots on each player's rack, and the one with the least number of dots wins.

Loading Dominoes

Before the game can be played, the Dominoes program has to be loaded from the companion disk. To do this, insert the disk in drive A: and click on FILE then on RUN. Type A:DOMINOES and press the Enter key. Alternatively in version 3.1 the file can be selected using the Browse option as described earlier. The Dominoes program is a large one, and it may take a while before the board is displayed.

> If, when trying to load this program, a message appears saying that you need to be running in either standard or enhanced mode please refer to chapter 25 for information on these modes.

The playing board

After Dominoes has loaded, the screen will be similar to the one shown in figure 14.12.

Seven dominoes or tiles are dealt to each player. Your rack of tiles is shown in the centre of the screen. The tiles held by your opponent, the computer, are represented by the box labelled **My tiles**. You cannot see the computer's tiles, as this would give you an unfair advantage. Although, it may seem as if the computer can see your tiles, they are only displayed for you to see, and the computer does not look at them when deciding what to play. The box labelled **Tiles left** shows how many dominoes are still to be picked up. The bar at the bottom of the screen is the **information line**. On a colour monitor this line is yellow. The information line tells you what is currently happening in the game, and the move played by the computer. As the dominoes are played, they are displayed around the outside edge of the screen.

FUN WITH THE COMPANION DISK

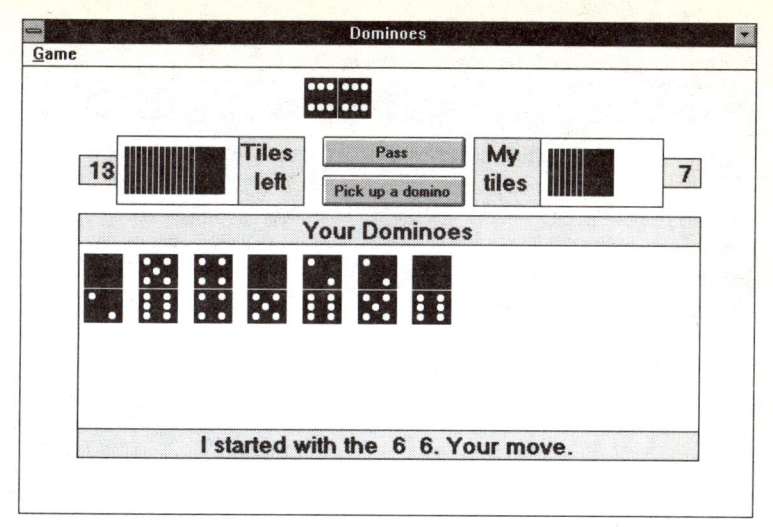

Figure 14.12

Starting the game

The game is started by the player with the highest double. Figure 14.12 shows that the game was started by the computer with double six, as this was the highest double held by either player. If you have the highest double, the line across the bottom of the screen will display: You have the highest double. You start.

To play a domino, click on the one you wish to play. It will automatically be played in the correct place. If the domino can be played at either end, it will be played at the left. Each player then plays in turn. If you are unable to play any dominoes, click on the Pick up a Domino button. If you cannot go and there are no dominoes left, click on the Pass button. In figure 14.13, there are no dominoes left and no tiles will go so the player has to pass.

If a situation arises during the game where neither player can go, the computer will count up the number of dots on the tiles in each rack and the player with the lowest number of dots wins. If you manage to beat the computer, the dialog box shown in figure 14.14 is displayed.

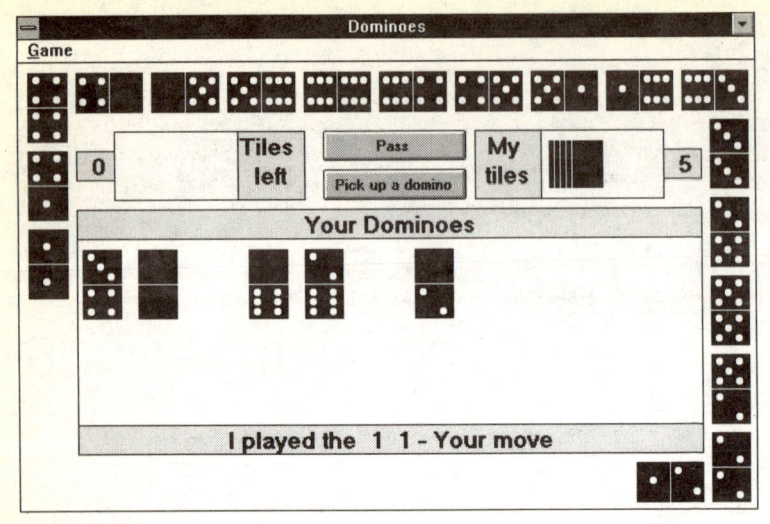

Figure 14.13

Figure 14.14

If you choose Yes, each player is given a new rack of dominoes and a new game is started. A new game can also be started at any time by clicking on GAME then on NEW or by pressing F2.

Hangman

This game is a computer version of the popular word game, Hangman. The game uses a dictionary containing a number of people, places, TV programmes, animals, etc.

FUN WITH THE COMPANION DISK

How to play Hangman

The idea behind the game is to guess the word that the computer chooses for you within a pre-set number of attempts by guessing letters. Any matching letters in the word are then displayed. Each wrong guess draws part of a gallows and a victim who is eventually hung and his head placed on a spike. A nasty violent game!

Loading Hangman

Before the game can be played, the Hangman program has to be loaded. Insert the disk in drive A: and click on FILE then on RUN. Type A:HANGMAN in the Command Line box and press the Enter key. In version 3.1 the file can be selected using the Browse option. When Hangman has loaded the screen shown in figure 14.15 will be displayed.

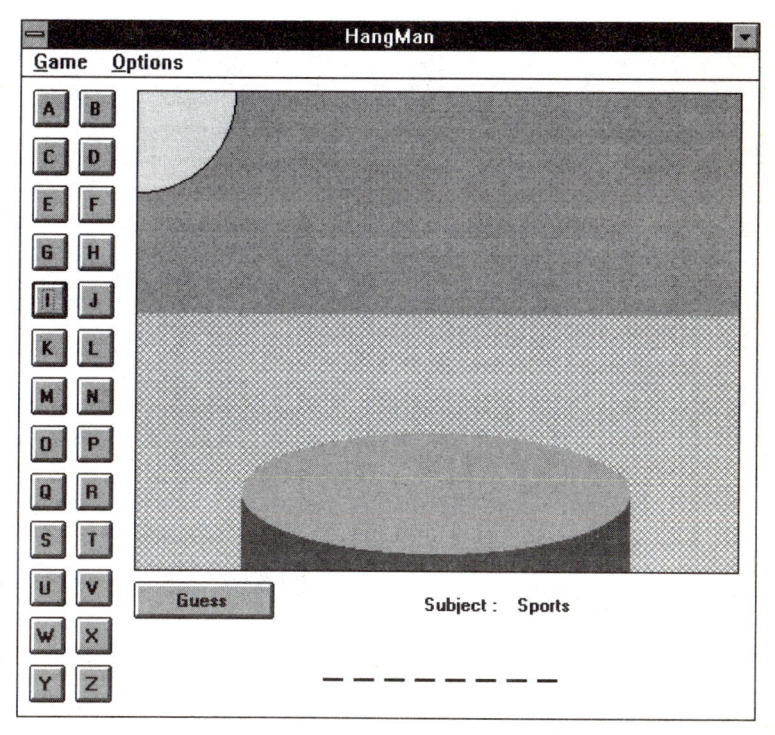

Figure 14.15

WINDOWS

NB If, when trying to load this program, a message appears saying that you need to be running in either standard or enhanced mode, refer to chapter 25 for information on these modes.

Starting a game

The word to be guessed is shown as a series of dashes at the bottom of the screen. Words and subjects are chosen at random. There may be more than one word, as in a name. You have to try and fill in all the letters of the word or words. Letters are guessed by clicking on the button that corresponds to the letter. When a letter has been selected, the corresponding button will be greyed out and cannot be selected again.

☺ The letter E is a good one to try first because it is the most commonly used letter in the English language.

NB The program has two lists of words, American and English. To change to the English list, click on OPTIONS and select ENGLISH.

If you guess a letter which is not in the word, the next part of the gallows or man is drawn. Figure 14.16 shows the gallows partly built. The letters which are in fainter type have already been guessed.

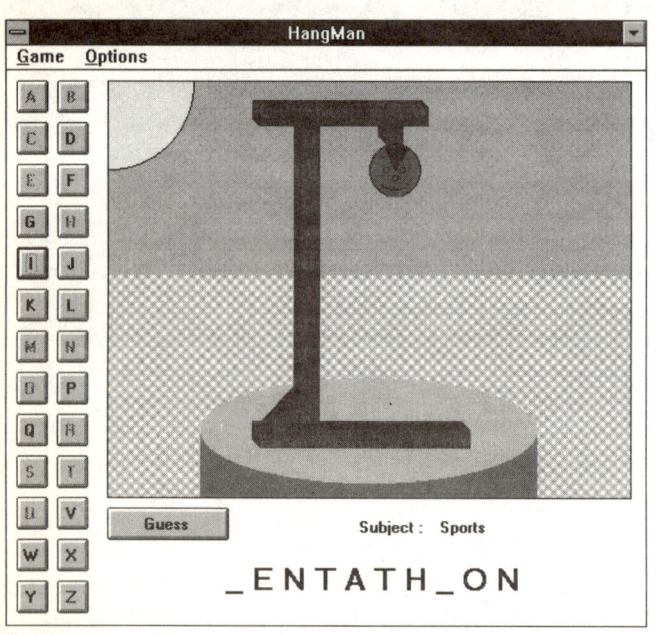

Figure 14.16

FUN WITH THE COMPANION DISK

If, as in figure 14.16, the word or name is obvious, you can click on the Guess button. This will display a box as in figure 14.17.

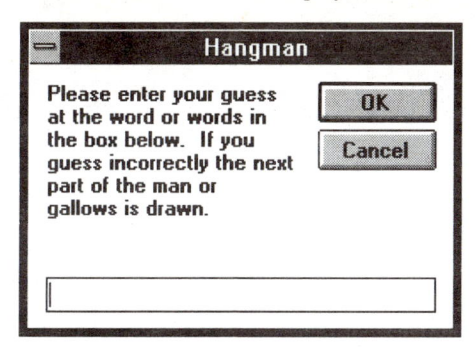

Figure 14.17

Type your guess for the word in the box. If your guess is wrong, another piece is added to the gallows. Continue guessing letters until either the man is hung or you have filled in all the letters and guessed the word. After you have had nine incorrect tries, you have failed and the screen will look like figure 14.18.

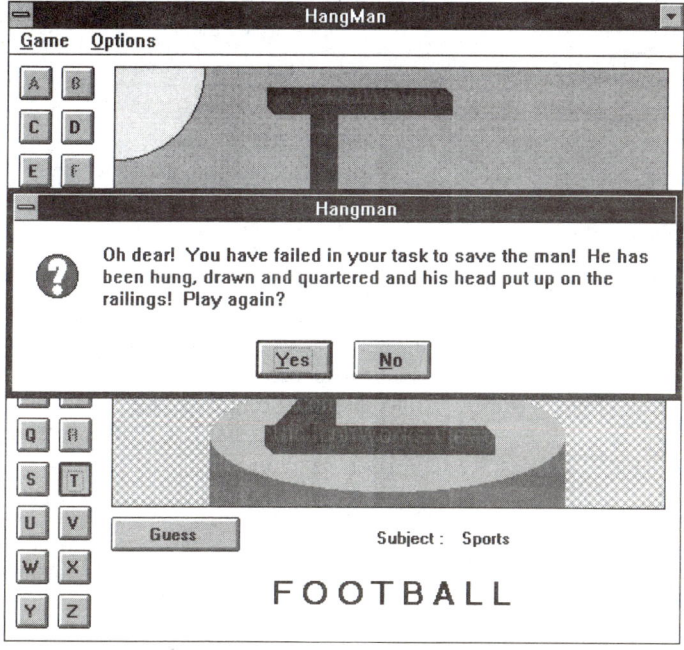

Figure 14.18

— 149 —

WINDOWS

Checkers

This game which is supplied on the companion disk version of the book is the game of Checkers or Draughts. This program plays a very strong game of checkers, even on its lowest level, so even good checkers players may struggle to win.

How to play Checkers

The basic idea of the game is to get into a position on the 8 × 8 board where you are the only player who has any pieces left. This is achieved by moving around the board, taking your opponent's pieces. The game is played on the black squares only of a chess style board. The twelve black playing pieces are at one end and the red pieces at the other. The pieces can only be moved along the black diagonals, the white squares are not used at all. When moving a piece, you can choose to move any of your pieces one space forward along a diagonal. If it is possible to take one of your opponent's pieces, then you **must** take it. Taking is done by jumping over the other piece and removing it from the board. You may make more than one jump and take more than one of your opponent's pieces in a turn. After one player has completed their move the other player has a turn. If you manage to get a playing piece to the back line, then this turns into a king. A king acts like a normal piece, except it can move and jump backwards as well as forwards.

Loading Checkers

Before the game can be played, the program has to be loaded. Insert the disk in drive A: and click on FILE then on RUN. In the box, type A:CHECKERS and press the Enter key. Alternatively, the file can be selected using the Browse option. After Checkers has loaded, the screen shown in figure 14.19 will be displayed.

To move a piece, you click on it, which gives it a border, and then click on the space to move to. The computer then makes its move. Be careful. The computer plays a very mean game of checkers, even on the lowest level.

The Level menu allows you to set the level. There are five different

FUN WITH THE COMPANION DISK

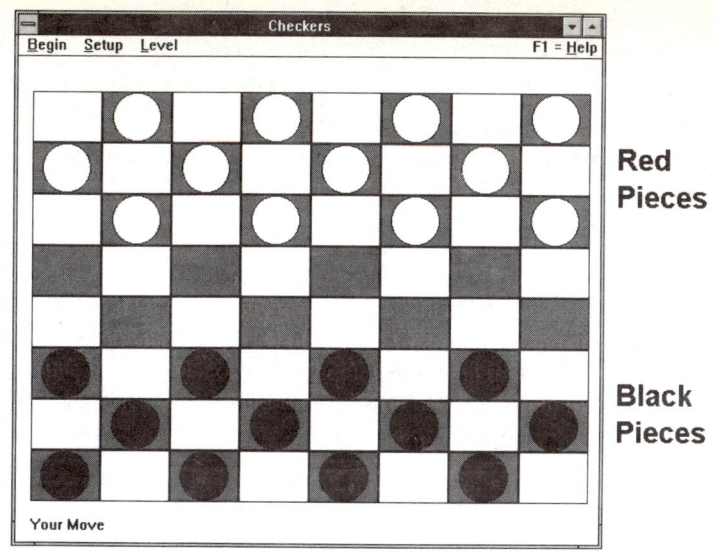

Figure 14.19

levels of play, from beginner to master level. The game is won when one player has no pieces left, as shown in figure 14.20. The black playing piece with a ring around it is known as a **king**. You get a king when a piece reaches the back line.

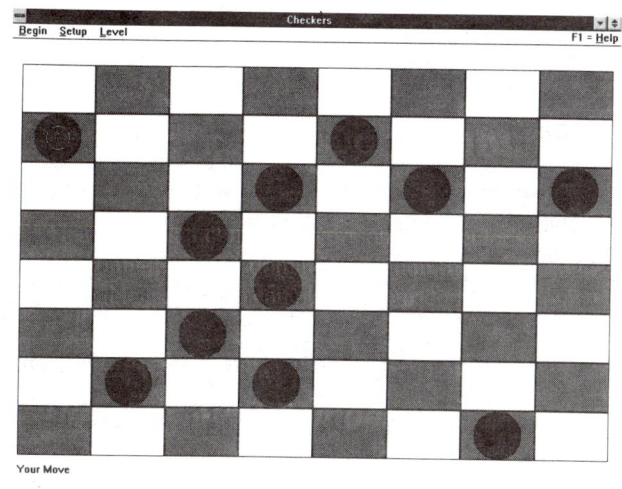

Figure 14.20

— 151 —

There are options in the game to choose the playing colours, to allow two players to play, and to play the computer against itself. These options are accessed from the Setup menu. To start a new game, click on BEGIN then on NEW GAME or press F2.

This game is hard to beat! We have only beaten it once on Novice level!

Summary

In this chapter you have learnt how to

- design and draw icons using IconWorks;
- save and load icon files;
- add and change icons in Program Manager;
- play Dominoes;
- play Hangman;
- play Checkers.

REFERENCE SECTION

This part of the book comprises ten chapters of reference material covering Program Manager and the main Accessories, plus a chapter on installing and setting up Windows to run on your computer. The Reference section aims to cover the main features of each topic to enable users to extract the required information quickly and easily. Some of the more advanced features are outside the scope of this book. Information on these can be found in the Microsoft Windows User Guide supplied with the Windows package.

15
– PROGRAM MANAGER –

This chapter contains reference material for the basic use of Program Manager and organising the windows and icons.

Program Manager

Program Manager is used to load and run other programs and applications. The Program Manager window will be different according to the software applications installed on the computer. After Windows has been installed on a computer which has some existing software, the Program Manager window will be similar to that shown in figure 15.1. The Windows Setup program has detected programs already on the disk and grouped them in the **Windows Applications group** or the **Non-Windows Applications group**, according to whether they are Windows based or DOS based programs.

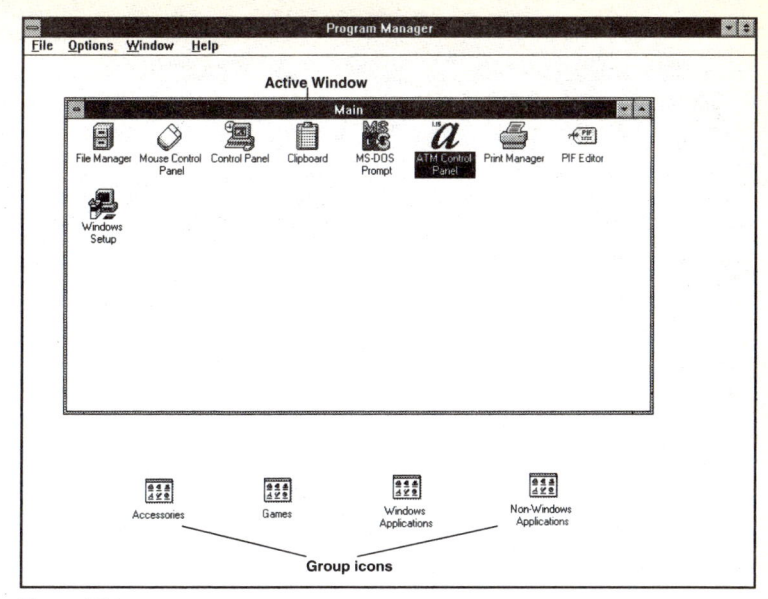

Figure 15.1

Opening a window

The group icons at the bottom of the screen are **minimised**. They can be opened up into a window by:

- double clicking on the icon;

or
- clicking once to highlight the icon and display the Control menu box then selecting RESTORE;

or
- clicking once to highlight the icon and display the Control menu box then pressing Enter;

or
- clicking once to highlight the icon and display the Control menu box then pressing R for RESTORE.

Features of the Program Manager window

The components of the Program Manager window are shown in figure 15.2.

WINDOWS

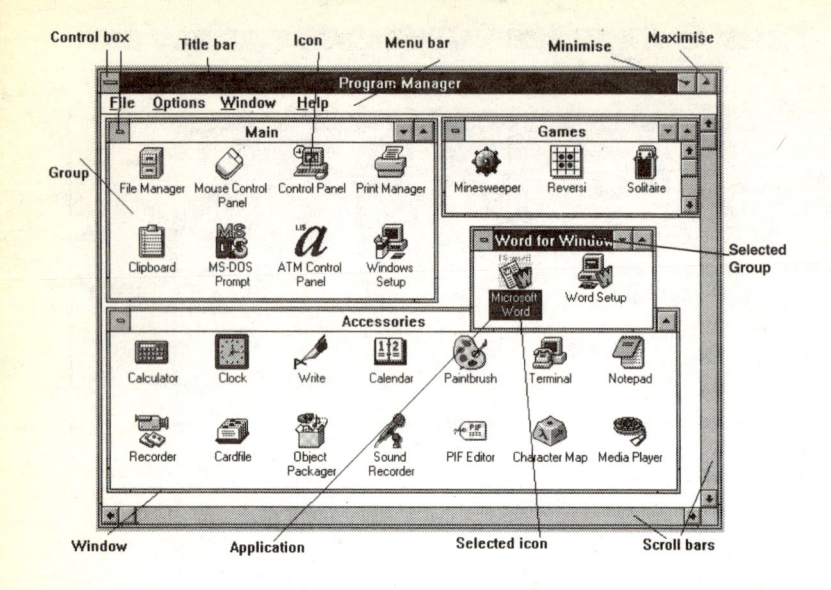

Figure 15.2

Window

Each separate area on the desktop is a **window**. Windows can be sized and moved around the desktop to suit the requirements of individual users. There are three main kinds of window: group windows, application windows and, within some applications, document windows. A **group window** contains **icons** representing the applications in the group. An **application window** is the window in which a program or application runs. A **document window** is the space occupied by an open document in Windows applications, such as Word, which allow more than one document to be open at the same time. The standard Windows accessories do not allow more than one file to be open at the same time, so document windows are not included in this chapter. In general, a document window behaves in a similar way to a group window.

Title Bar

The Title Bar is the name given to the top line of a window. This line is coloured blue on a colour monitor and a different shade of grey on a mono monitor. The Title Bar tells you the group, program or document that is currently in use. The Title Bar in figure 15.2 shows Program Manager.

Program group

Icons can be arranged in separate **groups** for different types of programs. You can create your own groups or use the standard groups supplied with Windows. When Windows is installed, it creates five program groups: Main, Accessories, Applications, Games and, in version 3.1 only, Start Up. Windows applications create their own program group during the installation process.

Menu Bar

<u>F</u>ile   <u>O</u>ptions   <u>W</u>indow   <u>H</u>elp

Figure 15.3

In all Windows programs there is a Menu Bar across the top of the screen, as shown in figure 15.3. This enables menus to be 'pulled down' to accomplish various commands and operations within the program you are using.

To pull down a menu:

- Click on the menu name on the bar.

or

- Hold down the Alt key and press the underlined letter in the menu title. For example, Alt F pulls down the File menu. Options can be selected from a menu in the same way, so pressing X selects Exit.

Minimise button

The Minimise button is the arrow pointing downwards at the top right hand corner of the desktop. It is used to remove the program window from the screen, usually to perform another task using a different part of Windows or another program. The minimised program appears as an icon at the bottom of the screen. This area is known as the **Icon Bar**. The program is still running when it is minimised, and no data will be lost. If you minimise a group window, it appears as a group icon at the bottom of the Program Manager window.

Maximise button

The Maximise button is the arrow pointing upwards at the top right hand corner of the window. It is used to make the window occupy the

maximum area, so that there is more space in the window in which to work. If you maximise an application window it will fill the whole screen.

Restore button

If the Maximise button has been clicked, there will be a Restore button in its place. If this Restore button is clicked, the window will return to the size it was before it was maximised.

Control Menu box

The Control menu box is the grey box at the top left of the window. It is used to pull down the Control Menu. Figure 15.4 shows the Control Menu for an application window on the left, and the Control Menu for a group window on the right.

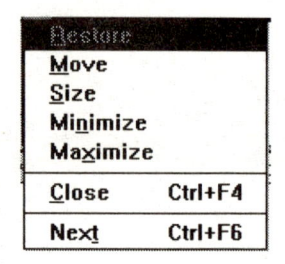

```
Restore
Move
Size
Minimize
Maximize
Close           Alt+F4
Switch To...   Ctrl+Esc
Run...
```

```
Restore
Move
Size
Minimize
Maximize
Close      Ctrl+F4
Next       Ctrl+F6
```

Figure 15.4

This menu enables windows to be restored, maximised or minimised, allows windows to be moved or sized and also enables you to close the window and exit from a program.

To display the Control Menu box:

- Click the left hand mouse button on the box.

or

- For an application window   press Alt SpaceBar.

or

- For a group window   press Alt Hyphen.

Working with application windows

An application window is a window in which a program runs: for example, the Program Manager window or the Write window.

Maximising a window

Maximising a window means making the window occupy the maximum space. This makes the maximum space available for working in the application. There are a number of ways of achieving this:

- Click on the Maximise button at the corner of the window.

or
- Click on the Control Menu box and select MAXIMISE.

or
- Press Alt SpaceBar to display the Control Menu box for the application window. Select MAXIMISE or press X.

Restoring a window

Restoring a window means returning the window to the size it was before maximising or minimising.

- Click on the Restore button in the corner of the window.

or
- Click on the Control Menu box and select RESTORE.

or
- Press Alt SpaceBar to display the Control Menu box for the window. Select RESTORE or press R.

Minimising a window

Minimising a window means reducing it to an icon on the Icon Bar.

- Click on the Minimise button in the corner of the window.

or
- Click on Control Menu box and select MINIMISE.

or
- Press Alt SpaceBar to display the Control Menu box for the window. Select MINIMISE or press N.

WINDOWS

Switching between windows

The current or **active** window is the window in which you are working. To change the active window

- Click anywhere in the required window, if it is visible on the screen.

or

- Press Ctrl Escape to display the **Task List**. Task List shows all the open applications. Double click on the required application, or click once to highlight the application then click on Switch To.

or

- Hold down Alt and press Tab until the required application name appears, then release the Alt key. Alt Tab will cycle through all the open applications.

Closing an application window

Closing the application window closes the application running in the window. Any unsaved data will be lost.

- Double click on the Control Menu box.
- Click on the Control Menu box of the window to be closed then select CLOSE.

or

- Press Ctrl Escape to display the Task List, highlight the task to be closed and click on End Task.

or

- Press Alt SpaceBar and select CLOSE.

or

- Press Alt F4.

—— Working with group windows ——

Group windows contain icons representing the programs in the group. The icons in a group window can be rearranged, added to, or icons can be removed if the programs are not used.

PROGRAM MANAGER

Arranging windows

Windows provides two standard layouts for the Program Manager window, **Tile** and **Cascade**. Figure 15.5 shows the two layouts.

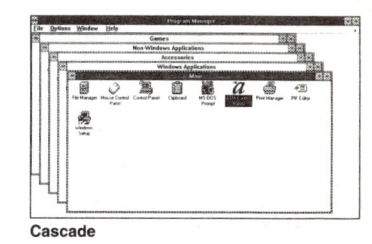

Tile   Cascade

Figure 15.5

As well as these standard options, each of the group windows can be sized individually and placed anywhere in Program Manager to give a layout like the one shown in figure 15.6.

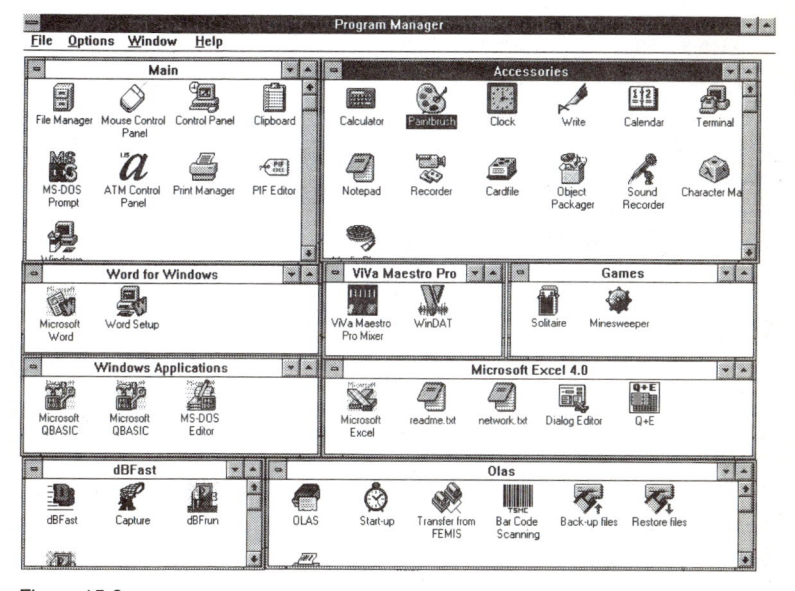

Figure 15.6

— 161 —

Switching between group windows

The current or **active** window is the window with the highlighted Title Bar. To change the active window

- Click anywhere in the required window.

or

- Press Ctrl Tab until the required window is active.

or

- Click on WINDOW on the Menu Bar to display the Window menu options shown in figure 15.7.

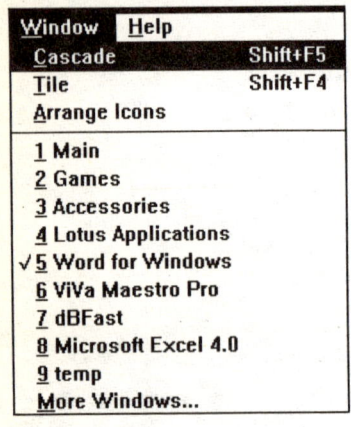

```
Window   Help
Cascade              Shift+F5
Tile                 Shift+F4
Arrange Icons

1 Main
2 Games
3 Accessories
4 Lotus Applications
√ 5 Word for Windows
6 ViVa Maestro Pro
7 dBFast
8 Microsoft Excel 4.0
9 temp
More Windows...
```

Figure 15.7

If there are more windows than space available, the bottom option will be MORE WINDOWS. Clicking on this option displays the Select Window box as shown in figure 15.8.

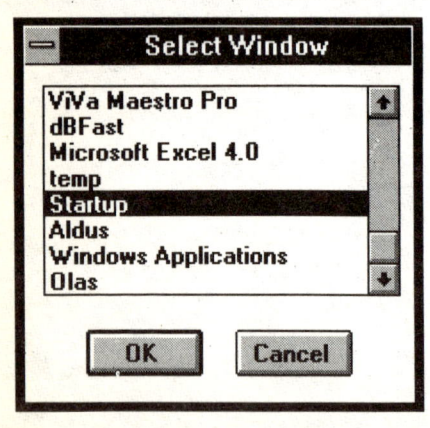

```
Select Window

ViVa Maestro Pro
dBFast
Microsoft Excel 4.0
temp
Startup
Aldus
Windows Applications
Olas

    OK        Cancel
```

Figure 15.8

— 162 —

Maximising a group window

Maximising a window means making the window occupy the maximum space. This is useful if the window contains many icons. There are a number of ways of achieving this:

- Double click on the Title Bar of the window.

or
- Click on the Maximise button at the corner of the window.

or
- Click on the Control Menu box and select MAXIMISE.

or
- Press Ctrl Tab until the required window is active. Press Alt Hyphen to display the Control Menu. Select MAXIMISE or press X.

Restoring a group window

- Click on the Restore button in the corner of the window.

or
- Click on the Control Menu box and select RESTORE.

or
- Click on Window then on the required group window. This will restore a minimised group to its previous position in the Program Manager window.

or
- Press Alt Hyphen to display the Control Menu for the window. Select RESTORE or press R.

Minimising a group window

- Click on the Minimise button in the corner of the window.

or
- Click on the Control Menu box and select MINIMISE.

or
- Press Alt Hyphen to display the Control Menu box for the window. Select MINIMISE or press N.

Sizing a group window

- Click on any of the edges of the window or on any of the corners. The pointer changes to a sizing icon. The frame can now be dragged to any required shape and size.

or
- Click on the Control Menu box and select SIZE. A sizing arrow appears. Use the arrow keys or drag with the mouse to move the edges of the box until the window is the required size and shape then press Enter.

Moving a group window

Group windows can be moved to any location in the Program Manager window. Click on the window to be moved to make it the active window.

- Click on the title bar and hold down the button to drag the window to its new location.

or
- Click on the Control Menu box and select MOVE. A moving arrow appears. Use the arrow keys or drag with the mouse to move the window to the required position then press Enter.

Closing a group window

A window can be closed so it does not appear on the desktop. It will appear as a group icon as shown in figure 15.1 on page 155. The program group still exists and can be re-opened at any time.

- Click on the Control Menu box of the window to be closed then select CLOSE.

or
- Press Alt Hyphen and select CLOSE.

Arranging icons in a group

With the group window, icons can be moved to any location by clicking on the icon and dragging it to the new location. In the same way, icons can also be moved into any other group in Program Manager. Windows can automatically arrange the icons in neat rows. Click on WINDOW then ARRANGE ICONS. The Auto Arrange option in the Options menu, if switched on, will maintain the icons in their neat rows.

Creating program groups

A standard Windows installation contains the following program groups.

Main	contains the important programs which are required for Windows to run
Games	contains two games
Startup	contains any applications to be automatically run when Windows is started

3.1 only

Accessories	contains a number of useful programs, which aid many tasks in Windows
Applications	contains any programs which Windows identified at installation (see chapter 25)
Network	contains programs used on the network (version 3.11 only)

Each group contains icons which represent programs. The programs making up a particular group are usually related in some way. Icons can be moved between different groups and new icons can be added to groups. You would want to add a new icon if you had obtained a new package and wanted to set up an icon for it in a group. This can be done for both Windows applications and non-Windows programs, although Windows applications usually set up their own group and icon when they are installed.

Click on FILE then on NEW and select Program Group from the dialog box. This displays the Program Group Properties box as shown in figure 15.9.

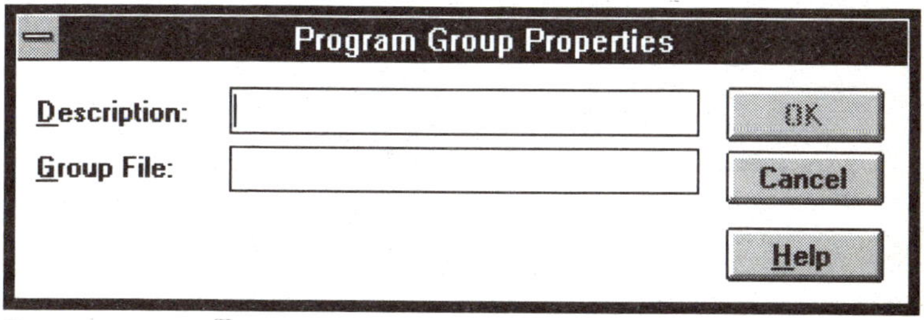

Figure 15.9

Windows creates a **group file** in the WINDOWS directory for each group. The group file has the extension GRP. It contains information about the programs that comprise the group, the icons which represent the programs and their location in the window plus any special settings for the execution of the program. The settings in the Program Group Properties box define the group file to Windows.

Description is the title of the group which will be displayed on the Title Bar of the window. **Group File** is the name to be used for the group file on the disk. If this is left blank, Windows will use the description as the name. Only the first eight characters will be used, and any spaces will be removed.

Deleting a program group

If a group is no longer required, it can be removed from Program Manager. Make the window to be removed the active window. Click on one of the icons. Click on FILE then on DELETE and press Y to confirm. Repeat the process for all the icons in the window. When the window is empty, it can be removed by clicking on FILE then DELETE. This time you will be asked to confirm that the group is to be deleted.

or

Highlight the icon to be removed. Press the Delete key then press Y to confirm.

Adding a new item to a group

To add a new item to a group, click on the group window to make it the active window, click on FILE then on NEW to display the New Program Object box shown in figure 15.10.

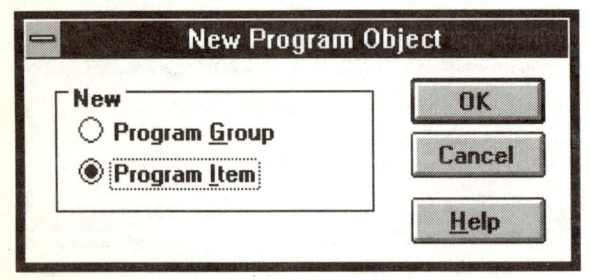

Figure 15.10

PROGRAM MANAGER

Click on OK to display the Program Item Properties box shown in figure 15.11.

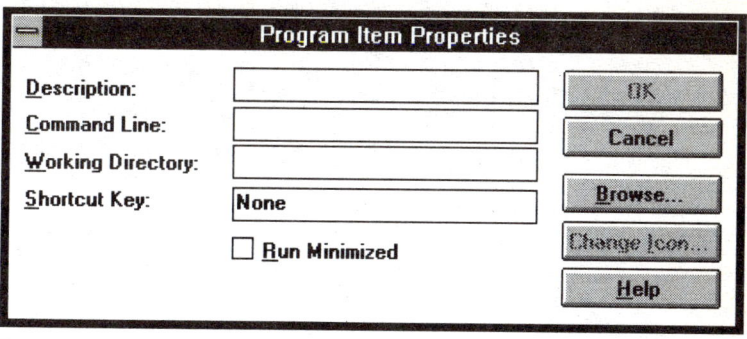

Figure 15.11

Option **Effect**
Description The text which will appear underneath the icon in Program Manager.

It is a good idea to keep the icon title fairly short, particularly if you are using version 3.0, as this allows only a single line for the title. Version 3.1 allows for the icon title to be wrapped to a second line.

Command Line The command line contains the file name of the main program file. If the program is not in the WINDOWS directory this line should also specify the directory containing the file.

Working Directory The directory which Windows will use to look for files while the program is running. This only needs to be specified if the working directory is not the same as the directory in the command line.

3.1 only

Shortcut Key The key combination which can be used to load the application quickly. This is useful for programs that you use frequently.

3.1 only

Run Minimised Whether the program is loaded in a window or as an icon. When it is checked the program loads as an icon.

3.1 only

WINDOWS

Loading and running programs

Move the pointer to the icon representing the required program. Open the program using one of the following methods.

- Double click on the icon.

or

- Click on the icon to highlight it then press Enter.

or

- Click on FILE then on RUN. Type the directory and file name and click on OK.

or

3.1 only

- Click on FILE then on RUN. Click on Browse, Select the required directory then double click on the program name.

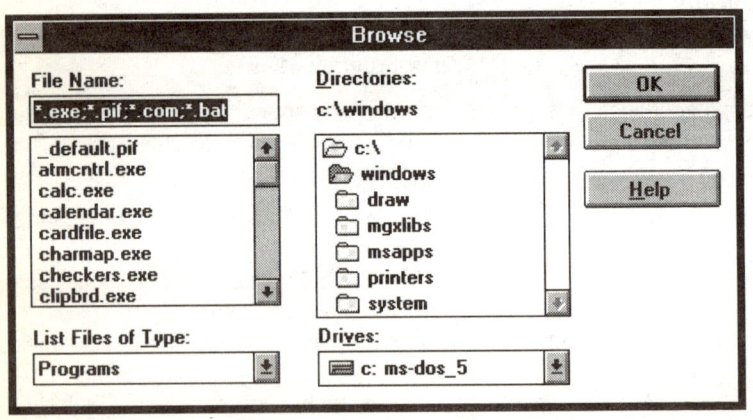

Figure 15.12

The pointer changes to an hour glass symbol to indicate that you should wait until the action has been completed.

Running non-Windows applications

Non-Windows applications can also be run under Windows. The program will be represented by a DOS icon. When the program is opened using any of the normal Windows methods, it runs in a DOS window on the desktop. The program will look and behave exactly as it does when running from the DOS prompt.

Properties

The Properties option allows changes to be made to window and icon titles, and different icons to be selected. Any of the available icons can be selected and used in place of the standard icon. In addition it is possible to purchase icons from a number of sources or to create your own from icon editors.

The companion disk contains an icon editor. Chapter 14 describes how to use it to design your own icons.

Highlight the icon representing the program to be changed. Click on FILE then on PROPERTIES to display the Program Item Properties box shown in figure 15.11.

Changing icons

Windows attaches an icon to each application according to its type. An icon can be replaced with any other icon to suit individual tastes. There are a number of icons in the file PROGMAN.EXE in the WINDOWS directory. Version 3.1 has another file (called MORICONS.DLL) which contains icons. Figure 15.13 shows a few of the icons in PROGMAN.EXE.

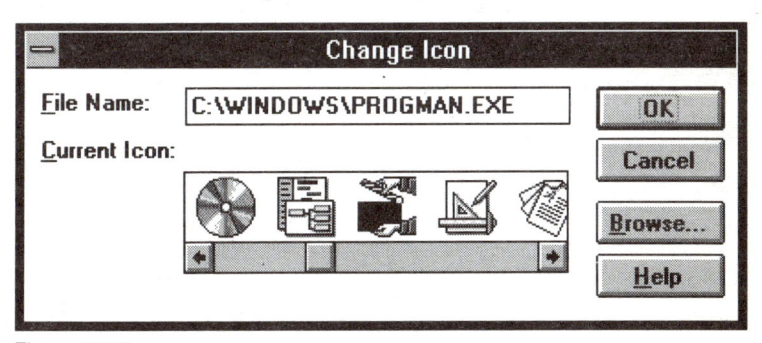

Figure 15.13

WINDOWS

Saving changes

Any changes you have made to Program Manager, such as the layout of the windows on the desktop, or changes to program properties, need to be saved so that the changes will still be effective the next time Windows is used.

3.1 only

Click on OPTIONS then on SAVE SETTINGS ON EXIT. Exit from Windows. The option, once switched on, will remain switched on.

3.0 only

Use any of the methods listed in the next section to exit from Windows. Check the Save Settings check box to save any changes you have made.

Exiting from Windows

There are a number of ways to exit from Windows.

- Click on FILE to pull down the File menu then click on EXIT.

or

- Click on the Control Menu box at the top left hand corner of the Program Manager window to display the Control Menu. Click on the CLOSE option.

or

- Double click on the Control Menu box at the top left hand corner of the Program Manager window.

or

- Hold down Alt and press F4.

or

- Hold down Alt and press F for the File menu then X for Exit.

All these methods will display the Exit Windows box shown in figure 15.14. The figure shows the Windows 3.1 Exit Windows box. The Windows 3.0 Exit box has a Save Settings check box, which, if checked, will save any changes to the layout of group windows on the desktop, so that the new layout will still be there the next time Windows is used.

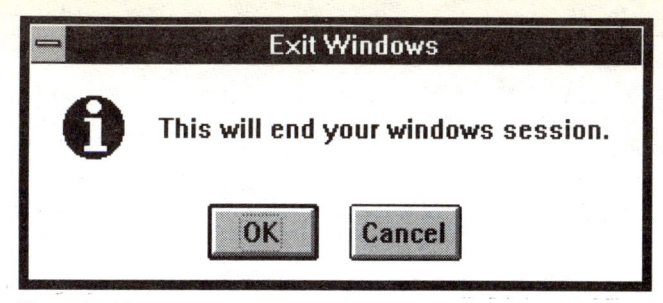

Figure 15.14

This is an example of a Windows **dialog box**. Dialog boxes are used extensively throughout Windows to pass information from Windows to the user, or to select an option. Dialog boxes always have at least one button, and often more. In this case, there are two buttons, the OK button and the Cancel button. These two buttons will be present on practically all dialog boxes. There will often be a Help option as well. The option is selected by clicking the required button. As you might expect, clicking OK confirms the selection, clicking Cancel cancels the selection.

A dialog box can also be used with key presses instead of the mouse if required. One of the buttons in the dialog box will have a dark outline. This indicates that it is the default choice and can be selected by pressing the Enter key. The other options can be selected by pressing the Tab key until the required button is highlighted and then pressing the Enter key.

Click on OK to confirm that you wish to exit from Windows. If you have any active applications which have unsaved data, Windows will remind you of this, and ask whether the data is to be saved before exiting. You will be returned to DOS or DOS-shell in the same position as when Windows was loaded.

Summary

This chapter has described

- the features of the Windows desktop;
- use of menus;
- working with applications windows;

- working with group windows;
- maximising, minimising and restoring windows;
- sizing and moving windows;
- arranging windows and icons;
- windows and icons;
- opening and closing windows;
- creating and deleting program groups;
- adding new items;
- loading and running programs;
- changing program properties;
- changing icons;
- exiting from Windows.

16
—— WINDOWS HELP ——

This chapter describes the facilities offered by Windows on-line Help. The built-in Help is one of the big advantages offered by Windows. Help is available to assist you at almost every stage of working within Windows. There is often a tutorial to enable new users to learn the basic features of the package. Help can be accessed whenever there is a Help option on the menu bar. The Help facilities offered are comprehensive and easy to learn and use. Windows also offers an excellent Glossary. Most Windows applications have followed this example and include extensive Help facilities within the programs.

The Help menus are different in versions 3.1 and 3.0. The basic features are the same but they are accessed in different ways. Version 3.0 does not have a tutorial. The Help screens shown in this chapter are mainly from version 3.1.

———— Accessing Help ————

Help can be accessed by any of the following methods:

- Click on HELP on the Menu Bar to pull down the Help menu, as shown shown in figure 16.1.

or

- Press Alt H to pull down the Help menu.

or

- Press F1 to go straight into Windows Help.

Figure 16.1 shows the Help menu in versions 3.0 and 3.1.

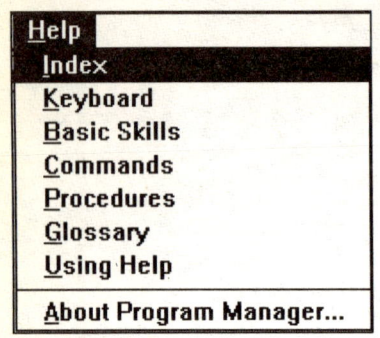

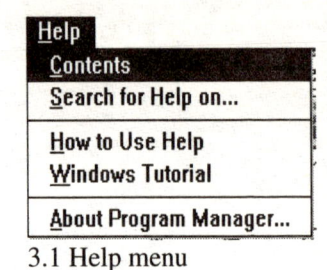

```
Help
 Index
 Keyboard
 Basic Skills
 Commands
 Procedures
 Glossary
 Using Help
 About Program Manager...
```
3.0 Help menu

```
Help
 Contents
 Search for Help on...
 How to Use Help
 Windows Tutorial
 About Program Manager...
```
3.1 Help menu

Figure 16.1

The main Help facilities consist of a large number of screens of information with a list of contents which can be browsed and searched to obtain help on any required topic. In addition any Help screen can be printed for future reference.

Windows tutorial

3.1 only

The Windows tutorial introduces the use of a mouse and the basic techniques of Windows. Details of how to use the tutorial can be found in chapter 3.

The 'About' dialog box

Almost every Windows program has an About option on the Help menu, which gives information about the program. The About option on the Program Manager Help menu gives information about Program Manager, as shown in figure 16.2.

WINDOWS HELP

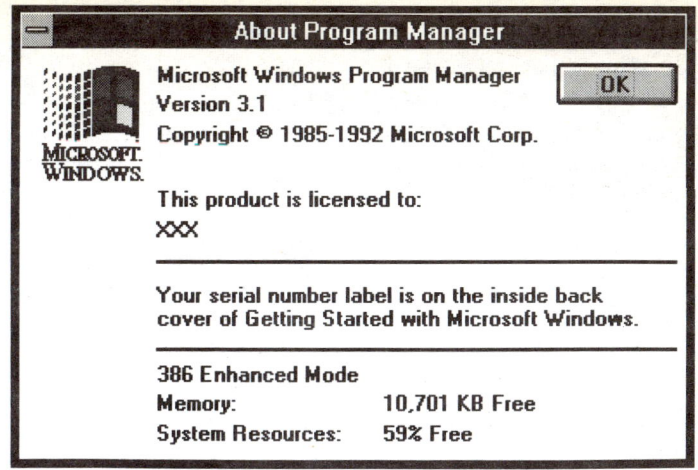

```
┌─────────────── About Program Manager ───────────────┐
│                                                      │
│   ▓▓▓▓   Microsoft Windows Program Manager  ┌─────┐ │
│   ▓▓▓▓   Version 3.1                        │ OK  │ │
│   ▓▓▓▓   Copyright © 1985-1992 Microsoft Corp.└───┘ │
│ MICROSOFT.                                           │
│ WINDOWS.                                             │
│                                                      │
│          This product is licensed to:                │
│          xxx                                         │
│          ─────────────────────────────────────       │
│                                                      │
│          Your serial number label is on the inside back│
│          cover of Getting Started with Microsoft Windows.│
│          ─────────────────────────────────────       │
│                                                      │
│          386 Enhanced Mode                           │
│          Memory:             10,701 KB Free          │
│          System Resources:   59% Free                │
└──────────────────────────────────────────────────────┘
```

Figure 16.2

Windows Help contents

Selecting the Contents option from the Help menu will display the Program Manager Help contents. Figure 16.3 shows the Windows 3.1 Help contents.

```
┌──────────────────── Program Manager Help ─────────────┐
│ File  Edit  Bookmark  Help                            │
│ ┌────────┬────────┬──────┬─────────┬──────────┐       │
│ │Contents│ Search │ Back │ History │ Glossary │       │
│ └────────┴────────┴──────┴─────────┴──────────┘       │
│                                                        │
│  Contents for Program Manager Help                    │
│                                                        │
│  Windows Program Manager is a tool you can use to easily start applications, and │
│  organize your applications and files into logical groups. │
│  To learn how to use Help, press F1.                  │
│                                                        │
│  How To...                                            │
│  Arrange Windows and Icons                            │
│  Change an Icon                                       │
│  Organize Applications and Documents                  │
│  Quit Windows                                         │
│  Start an Application                                 │
│  Switch Between Applications                          │
│                                                        │
│  Commands                                             │
│  File Menu Commands                                   │
│  Options Menu Commands                                │
│  Window Menu Commands                                 │
└────────────────────────────────────────────────────────┘
```

Figure 16.3

— 175 —

Topics which are underlined are **hot links** and can be clicked on to display the related Help topic. A solid underline brings up another list of topics. A dotted underline displays the Glossary entry which gives information on the underlined word. There may be several layers of hot links taking you through related topics to the required Help screen which contains the information. Some sample Help screens are shown in figures 16.4 and 16.5.

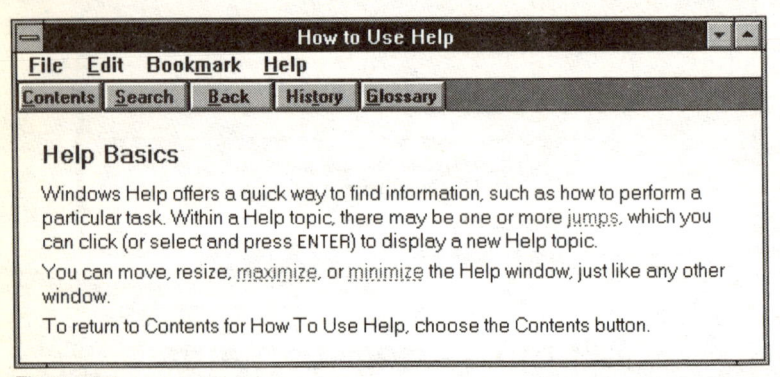

Figure 16.4

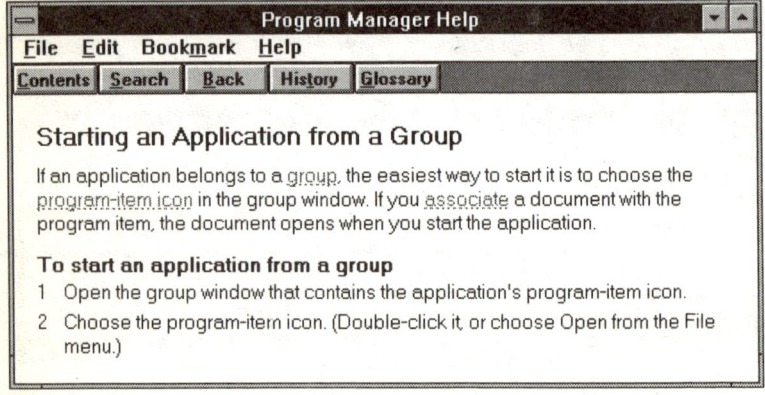

Figure 16.5

The screen can be copied to the Clipboard for use elsewhere in Windows or, more usefully, can be printed to provide a written help sheet.

Printing Help screens

The Help screen can be printed by clicking on FILE then selecting PRINT TOPIC.

Help options

The Help window has its own Menu Bar and a row of buttons, as shown in figure 16.6, which allow you to navigate around the Help screens.

Figure 16.6

Glossary

The Windows Glossary is a list of Windows words and their explanations. Click on Glossary to display the Glossary box as shown in figure 16.7. All these words are hot links and can be clicked to display the explanation. In version 3.0, the Glossary is accessed directly from the Help menu. In this version it is necessary to hold down the mouse button to view the explanation. Figure 16.7 shows a sample glossary entry explaining the term **application window**.

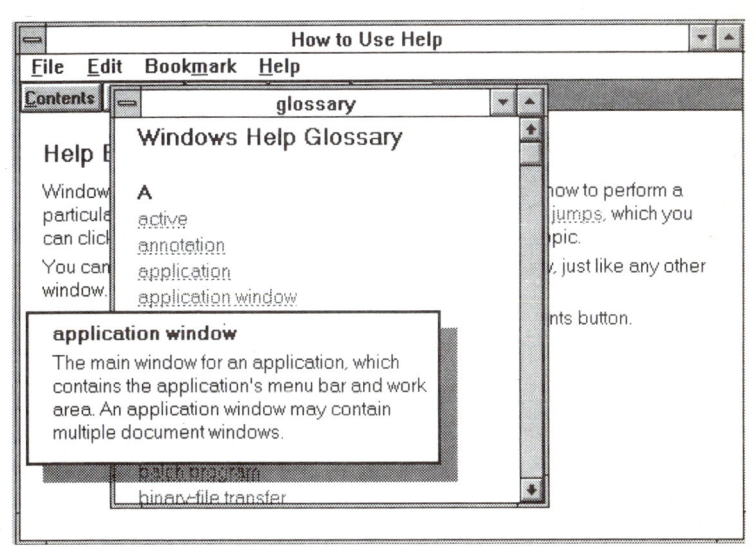

Figure 16.7

There is also a glossary at the back of this book.

Searching in Help

Often you will require help on a particular topic. Windows Help offers a search facility as a quick way of doing this. Search can be accessed from the button bar shown above or, in version 3.1, directly from the Help menu. Both methods will display the Search box as shown in figure 16.8.

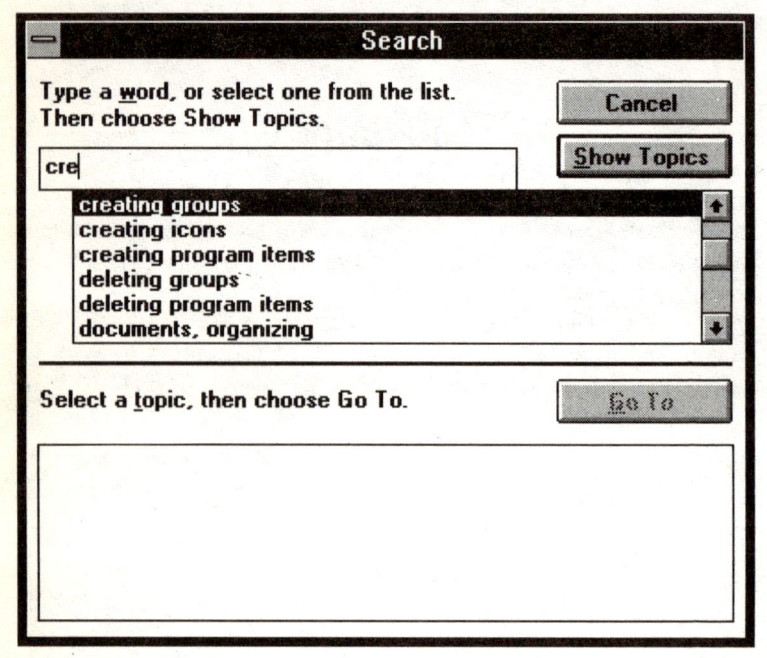

Figure 16.8

Type the topic you require in the box. As soon as you start to type, Windows Help will display the topics which match what you have typed. If the topic is not in the list, you can re-enter the required topic phrased in a different way or browse the list using the scroll bars. When the topic you require is shown in the list, click on it to highlight, then click on Show Topics. This will display the names of the related screens. Hopefully one of these will be the one you want! Click on it and then click on Go To to display the Help screen. This sounds a very long complicated process but with a little practice, particular help screens can be accessed very quickly using Search. The Back button will take you back to the previous screen, usually back to the Contents list.

Help history
3.1 only

The History button displays a History box, as shown in figure 16.9, which keeps a record of your use of the Help facilities. Double clicking any of the topics brings up the relevant screen for you to view.

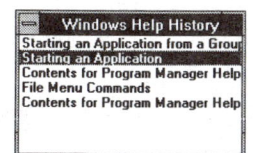

```
Windows Help History
Starting an Application from a Group
Starting an Application
Contents for Program Manager Help
File Menu Commands
Contents for Program Manager Help
```

Figure 16.9

Context sensitive help
3.1 only

Context sensitive help is help on the particular function or operation which you are carrying out. This is available in many Windows programs in version 3.1. For example, if Printers in Control Panel is highlighted, you can press F1 to display a screen of information on printers, as shown in figure 16.10.

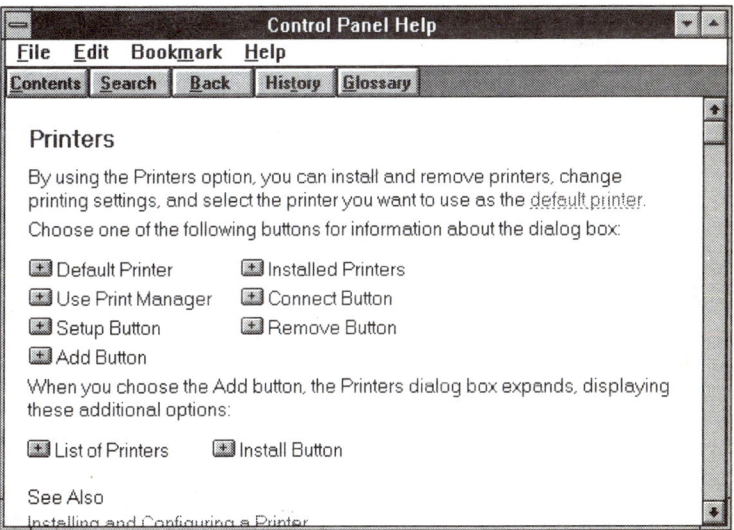

Figure 16.10

Summary

This chapter has described
- Windows on-line help features;
- how to access Windows Help;
- the Windows tutorial;
- About boxes;
- using the Help contents list;
- hot links;
- printing Help topics;
- searching in Help;
- accessing and using the Glossary;
- using Help history;
- using context sensitive help.

17
FILE MANAGER

This chapter contains reference material for File Manager. File Manager is a useful utility for general maintenance and control of the files on your disks. File Manager enables you to view and store files on your disks, copy and rename files, deletes files no longer wanted and format floppy disks. In addition, File Manager can be used to start and run programs under Windows.

File Manager was one of the features of Windows version 3.0 which underwent major changes for version 3.1. This chapter describes the features and uses screen dumps from version 3.1. Most of the features are available in version 3.0, but the details of the screens and menus are usually different.

Data storage

The amount of data which can be stored on the hard disks in desktop computers normally ranges from around 40 MB (megabytes) to 300 MB or even more. Windows applications tend to be large and, in practice, at least a 100 MB hard disk will be required if you plan to use Windows regularly. This is a large amount of storage space and needs to be managed properly. This is achieved by storing each application in its own area of the disk. This area is known as a **directory**. The directory will contain all the program files, together with any files which you create when working in the application.

The organisation of directories on the disk is in a **tree structure**, as shown in figure 17.1. The top level is known as the **root directory**. The root directory contains the system configuration files and the names of the directories at the next level.

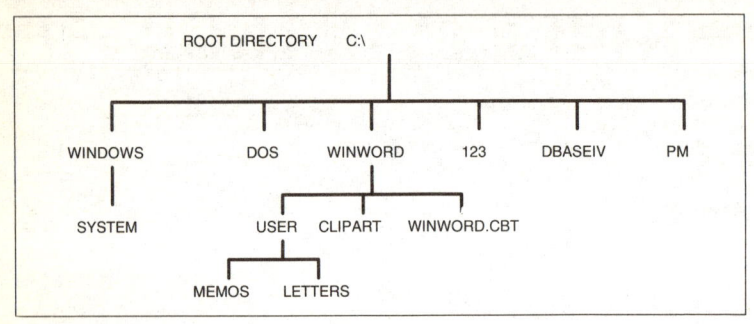

```
                    ROOT DIRECTORY    C:\
       ┌──────┬──────────┬──────────┬──────┬──────────┬──────┐
    WINDOWS   DOS     WINWORD      123   DBASEIV     PM
       │              ┌────┼────────┐
    SYSTEM          USER CLIPART WINWORD.CBT
                   ┌──┴──┐
                 MEMOS LETTERS
```

Figure 17.1

Programs create their own directories as they are installed. For example, Windows creates its basic WINDOWS directory and a sub-directory of Windows called SYSTEM, as shown in figure 17.1. Directories can be created within directories to as many levels as required. In practice, two or three levels give the greatest efficiency. The more levels you have, the more difficult it can be to find the file you are looking for.

In File Manager, different types of files have different icons. These are the same in both Windows 3.0 and 3.1. The icons are shown in figure 17.2.

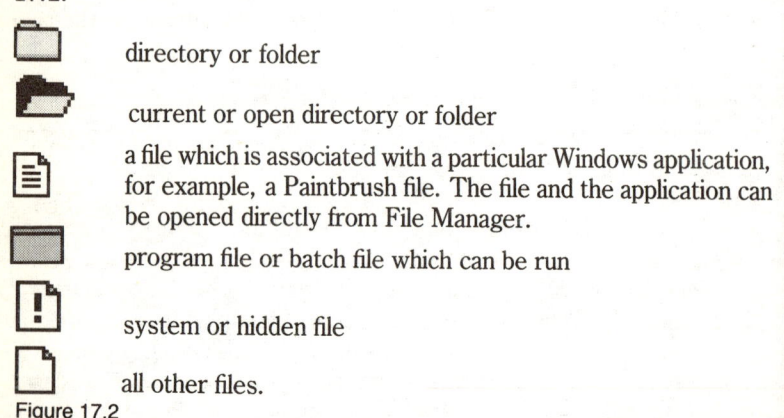

📁 directory or folder

📂 current or open directory or folder

📄 a file which is associated with a particular Windows application, for example, a Paintbrush file. The file and the application can be opened directly from File Manager.

▭ program file or batch file which can be run

[!] system or hidden file

▯ all other files.

Figure 17.2

FILE MANAGER

Starting File Manager

File Manager is in the Main window. Double click on the File Manager icon to load File Manager. Figure 17.3 shows the Windows 3.1 File Manager screen.

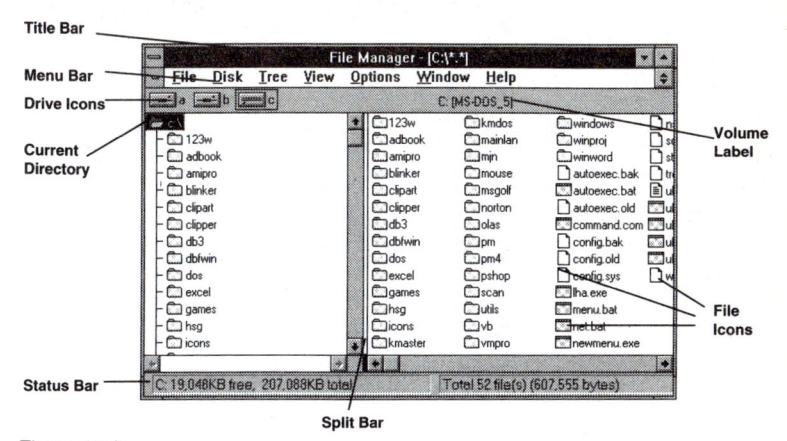

Figure 17.3

This display is known as a **directory window**. It is a pictorial representation of the files on the current drive. In version 3.1, the screen is split vertically down the middle. The left-hand side of the window shows the directory structure of the current drive (usually drive C). The current directory is shown as an open folder icon. By default, only the directories at the top level in figure 17.1 are shown. The right hand side of the screen shows the files in the current directory which, in this case, is the root directory.

The main elements of the window are described below.

Drive Icon	Drive icons represent the drives available on your computer.
Title Bar	The top line of the window showing File Manager.
Volume Label	A volume label is an optional name assigned to a disk.
Status Bar	The bottom line of the window. The Status Bar is used by File Manager to display information about the files and directories.

— 183 —

WINDOWS

Current Directory Icon	The open folder icon.
Up Icon 🖿	Double clicking on the up icon moves up to the directory at the next higher level.
Split Bar **3.1 only**	The vertical line dividing the screen into two halves.
File Icons	Different icons representing the types of files in the directory.
Tool Bar (version 3.11)	Icons representing View options, shown in figure 17.4.

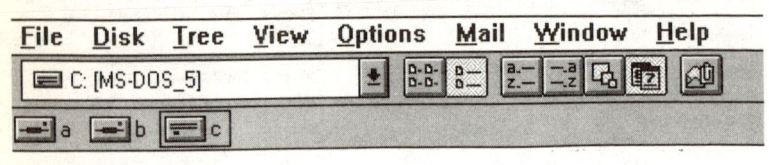

Figure 17.4

Changing views
3.1 only

The directory display window can be changed so that it only shows one of the two elements in figure 17.3. Click on VIEW then on TREE ONLY to display only the directory tree. Click on VIEW then DIRECTORY ONLY to display only the contents of the current directory.

Changing directory

Double click on the required directory to open the folder. If the directory contains any sub-directories, these will be displayed, as shown in figure 17.5. The directory is then said to be **expanded**.

The default display is to show directories as **collapsed** until the directory is opened. This can be changed so that all sub-directories are visible by changing the settings in the Tree menu.

The Tree menu options are:

Option | **Effect**
Expand One Level | Expands current directory so that the first level sub-directories are

FILE MANAGER

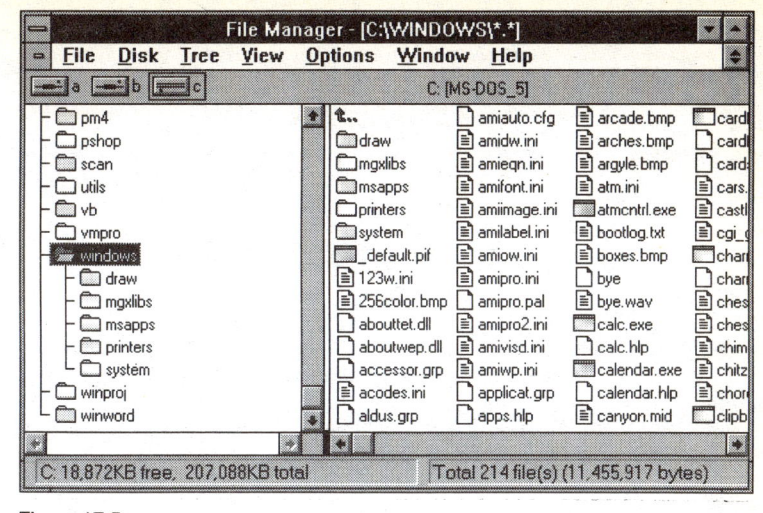

Figure 17.5

	shown. This has the same effect as double clicking on the directory icon.
Expand Branch	Expands the current directory so that all sub-directories at all levels are indicated.
Expand All	Expands all directory branches.
Collapse Branch	Collapses the branch so that sub-directories are not shown.
Indicate Expandable Branches **3.1 only**	Marks each directory which has sub directories with a + sign.

⎯⎯ Displaying file information ⎯⎯

By default, only the name of the file is shown. This can be changed to show the file size, the date and time the file was saved, and the file attributes, as shown in figure 17.6. To display these extra details, click on VIEW then select ALL FILE DETAILS. In version 3.11 you can also do this by clicking on the ▦ icon on the Tool bar. This gives more information but reduces the number of files which can be displayed at the same time.

— 185 —

chap12.doc	479678	10/04/93	00:36:34	a
chap13.doc	890555	10/04/93	14:01:42	a
chap14.doc	3633483	10/04/93	22:02:20	a
chap15.doc	2326228	11/04/93	00:02:24	a
chap16.doc	2348253	11/04/93	00:47:28	a

Figure 17.6

Arranging files

By default the files in the directory are listed in alphabetical order. The other options are listed below. To change the display, click on VIEW then on the option required. Version 3.11 also has icons on the Tool bar to change the display.

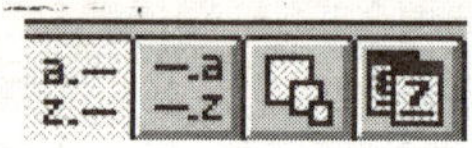

Option **Effect**

By Date   Arranges files in date order, starting with the newest.

3.1 only

By Type   Arranges files so that all files with the same extension are together. This means that all the BMP, DOC, etc. files are together. The files are then listed in alphabetical order of file name.

By Size   Arranges files in descending order of size.

3.1 only

Returning to higher levels

- Double click on the Up icon in 3.1 or the .. in 3.0 to move up one directory level.

or

- Click on the required directory icon to move any number of levels.

or

- Click on C:\ at the top of the directory tree to return to the root directory.

Changing drives

The drives available on your computer are shown across the top of the screen under the Title Bar as shown in figure 17.7.

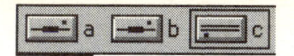

Figure 17.7

Drives a and b are floppy disk drives. If your computer has only one floppy disk drive, there will be no b icon. Drive c and any further letters represent fixed drives available on your computer. Drive c will nearly always be present but there may be further drives if you have a hard disk which has been divided or partitioned into different drives, or if you are working on a network which may have many different drives.

Saving options

In version 3.1, File Manager automatically saves the new settings so that they will still be in effect when next used. In version 3.0, you will be asked if any changes are to be saved.

Creating directories

Programs create their own directories when they are installed. It may be necessary or desirable to create further directories or sub-directories to store particular groups of files.

The directory will be created as a sub-directory of the current directory. Ensure you are in the correct place before starting.

Click on FILE then on CREATE DIRECTORY. This displays the dialog box shown in figure 17.8.

Figure 17.8

Type a name for the new directory. The rules for naming directories are the same as for files: up to eight characters and no spaces. Click on OK.

File operations

The term file operations means all the general tasks needed to keep your hard and floppy disks tidy. These include tidying disks by deleting files no longer wanted, making copies of files, moving files between disks and directories, renaming files, and formatting and copying floppy disks.

Selecting files

The file or files have to be selected before they can be moved, copied, or deleted.

Files required	**Method**
Single file.	Click on the required file. This will be highlighted to show it is selected.
Group of files that are next to each other.	Click on the first file. Hold down the Shift key and click on the last file. All the files between the first and last will be highlighted.
Number of files which are not together.	Click on the first file. Hold down Ctrl while clicking on the other files.
Number of groups of files.	Click on the first file. Hold down both Ctrl and Shift while highlighting the files.

Figure 17.9 shows three files selected.

Moving files

The highlighted files can then be moved to a different directory, another drive or to any of the sub-directories in the current directory. The original location of the file is known as the **source**. The new location is known as the **destination**.

Moving by dragging

Files can be moved by dragging. To drag a file, both the source and destination directories need to be visible.

FILE MANAGER

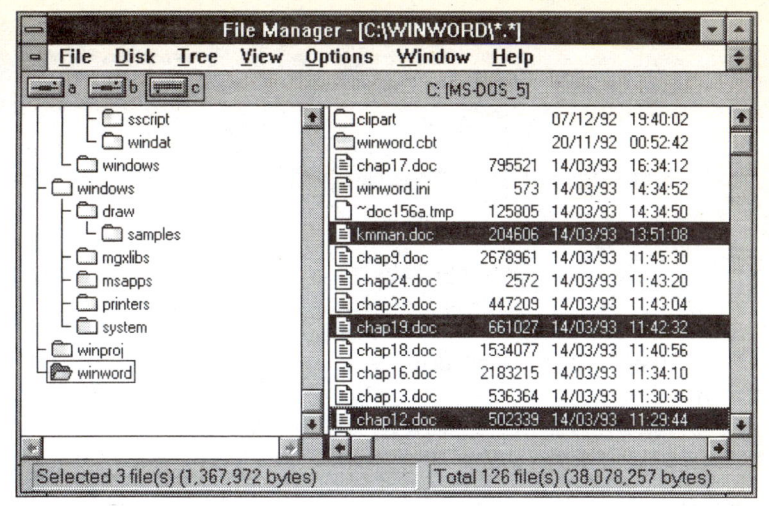

Figure 17.9

Click on one of the highlighted files. The mouse pointer changes to a file or files icon. Drag this icon to the required drive or directory. File Manager will ask for confirmation before moving the files. If you try to move the file to a new drive, perhaps to a floppy disk, File Manager will copy the file instead of moving it. Files can be moved to another drive by holding down the Shift key while dragging the files to the required drive icon.

Moving using menus

Files can also be moved using the File menu. Click on FILE then on MOVE to display the Move dialog box as shown in figure 17.10.

Figure 17.10

The name of the selected file is displayed in the From box. Type the destination directory in the To box. The file can be renamed as it is moved by typing a destination file name after the destination directory.

Opening more than one directory

Having more than one directory open can make it easier to move and copy files, especially between sub-directories. To open the second directory window, hold down the Shift key and double click on the required directory icon. This will open a second window. Click on WINDOW then TILE to arrange the windows. You may find that both windows show the same directory. If this is the case, change one of the windows by clicking on the required folder. Figure 17.11 shows two directories open at the same time.

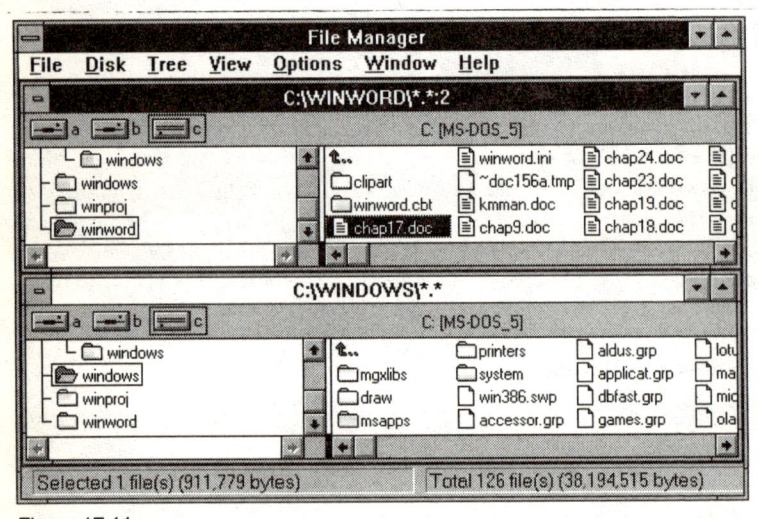

Figure 17.11

3.1 only

Version 3.1 offers an alternative method. Click on WINDOW then on NEW WINDOW. This displays the normal directory window, split between the directory tree and the files in the current directory. The required directory can then be opened to display the files. The directory windows can be arranged using the TILE or CASCADE options from the WINDOW menu.

Copying files and directories

Copying is very similar to moving. The difference is that, when copying, the file or files remain in the source directory after they have been copied to the destination directory. After files have been moved, they only appear in the destination directory.

Copying by dragging

Click on the required file and drag to the new location while holding down the Ctrl key. Release the mouse button and then release the Ctrl key. Click on OK to confirm the copy. More than one file can be copied at the same time by highlighting all the required files as described earlier.

Files can be copied to another drive by dragging the files to the required drive icon with the mouse. No keys need to be pressed to do this.

Copying using menus

Files can also be copied from the File menu. Click on FILE then on COPY to display the Copy dialog box as shown in figure 17.12.

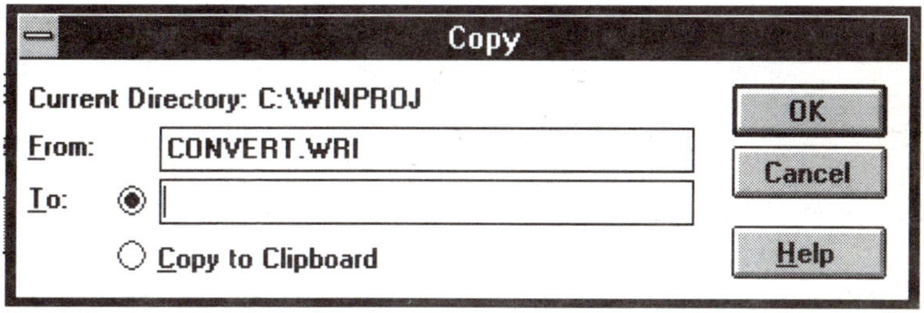

Figure 17.12

The name of the selected file is displayed in the From box. Type the destination directory in the To box. The file can be renamed as it is copied by typing a destination file name after the destination directory.

Copying to the Clipboard

Select the file as described previously, then click on FILE, then on COPY. Enter the From and To options as above, then click on Copy to Clipboard. Click on OK. The information in the file can then be used anywhere within Windows.

Searching for files and directories

It can be very useful to search for a particular file or a group of related files. The search can be extended so that more than the current directory is searched. Click on FILE then on SEARCH to display the Search dialog box, as shown in figure 17.13.

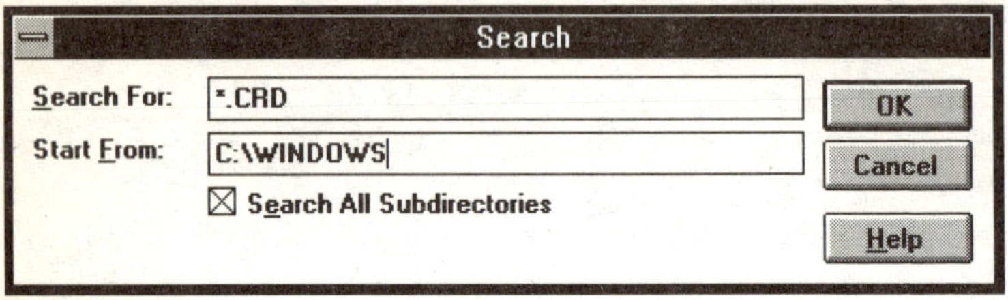

Figure 17.13

In the Search For box, type the name of the file or directory. To search for groups of files which have similar names or extensions, you can use **wild card** characters. A wild card is a character which stands for any other character or any group of characters. The character ? stands for any single character so TASK? will stand for any file name beginning TASK and followed by a single character or no characters: for example TASK, TASKA, TASK1, etc. The wild card character * stands for any group of characters so H* searches for any files beginning with the letter H. In the example in figure 17.13, *.CRD will search for all files with the CRD extension.

The search starts from the current directory, which is shown in the Start From box. By default, File Manager will search all sub-directories of the current directory. The check box can be switched off if required. Click on OK to start the search. The files found by the search are displayed in the Search Results window, shown in figure 17.14.

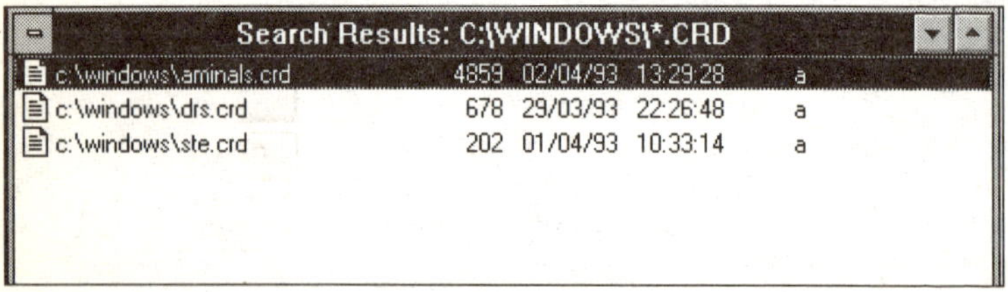

Figure 17.14

FILE MANAGER

Renaming files

A file or directory can be renamed if required. Highlight the file or directory to be renamed. Click on FILE then on RENAME to display the Rename dialog box shown in figure 17.15.

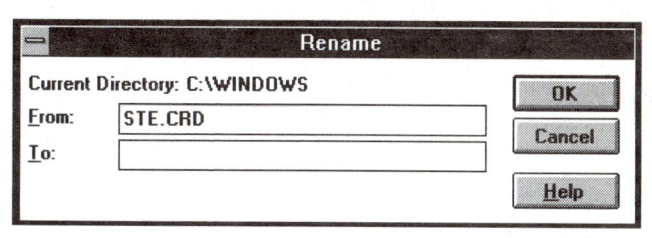

Figure 17.15

The name of the file or directory is shown in the From box. Type the new name in the To box and click on OK. The file or directory name must not already exist. If it does, File Manager will display an error box and ask you to re-enter the file names.

Deleting files

Files no longer required can be deleted from the disk. Directories can also be deleted.

This facility should be used with caution. Deleting a directory also deletes all sub-directories and files within them. NB

Highlight the file(s) or directories to be deleted. Click on FILE then on DELETE to display the Delete dialog box, as shown in figure 17.16. Click on OK to delete the selected files. File Manager will ask for confirmation before deleting the files.

Figure 17.16

— 193 —

Formatting floppy disks

Formatting is the process of making a floppy disk ready for use. This can be done from MS-DOS Prompt or from within File Manager.

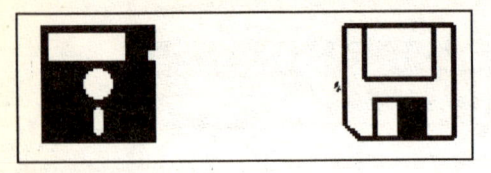

Figure 17.17

Floppy disks come in different sizes and capacities. The original floppy disk was the 5.25" disk shown on the left in figure 17.17. These are still used and are now available in two forms: double and high density. This type of disk is susceptible to damage from heat, scratching and bending. The smaller 3.5" diskette or micro disk, shown on the right in figure 17.17, has now become the standard for the PC. This type of disk is more resistant to damage and easier to transport. The 3.5" disk also comes in different forms: double density and high density. The latest high density micro disks can now store up to 2.8 MB. The storage capacities (in kilobytes or megabytes) of the various disk types are shown in the table below.

Size	Low Density	High Density
5.25"	360 KB	1.2 MB
3.5"	720 KB	1.44 MB

NB Formatting a disk removes any files on the disk. There is no way of recovering such files. Always ensure that you have the correct disk in the drive before formatting!

To format a disk:

- Insert the disk to be formatted in the correct drive.
- Click on DISK then on FORMAT DISK to display the Format Disk dialog box, shown in figure 17.18.
- Select the required drive and capacity.
- Enter the text for a disk label if required.
- Click on DISK then on FORMAT DISK to display the Format Disk dialog box, shown in figure 17.18.

NB A Quick Format can only be performed on a disk which has previously been formatted.

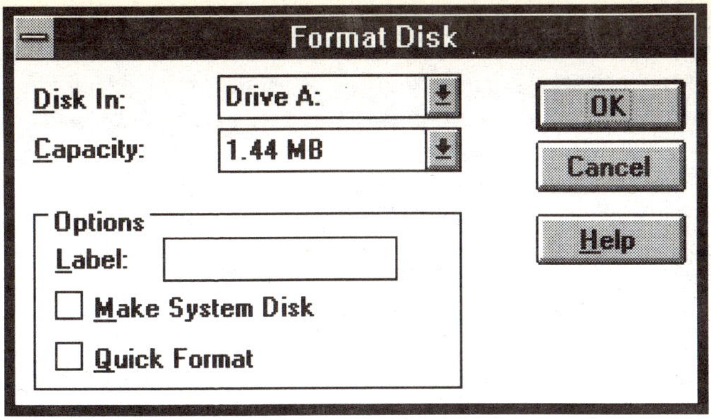

Figure 17.18

Creating a system disk

A system disk contains the basic DOS files which are required to enable the computer to be started up. Checking this box means that the disk will be formatted to receive these files and the files will be copied onto it during the formatting process. The disk can then be used to start up the computer.

Copying floppy disks

Floppy disks can be copied to make back-up disks. The source and destination disks must be of the same type.

Click on DISK then on COPY DISK to display the Copy Disk dialog box as shown in figure 17.19. Select the required drive. If your computer has more than one floppy drive, you will be asked to select the drives to be

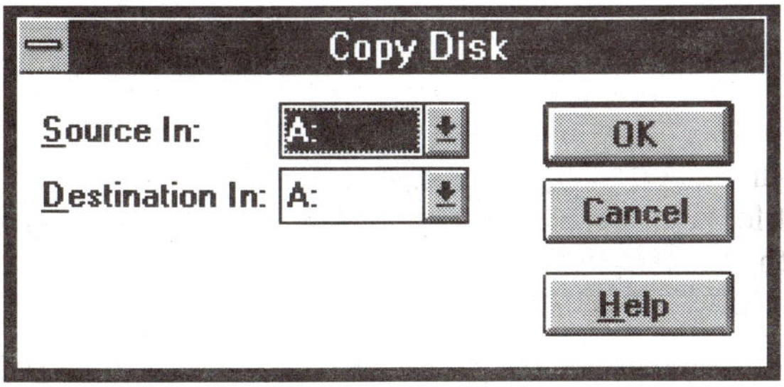

Figure 17.19

used for source and destination. It is still possible to copy disks with only a single floppy disk drive by entering the drive letter in both Source and Destination boxes as shown in the figure. File Manager will prompt you to insert the source and destination disks as required and will ask for confirmation before copying the disk.

NB Using Copy Disk will overwrite any existing contents of the destination disk. There is no way of recovering any lost data.

- Starting programs from File Manager -

File Manager can also be used to run programs. Double clicking on any executable program file will cause the program to load and run. As well as program files, it is possible to load other files, for example, Paintbrush files or Write document files. Double clicking on a BMP or PCX file will cause the Paintbrush application to load and run and will also load the picture file ready for you to use. This is known as an **association**. If you try to run a file without an association, File Manager will display an error box.

Click on FILE then on ASSOCIATE to display the box shown in figure 17.20. This allows you to associate files of a particular extension with an application. When the file is then 'run', the associated application is opened and the file loaded into it.

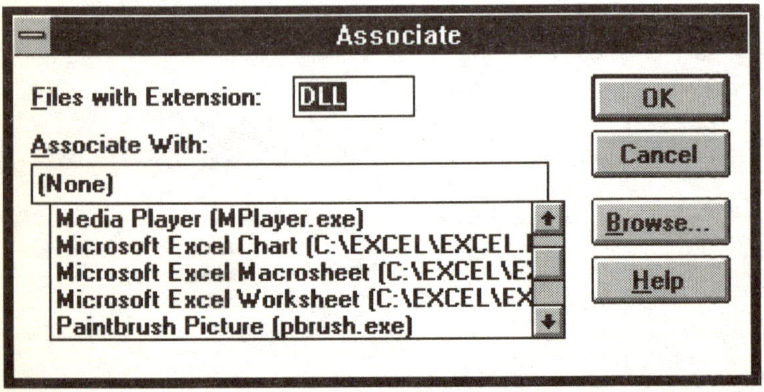

Figure 17.20

Drag and drop printing

Drag and drop printing is a quick way of printing a file. It only works for files which have associations. Print Manager must be open at the bottom of the screen on the icon bar. Select the file to be printed and drag the file icon onto the Print Manager icon at the bottom of the screen. The application to which the file belongs is automatically opened, and the file is sent to Print Manager. The application then closes and returns to File Manager.

Exiting from File Manager

This can be done in a number of ways.

- Click on FILE then on EXIT.

or
- Click on the Control Menu box then on CLOSE.

or
- Double click on the Control Menu box.

or
- Press Alt F then X for Exit.

or
- Press Alt then F4.

Any of these methods will close the File Manager window and return to Program Manager.

Summary

This chapter has described the facilities available within File Manager for

- organising the hard disk;
- creating directories;
- searching for files;
- moving files;
- copying files;
- deleting files;
- formatting disks;
- copying disks;
- starting applications.

18

CONTROL PANEL

This chapter looks at the Windows Control Panel, which controls the set up of Windows on the computer. Control Panel has a series of options which each affect a different aspect of the system. The Windows 3.0 and 3.1 Control Panel windows are shown in figure 18.1. The Control Panel windows are largely the same, except that some of the icons are slightly different and version 3.1 has an extra icon for Drivers. Version 3.11 has an extra icon for Fax.

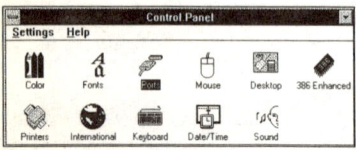

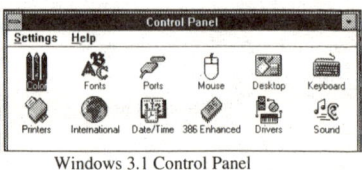

Windows 3.0 Control Panel   Windows 3.1 Control Panel

Figure 18.1

Colours

The Color option allows you to change the colours used on the desktop. Double click on the Color icon to display the Color box. At this stage, only the left hand side of the box in figure 18.2 is displayed.

The Windows default colours are white windows with grey scroll bars on a grey background. The active window has a blue Title Bar. The Color box offers a number of different colour schemes or you can define your

CONTROL PANEL

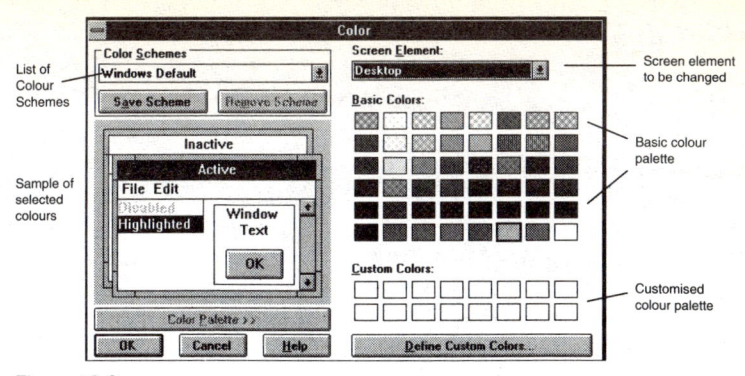

Figure 18.2

own. Some colour schemes are very bright and colourful, others are much more restful. Some colour schemes are specially designed for LCD screens such as are found on laptops and notebook computers.

Click on the Color Schemes list box to display the preset schemes. Select the required scheme. A sample of the selected scheme is shown in the box in the left of the Color window shown in figure 18.2.

Changing colour schemes

The standard colour schemes can be customised to your own tastes.

Click on Color Palette. This extends the Color box to include the palette area, shown on the right of figure 18.2. This figure is in black and white but still gives an idea of the scope of the operation. Select the screen element you wish to change from the list box.

This can also be done by clicking in the required area. Clicking on a scroll bar will set the colour for scroll bars, clicking on the active Title Bar will set colours for active Title Bars, and so on. The selected screen element will be displayed in the box.

Select the required colour from the palette.

Selecting solid colours and not having too many different colours will allow Windows to re-draw your desktop more quickly.

Repeat the process for all the required elements of the screen. Type a name for your new colour scheme and click on OK.

— 199 —

Creating your own colours

Click on Define Custom Colors to display the Custom Color Selector box, as shown in figure 18.3.

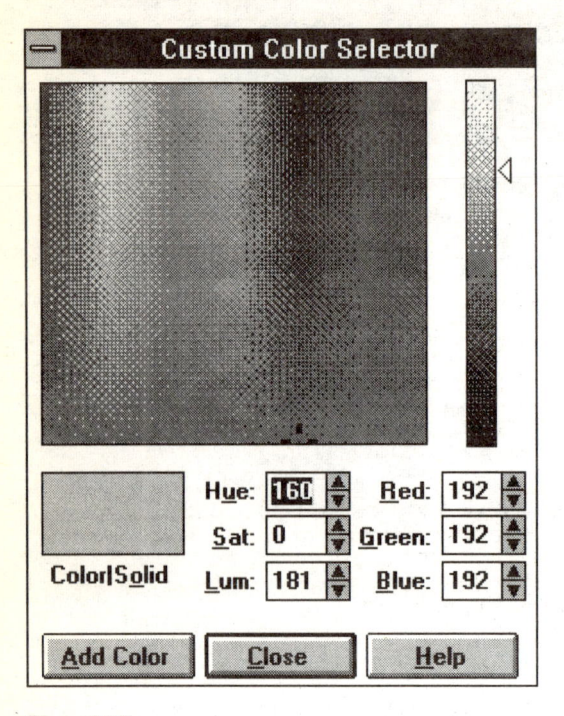

Figure 18.3

- Click on the Red, Green and Blue boxes to reduce or increase the amounts of each colour.

or

- Click in the main block of colour to select a colour. You can then select the density of the colour using the bar at the right of the main block. The red, green and blue indicators will change to reflect the colour you have selected.

The results will be shown in the Color box to the lower left of the coloured area.

☺ Remember, you can click on Help at any time to explain the various buttons in the dialog boxes. Clicking on the Help button in figure 18.3

displays a Help screen with a number of related topics. Clicking on Color/Solid displays the Help screen shown in figure 18.4. This gives information on the Color box which displays the results of your colour changes.

Color/Solid Box

This box shows the changes you make to the hue, saturation, and luminosity of a color. As you make changes, the new nonsolid color is displayed on the left side of the box. The right side of the box shows the solid color closest to the selected color.

▶ Double-click the right side of the box to select the solid color.

Figure 18.4

Fonts

If you have installed a printer, any fonts in the printer would have been made available for Windows to use. This option allows you to install extra fonts which you may wish to add to your system.

Double click on the Fonts icon to display the Fonts option box, as shown in figure 18.5. The Windows 3.0 screen is slightly different, but the main differences are due to the addition of TrueType fonts in version 3.1. The Fonts box shows a list of all the fonts currently installed in your system. Selecting any font will display part of the font in the Sample box. Below the sample box there is a description of the characteristic of the font.

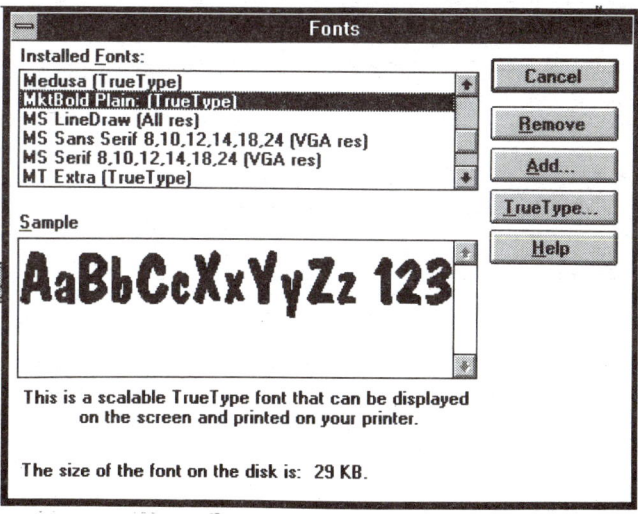

Figure 18.5

Installing new fonts

Click on Add to display the Add Fonts box, as shown in figure 18.6.

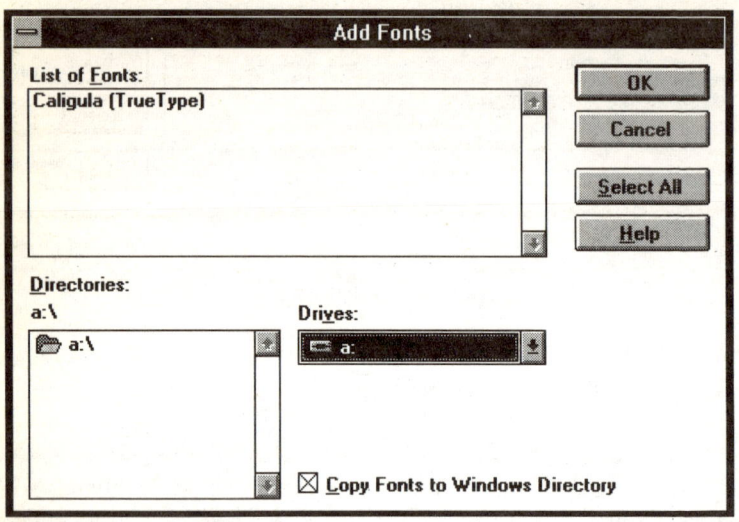

Figure 18.6

Click on the required drive and directory. All fonts found on the required drive and directory will be listed. Any or all of the fonts in the list can be transferred. Highlight the font(s) to be transferred and click on OK.

☺ More than one font can be installed at the same time by holding down the Shift key while highlighting the fonts. Click on Select All to highlight all the fonts.

If the check box at the bottom is checked, the fonts will then be transferred to the Windows System directory ready for you to use.

TrueType setting
3.1 only

TrueType fonts are normally stored with the TrueType facilities enabled. This requires extra memory. The TrueType setting can be switched off to store the font as a non-TrueType font which uses less memory.

To store a font as a non-TrueType font, click on TrueType to display the TrueType box, as in figure 18.7. Click on Enable TrueType Fonts to clear the check box and click on OK. The fonts are not removed from the system. They can be enabled again at any time.

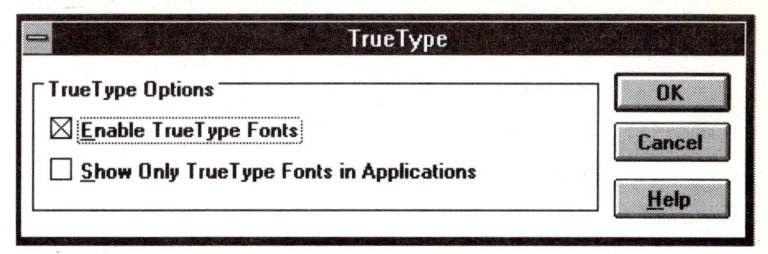

Figure 18.7

This option does not take effect until Windows is re-started.

Removing fonts

You may wish to remove fonts which you do not use to save disk space. Click on Fonts. Highlight the font(s) to be removed. Click on Remove to display the Remove Font dialog box, shown in figure 18.8. Check the Delete Font File box if the font is to be removed from the disk to release its storage space then click on Yes to remove the font(s).

Figure 18.8

Ports

This option allows you to set up the parameters for the serial ports of your computer. Most computers have two serial ports, COM1 and COM2. The mouse is usually connected to COM1. The most likely use for COM2 is a modem, which should be set up from within Windows Terminal (see chapter 23).

Mouse

The Mouse option in Control Panel allows you to change the way that the mouse is used. The most likely use of this is to switch the left and right buttons for left handed use.

Double click on the Mouse icon to display the Mouse dialog box, as in figure 18.9. Click on Swap Left/Right Buttons then click on OK.

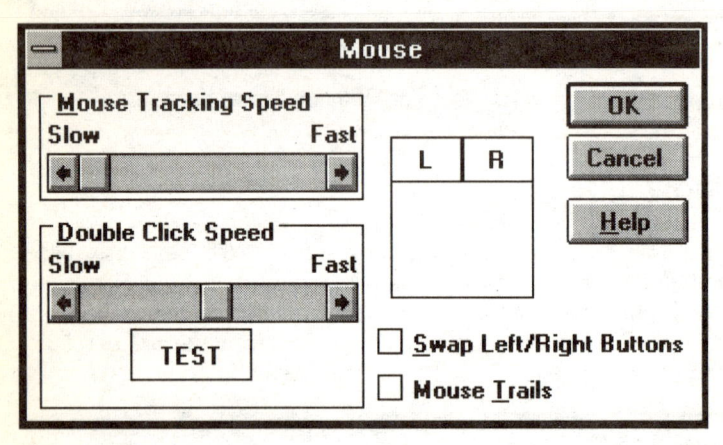

Figure 18.9

If you swap the left and right mouse buttons, you will need to remember this when working through the book. When the instruction is to click or hold down the left mouse button, you will need to use the right mouse button instead.

Enabling Mouse Trails causes visible trail to appear on the screen as the mouse is moved around.

The other settings allow you to adjust the speed at which the mouse pointer moves across the screen and the speed of double clicking. If you experience difficulties in these areas, it is worth experimenting with the settings to see if they make it any easier.

Desktop

The Desktop option allows you to change various aspects of the display to suit individual preferences. In Windows 3.1, the aspects that can be changed are the pattern of the desktop background, the screen saver to be used, the way in which icons are displayed, and other settings such as the width of the window border and the rate at which the cursor blinks. Windows 3.0 offers the same range of options except for screen savers.

Double click on the Desktop icon to display the Desktop dialog box, as in figure 18.10.

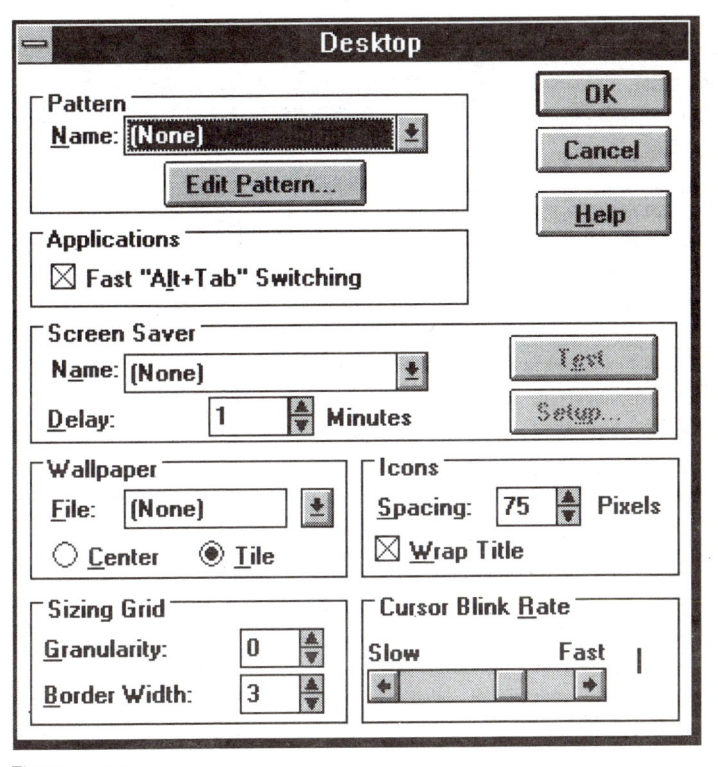

Figure 18.10

Patterns

Windows offers a range of different patterns. The selected pattern will be used for the screen background. Click on the Pattern list box and select the required pattern.

Screen savers
3.1 only

A screen saver is a device which comes into action when the mouse has not been moved or a key has not been pressed for a set time. Its purpose is to save the screen from being burnt by continually displaying the same pattern of colour in the same place on the screen. The screen saver works by displaying continually moving blocks of colour or patterns instead of a static display. It is now possible to purchase screen savers for Windows which provide a vast range of effects, some of which are highly entertaining.

The standard screen savers in Windows 3.1 are:

Blank Screen	blank screen
Flying Windows	Windows 3.1 icons in different colours
Marquee	text banner moving across screen
Mystify	lines flowing around screen, changing shape as they move
Starfield Simulation	many coloured points of light that look like stars

Select the required screen saver from the list box. You can view the effect by clicking on the Test button. The time interval before the screen saver comes into effect can be changed by altering the Delay setting.

Click on Setup to display the Setup box. This allows you to change many of the features of the screen savers: Marquee, for example, can use any available font, size and colour of text, the background colour can be changed, the position and speed can be changed and you can even type your own message! A sample is displayed to reflect any changes that you make. The Setup options are different for each screen saver. The Setup option box for Marquee is shown in figure 18.11.

Setting passwords

A screen saver can be password protected so that only users knowing the password can go back into Windows. Check the Password Protection box

CONTROL PANEL

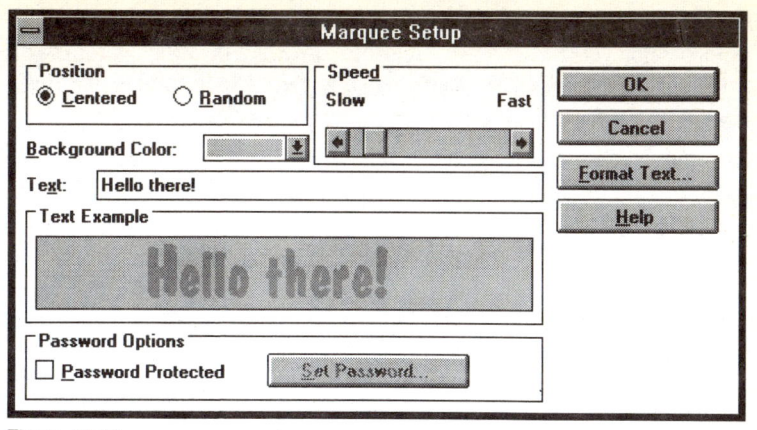

Figure 18.11

and then click on the Set Password button to display the Change Password box shown in figure 18.12.

Figure 18.12

You are required to enter your old password, if you have one, and then your new password twice to ensure you have entered it correctly. When password protection is in effect, the password has to be entered before Windows will return to the desktop.

Wallpaper

Wallpaper also colours the background of the desktop, as does a selected pattern. The difference is that wallpaper uses bit-mapped images stored in BMP files. There are a number of standard wallpapers supplied with Windows, or you can choose any other BMP file on your system. You could even draw your own masterpiece in Paintbrush, save it as a BMP file, and use it as screen wallpaper!

NB Note that screen savers, patterns and wallpaper all use memory. If you run out of memory while running programs you may need to remove some or all of these options.

Sizing grid

The Sizing Grid option allows an invisible grid to be switched on and sized to facilitate arranging icons on the desktop.

Icons

The Icons option allows the spacing between icons in the windows to be altered. In version 3.1 the icon title can extend to more than one line if necessary. This is achieved by the Wrap Title option being switched on by default. The Wrap Title option can be switched off. In version 3.0, icon titles can only occupy a single line.

Keyboard

The Keyboard option enables you to alter the rate at which characters are repeated when a key is held down. This is unlikely to need to be changed.

Printers

The Printers option allows you to install or remove printers, change the output port which the printer is using and choose a new default printer.

Double click on the Printers icon to display the Printers option box as shown in figure 18.13.

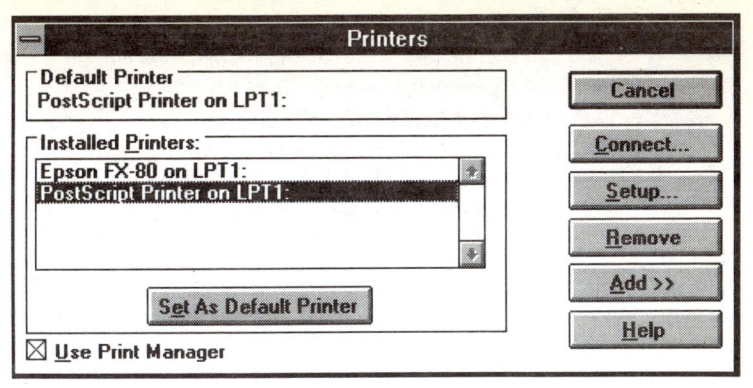

Figure 18.13

Windows asks for information about your printer(s) at the time it is installed. See chapter 25 for details of Windows installation. The Printers box shows the installed printers and the printer that has been selected as the default printer. In the set up shown here, the PostScript laser printer is the default printer, and there is an additional dot matrix printer. Both printers are connected to the parallel printer port (LPT1). In practice, this is achieved by use of a printer switch box which directs the output to the required printer.

The functions of the various buttons are described below.

Button   **Function**
Connect   This enables a printer to be connected to any required output port; the dot matrix printer, for example, could be connected to LPT2 (if the computer has a second parallel printer port), avoiding the need to have a switch box.

Setup   The Setup option allows you to set the paper size and orientation (portrait or landscape) and the number of copies required.

Remove   This option allows printers to be removed. Highlight the printer(s) to be removed then click on Remove. Windows will ask for confirmation before removing the printer.

Add   This is used to install a new printer for use with Windows. Clicking on Add extends the Printers box to display a long list of printers.

WINDOWS

> Scroll down the list and select the name of your printer. Click on Install. You will be prompted to insert the required Windows disk in order for Windows to copy the printer driver file into your Windows system directory. You will then be asked whether this is to be the new default printer.

NB Note that although the list of printers is extensive, your printer may not be in the list, particularly if it is an old printer or a very new model. In this case, a suitable driver can usually be found by selecting a model of the same type (laser, dot matrix, ink jet, etc.) from the same manufacturer. Alternatively, consult your printer manual to see if the printer emulates any other printers – these may well be in the list.

Set as Default Printer This allows you to select any of the installed printers in the list to be used as the default printer. Highlight the required printer and click the button. The printer name in the Default Printer box will change to the printer you have selected.

Use Print Manager Print Manager is a utility program which collects all the printed output from Windows and processes and prints it. The Use Print Manager option switches between sending output directly to the printer or sending it to Print Manager. Print Manager is discussed in more detail in the next chapter.

Click on Close to return to Control Panel.

International

The International option allows you to tell the computer in which country you live and which format of dates, currencies and times you require. The specified language is used in the dictionaries and for all dialog boxes. Metric measurements are now standard but this can be changed to Imperial if you wish.

CONTROL PANEL

Date and time

The Date/Time option allows you to change your system date and time. Double click on the Date/Time icon to display the Date & Time option box, as in figure 18.14.

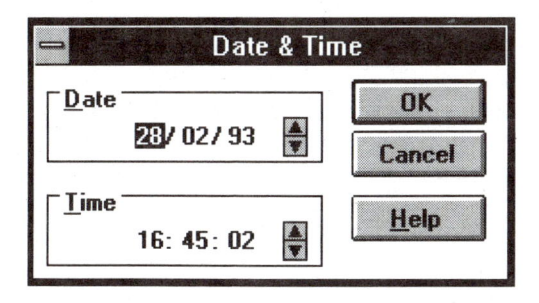

Figure 18.14

To change a value, select the part of the date or time to be changed, and type the new value. The settings will be stored in the computer for future use both by Windows and by DOS.

386 Enhanced

This option allows you to allocate Windows processing and memory to applications. The option can only be used if you have a 386 computer with enough memory to run Windows in 386 Enhanced mode. Chapter 25 contains more information on using 386 Enhanced mode.

Drivers

3.1 only

The Drivers option is one of the new features of Windows 3.1. Its purpose is to allow Windows to make full use of multimedia devices such as sound cards or CD-ROM drives. Such devices, although installed in your computer or connected to it, will not be automatically detected by Windows. Each device needs a **device driver**. A device driver is a program that controls a particular piece of hardware and the way it talks to Windows. Some drivers are supplied with Windows. Manufacturers of sound cards and other devices generally supply suitable device drivers with the hardware.

Sound

3.1 only

In Windows 3.0, the Sound option only allows you to disable the warning beep. In Windows 3.1, Sound provides options which enable users with a sound card to incorporate sound into their normal usage of Windows. You can select different sound effects for a number of events within Windows, such as starting and exiting Windows.

Double click on the Sound icon to display the Sound option box, as in figure 18.15.

This displays a list of the sound files supplied with Windows. Windows associates particular sounds from the list with various actions: for example, when Windows is started and Program Manager is displayed, the sound emitted is a Tada. The Sound dialog box enables you to change these sounds to suit your individual preference. If you do not have a sound card fitted, all the options will be greyed out and cannot be selected.

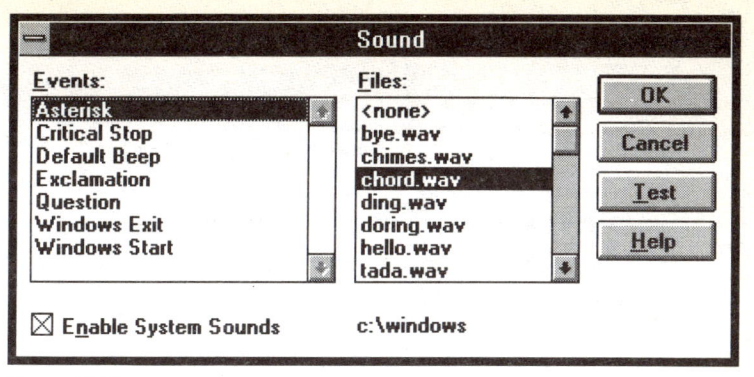

Figure 18.15

Summary

This chapter has discussed the use of the Windows Control Panel including:

- changing colours and desktop patterns;
- installing and removing fonts;
- changing mouse settings;
- installing and setting up printers;
- setting language, currency, date and time;
- installing device drivers;
- using sound cards.

19

— THE MAIN WINDOW —

This chapter contains reference material for the remaining programs in the Main Program Manager window. These are Print Manager, Windows setup, Dos Prompt, and Clipboard Viewer.

Print Manager

Print Manager is a utility program which intercepts all output sent to the printer from within Windows. The print jobs are then queued and printed by Print Manager.

The big advantage offered by Print Manager in 386 Enhanced mode is that it is able to work in the background, printing files, while you carry on working in the current program or any other program within Windows. You may well notice that the programs run quite a bit slower while Print Manager is active.

Printing documents

The appearance of your printed document depends on the fonts and sizes you have used within the document and the ability of your printer to reproduce these. The existence of TrueType fonts in Windows 3.1 has made it much easier to produce quality output on cheaper dot matrix printers. Fonts are discussed in greater detail in chapter 8.

MAIN WINDOW

All Windows programs contain the Print option on the File menu. This will usually send the output to Print Manager for processing and printing. Print Manager is the default printing method in Windows. However, it is also possible to send output directly to the printer from Windows applications. This method usually prints the output faster but prevents you from doing any other work until the document is printed.

3.1 only

Print Manager also makes it possible to install and remove printers, select the printer port and change the print setup. These functions and menus are identical to those described in the section on printers in chapter 18.

Non-Windows applications running under Windows print directly using their own printer drivers. They do not normally send their output to Print Manager. This means you will have to wait for the program to finish printing before you can continue working within Windows.

Double click on the icon to display the Print Manager window, as shown in figure 19.1. In this figure, Print Manager is shown processing two print jobs: one a bit-mapped (BMP) graphic file from Paintbrush and the a Word document (part of this book). The printer symbol next to the first job in the list indicates that this is the job currently being printed.

Figure 19.1, version 3.1

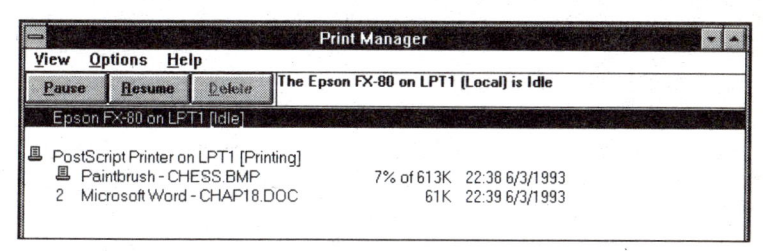

Figure 19.1, version 3.11

— 215 —

Print Manager shows you the names of the available printers, the name of the printer in use, the port it is connected to (usually LPT1) and the current status of the printer (printing, idle or stalled). This option box allows you to control the printing of the documents.

Effect	Action
Pause print queue	Click on Pause button or icon.
Resume print queue	Click on Resume button or icon.
Delete print job	Click on job name in print list then click on Delete button or icon.
Change order of printing	Click on job to be moved and drag to required place in the queue.

Print Manager menu options

The View menu allows you to change the way in which files are displayed. The default display is that Print Manager shows the file size and date and time the job joined the queue.

The Options menu allows you to change the priority and speed of printing, and, in Windows version 3.1, to set features specific to the particular printer that you are using. Changing the printing speed determines the proportion of time that Windows allows Print Manager to use. The default printing priority is Medium which is suitable for most situations. Occasionally, you may be working in an application which requires a lot of processing power, and it could be useful to reduce the printing priority so that more resources are available for the application. This will increase the time it takes for Print Manager to produce the printed output.

3.11 only

The Printer menu allows printing to be paused and restarted.

The Document menu allows individual documents to be deleted, or moved lower or higher in the queue.

Version 3.11 also has a Tool bar with icons to accomplish many of these functions.

Installing a printer

3.1 only

In version 3.1, the Options menu has a Printer Setup option, which will display the installed Printers box for your printer. A sample screen is shown in figure 19.2. The Printers box is the same box as is displayed by double clicking on Printers in the Windows Control Panel. In Windows 3.0, printers can only be installed and set up from within Control Panel.

The Printers box shows the names of the printers which have been installed on your system and the printer which has been selected as the default printer.

The options are:

Option   **Effect**
Connect   This enables a printer to be connected to any required output port, for example, a second printer could be connected to LPT2.

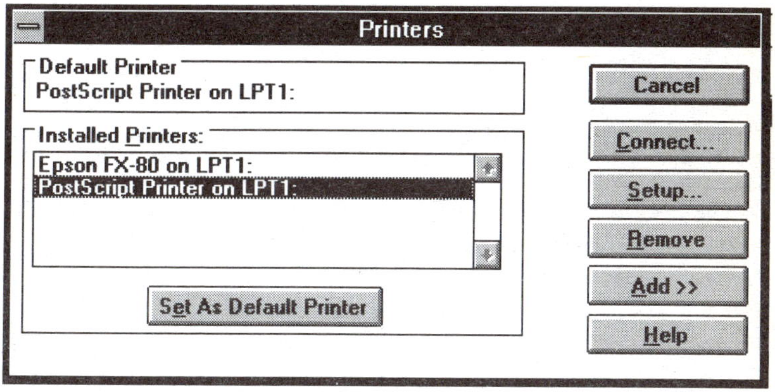

Figure 19.2

Remove   This allows printers to be removed. Highlight the printer(s) to be removed then click on Remove. Windows will ask for confirmation before removing the printer driver.
Add   This is used to install a new printer for use with Windows. Clicking on Add extends the Printers box to include a long list of printers. Scroll down

the list and select the name of your printer. Click on Install. You will be prompted to insert the required Windows disk in order for Windows to copy the printer driver file into your Windows system directory. You will then be asked whether this is to be the new default printer.

Set as Default allows you to select any of the installed printers in the list to be used as the main printer. Highlight the required printer and click the button. The printer name in the Default Printer box will change to the printer you have selected.

Use Print Manager switches between sending output directly to the printer or sending it to Print Manager.

NB Note that although a long list of printers is displayed, your printer may not be in the list, particularly if it is an old printer or a very new model. In this case, a suitable driver can usually be found by selecting a model of the same type (laser, dot matrix, ink jet etc.) from the same manufacturer. Alternatively, consult your printer manual to see if the printer emulates any other printers – these may well be in the list.

Printer setup options

The Setup screens for two printer types are shown in figures 19.3 and 19.4 below.

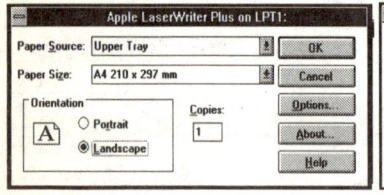

Figure 19.3   Figure 19.4

Option   **Action**
Paper source   Sets paper tray or paper feed method.
Paper size   Selects paper size.
Resolution   Sets intensity for graphic images. May be High, Medium or Low, or may be expressed in dots per inch (DPI).
Orientation   Selects Portrait or Landscape printing. Some printers cannot print in Landscape.

MAIN WINDOW

Options   The available options vary according to the selected printer.
Copies   Sets number of copies.
Help   Activates Print Manager Help.

Closing Print Manager

3.0 only

- Click on VIEW then EXIT.

3.1 only

- Click on OPTIONS then EXIT.

or

- Click on the Control Menu box in the corner of the Print Manager window.

Both methods will close Print Manager. If there are still jobs to be printed, Windows will ask for confirmation before closing Print Manager.

Windows Setup

Windows Setup is used to change your Windows system settings and to set up applications to work with Windows.

Windows Setup

Double click on the Windows Setup icon to display the Windows Setup dialog box shown in figure 19.5. This shows the current system settings for monitor, keyboard, mouse and any network that may be installed. The figure shows version 3.1. Version 3.0 has a further option called Swap File, which will show the type of swap file being used by your system. Chapter 25 discusses swap files in more detail.

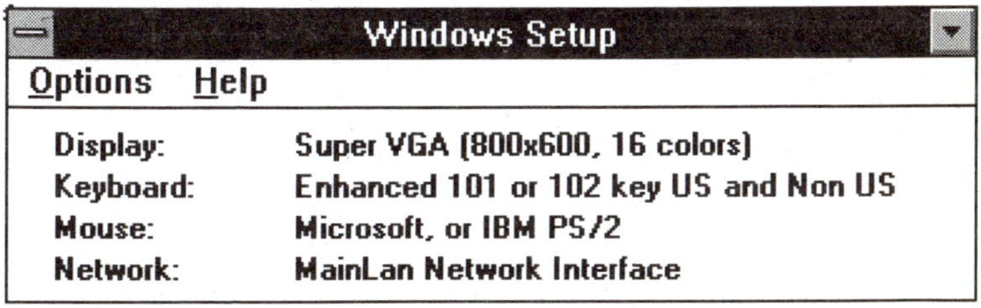

```
┌─────────────────────────────────────────────────────┐
│                   Windows Setup                  ▼  │
├─────────────────────────────────────────────────────┤
│ Options   Help                                      │
│                                                     │
│   Display:      Super VGA (800x600, 16 colors)      │
│   Keyboard:     Enhanced 101 or 102 key US and Non US│
│   Mouse:        Microsoft, or IBM PS/2              │
│   Network:      MainLan Network Interface           │
└─────────────────────────────────────────────────────┘
```

Figure 19.5

Click on OPTIONS to display the Options menu. This allows you to change system settings and set up applications. Windows 3.1 has an extra option which allows you to add or remove Windows components.

Changing system settings

The Change System Settings option provides a list box for each of the four settings from which you can highlight and select the required option. This is shown in figure 19.6 with the mouse list box displayed. Select the required setting and click on the Control Menu box to store the setting and close the window.

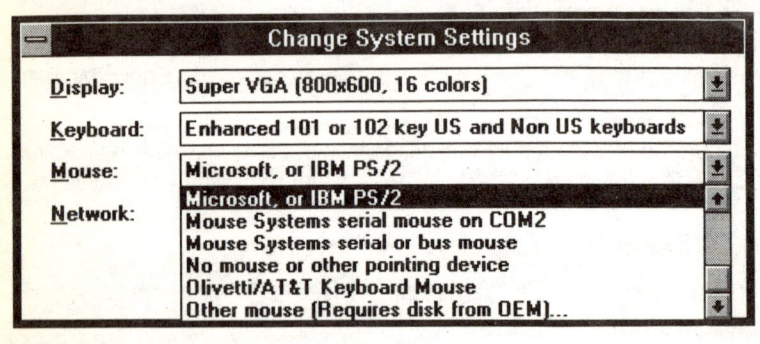

Figure 19.6

Setting up applications

Windows will recognise all of the common PC packages. Click on the SETUP APPLICATIONS option to initiate a search of your disk for programs which Windows can recognise. You can specify the part of the disk to be searched. A list of the identified applications will be displayed. Highlight the applications you wish to use or click on Select All to allow Windows to create a program icon and a suitable start up file for the selected programs.

Adding or removing components
3.1 only

Selecting Add or Remove components displays the screen shown in figure 19.7. This indicates which optional Windows elements have been installed in your system. The amount of disk space used by each of the elements is also shown. It may sometimes be necessary to remove some or all of these components to save disk space or to reduce the memory Windows requires when running. To remove a component, switch off the check box. To install a component, switch on the check box.

It is also possible to remove some of the files in each component: you could, for example, remove all the screen savers except for your favourite. To do this, click on Files and highlight the files to be removed or installed.

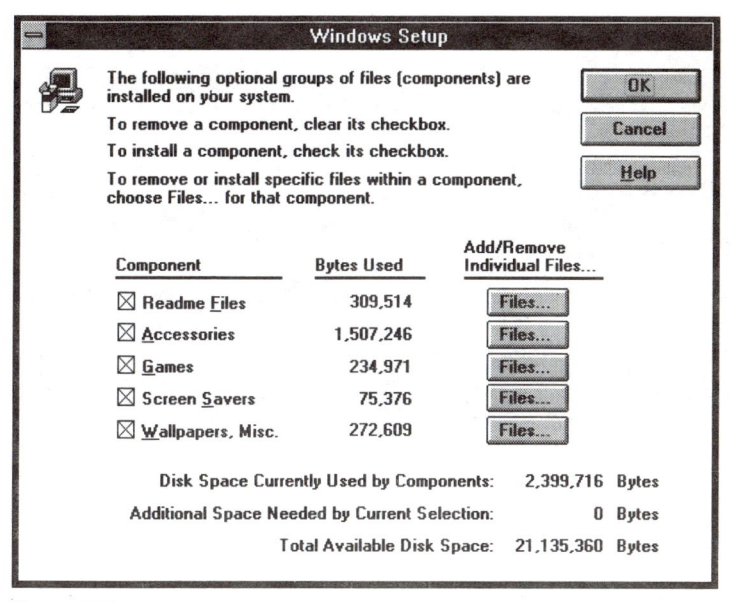

```
                        Windows Setup

    The following optional groups of files (components) are        OK
    installed on your system.
    To remove a component, clear its checkbox.                   Cancel
    To install a component, check its checkbox.
    To remove or install specific files within a component,       Help
    choose Files... for that component.

                                      Add/Remove
    Component           Bytes Used    Individual Files...

    ☒ Readme Files         309,514        Files...
    ☒ Accessories        1,507,246        Files...
    ☒ Games                234,971        Files...
    ☒ Screen Savers         75,376        Files...
    ☒ Wallpapers, Misc.    272,609        Files...

         Disk Space Currently Used by Components:   2,399,716 Bytes
         Additional Space Needed by Current Selection:      0 Bytes
                       Total Available Disk Space: 21,135,360 Bytes
```

Figure 19.7

MS-DOS Prompt

The MS-DOS Prompt icon provides a quick and easy way to exit from Windows to DOS in order to use a DOS command. Windows is still running and in control but temporarily shells to DOS. This facility will appeal to those users who are familiar with DOS and wish to continue using DOS to copy, delete or rename files or to format disks. These functions are all provided within Windows File Manager, which is described in chapter 16.

Double click on the MS-DOS Prompt icon to display the MS-DOS Prompt window with the DOS C:\> prompt shown in figure 19.8. Windows 3.1 provides some reminders as to the keys to use while you are using DOS prompt and how to return to Windows when you are finished. The version 3.0 COMMAND window is much less helpful and gives no such information!

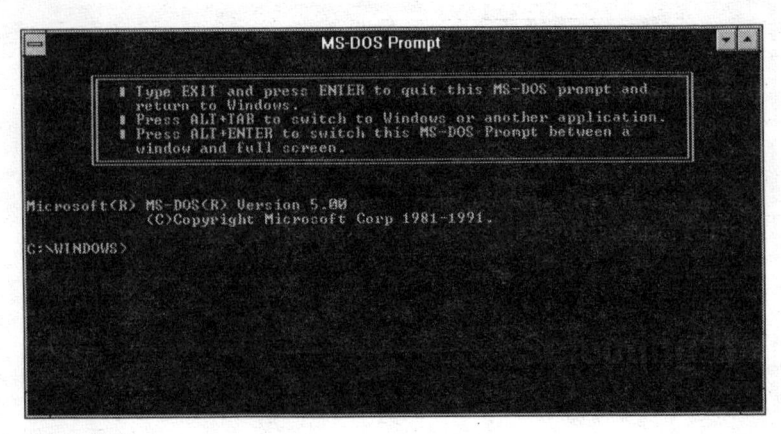

Figure 19.8

The mouse is no longer operative so you will need to use the key equivalents.

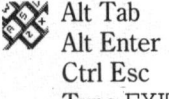

Alt Tab	switches to the next open Windows application
Alt Enter	switches between full screen and window display
Ctrl Esc	displays the task list
Type EXIT	closes MS-DOS Prompt window and returns to Windows

MAIN WINDOW

Clipboard viewer

The Windows Clipboard is a very powerful tool. The Clipboard is an area of memory which can be used to place sections of text or graphics from any Windows application. The text or graphic is then available to any other Windows application. The Clipboard is able to hold a considerable amount of information.

The Clipboard Viewer displays the current contents of the Clipboard. The Clipboard shown in figure 19.9 contains part of the Help text from Clipboard Viewer Help.

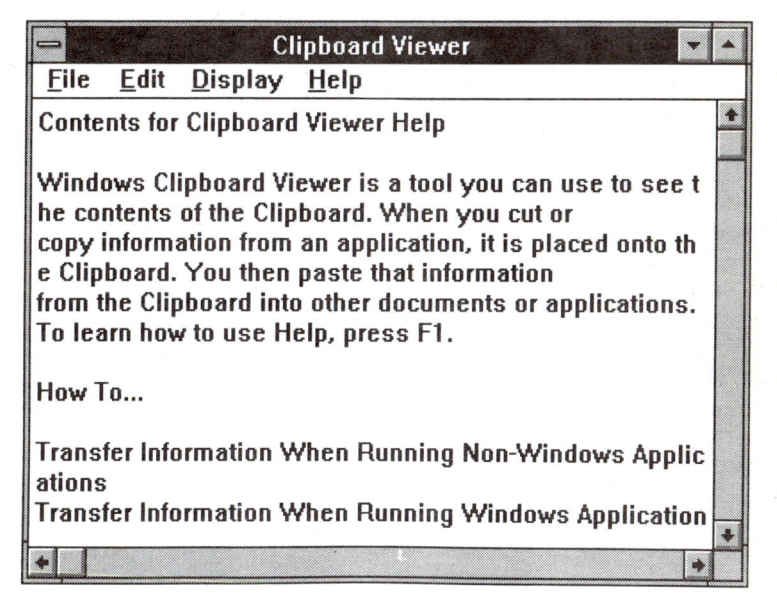

Figure 19.9

Saving Clipboard files

The main disadvantage with the Clipboard is that it can only contain one piece of data. This problem can be lessened by saving the contents of the Clipboard to disk. Click on FILE then on SAVE AS. Select the required drive and directory and specify a filename. By default, Clipboard files are stored in the WINDOWS directory and given an extension of CLP.

WINDOWS

ClipBook Viewer

The saved Clipboard file can be re-opened in Clipboard Viewer by clicking on FILE then on OPEN. Select the file to be opened. It can then be pasted into other Windows applications.

This disadvantage has been overcome in version 3.11. Clipboard Viewer has been renamed Clipbook Viewer with a new icon and the facility to store a number of Clipboards as pages in a book called a **Local Clipbook**. All or some of the Clipbook can be made available to other users on a network.

Data has to be cut or copied to the Clipboard in the normal way. It can then be transferred to the Clipbook by clicking on the Paste icon or selecting EDIT then PASTE.

The Clipbook Viewer screen display is shown in figure 19.10.

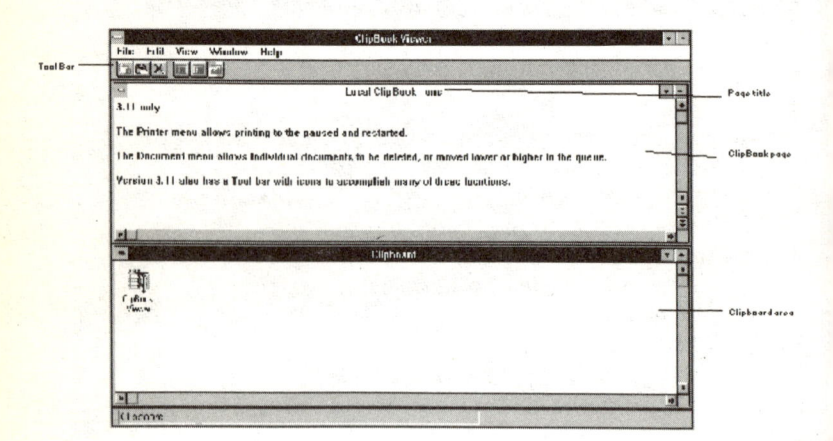

Figure 19.10

Summary

In this chapter, the following topics have been discussed:
- printing using Print Manager;
- installing and removing printers;
- setting up printers;

— 224 —

- changing Windows system settings;
- adding or removing optional components;
- using MS-DOS prompt;
- using the Clipboard Viewer.

20
ACCESSORIES 1
PAINTBRUSH

This chapter contains reference material for Paintbrush, the graphics program supplied with Microsoft Windows.

Double click on the Paintbrush icon in the Accessories window to display the Paintbrush screen, as shown in figure 20.1.

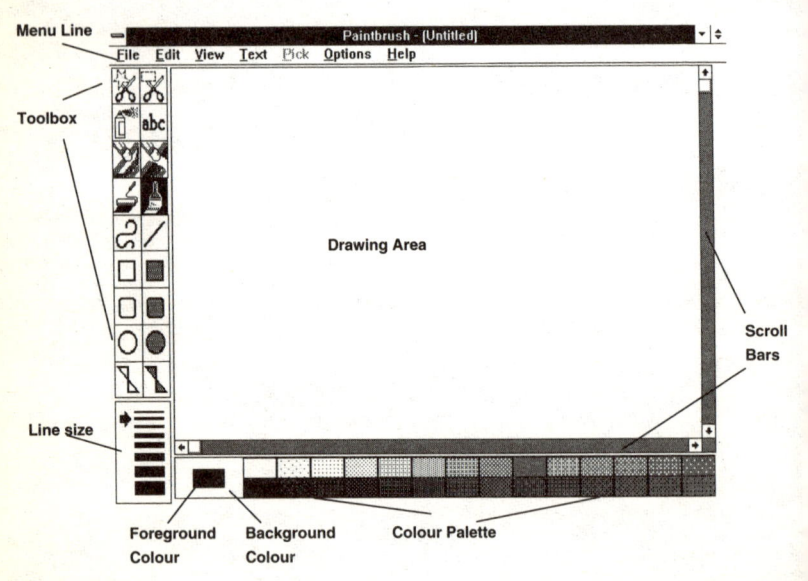

Figure 20.1

Starting a new file

Click on FILE then on NEW. Paintbrush will remind you if an existing file has not been saved and ask if you wish to save.

Opening an existing file

Click on FILE then on OPEN. By default, the Open dialog box displays all BMP files in the WINDOWS directory. The file type can be changed if required. Select the required directory and file name and click on OK.

The Paintbrush toolbox

The toolbox contains a number of different icons which produce particular shapes or effects. Click on the icon to select the tool. The functions of the various tools are described below.

ICON	TOOL	FUNCTION
/	Line tool	Draws lines. Move the crosshair cursor to the point where the line is to start. Drag the crosshair to the point where the line is to end.
	Normal eraser	The normal eraser turns everything to the background colour, effectively rubbing it out.
	Colour eraser	The colour eraser changes the foreground colour to the background colour.
	Box tools	Draws rectangles. Click at one corner and drag until the required rectangle is drawn. To draw a square, hold down the Shift key while dragging the mouse.
	Rounded corner box	Click at one corner and drag until the required rectangle is drawn. To draw a square, hold down the Shift key while dragging the mouse.

WINDOWS

	Circle tools	Click at the centre and drag until the required shape is drawn. To draw a circle, hold down the Shift key while dragging the mouse.
	Polygon A polygon is a closed shape with any number of sides.	Draw a line. Release the mouse button at the end of the line and draw a second line, starting at the end of the first line. Release the mouse button again. Repeat this until all the lines are in place. Double click at the last point. This finishes off the shape, joins up the last side and fills it with colour.
	Curved line	Draw a line. The line can then be bent in two ways. Single curve: click on the line and drag the line until the curve is correct. Click on the second end point of the line to fix the curve. Double curve: drag the line to produce the first curve. Click on the line again and drag to form the second curve. Release the mouse to fix the line.
	Brush	The brush tool is used for drawing solid blocks of colour in the selected foreground colour. Click and drag to draw.
	Airbrush	The airbrush tool sprays dots of the foreground colour on the picture. Click and drag the mouse to cover the area.
	Roller	The roller tool is used to fill areas of the picture with the foreground colour. Click in the area to be filled. The area will be filled up to any solid lines.
	Text tool	The text tool allows you to add text at any required place and in different sizes and styles. Click to make an insertion point and type the text.
	Selection tools or **cut-out tools**	These two tools are used to select part of a picture. The first tool is used when the part to be selected is close to other shapes and so has to be cut carefully. The second tool draws a rectangle around the shape. Drag the pointer so it draws an outline which completely encloses the shape(s). The selected area can now be moved, copied or deleted.

Saving the file

Click on FILE then on SAVE. If the file does not have a name, type a file name. Paintbrush files are saved in the WINDOWS directory as bit-mapped files with an extension of BMP. Paintbrush offers an alternative format of PCX which is a graphics format which can also be used in non-Windows packages. To save the file as a PCX file, click on the Save File as Type list box and select the PCX files option, as shown in figure 20.2. Click on SAVE or SAVE AS in the normal way.

Save File as Type:
PCX files (*.PCX)

Figure 20.2

Printing

Click on FILE then on PRINT. This displays the Print box shown in figure 20.3. The default settings are as shown. Change any required settings and click on OK.

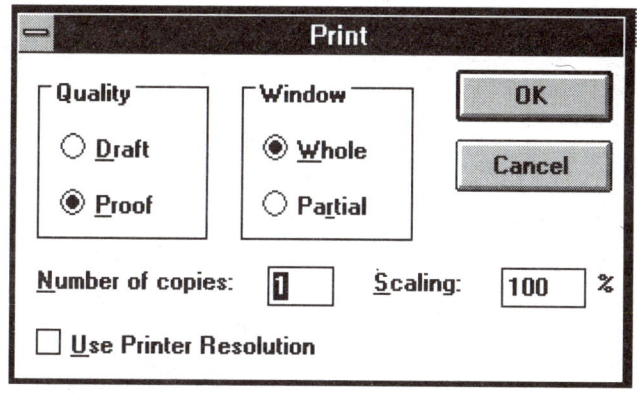

Figure 20.3

Changing printing size

Standard Paintbrush drawings using the visible drawing area occupy approximately the top half of a sheet of A4 in size. Part of a drawing may be printed by selecting Partial in the print box shown in figure 20.3, and

— 229 —

using the mouse to define the area to be printed. The Scaling option reduces or increases the overall size of the printed picture.

Changing the appearance of the picture

Changing line thickness

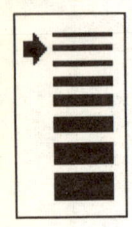

Figure 20.4

The line thickness setting determines the width of any lines drawn, the lines used for outlines of shapes, the width of the eraser tools, and the thickness of the brush and airbrush tools. Figure 20.4 shows the line thickness box. The arrow in the box points to the current line thickness. Click on the required line thickness.

Selecting colours

Figure 20.5

Figure 20.5 is a black and white version of the colour selection box. On a colour screen, each of the boxes shows a different colour. The box at the left shows the currently selected colours. Different colours can be selected for the foreground and the background. The default colours are black foreground and white background. The foreground colour is used for the colour of any lines, the colour of any filled boxes, the brush and roller colours and the colour for the colour eraser.

- To select a **foreground colour** from the box, click on the colour with the **left** mouse button.
- To select a **background colour** from the box, click on the colour with the **right** mouse button.

Editing colours

As well as the colours in the colour selection box, you can produce your own colours. Double click on the colour palette or click on OPTIONS then on EDIT COLOURS to display the Edit Colors box shown in figure 20.6. This box enables the three basic colours, red, blue and green, to be mixed in varying proportions to create the colour you require. A sample of the colour is shown in the box at the right as you mix the colours.

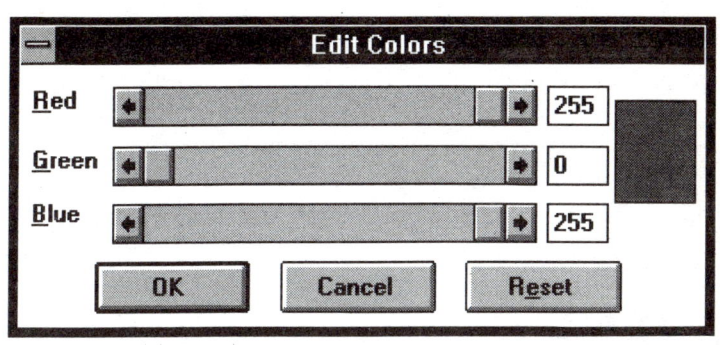

Figure 20.6

Changing brush shape

Double click on the brush tool in the tool bar or click on OPTIONS then on BRUSH SHAPES to display the Brush Shapes box, as shown in figure 20.7. The brush can be a line, or a round or square-headed brush. Click on the required brush shape then click on OK.

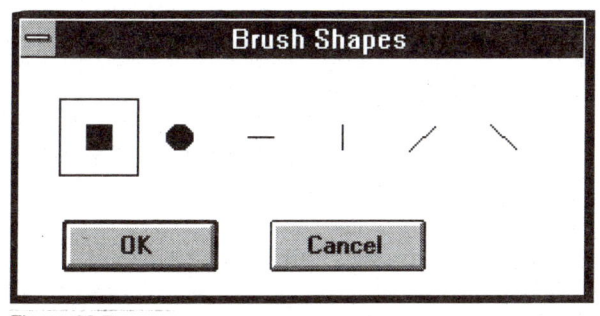

Figure 20.7

Changing the appearance of text

3.0 only

Version 3.0 uses three separate menus to control the appearance of the text.

- Click FONT to select the font.
- Click on STYLE to select the text style.
- Click on SIZE to select the size of the text.

3.1 only

In version 3.1, the text features are all found on one menu, the Text menu. Click on TEXT on the Menu Bar to display the Text menu, as shown in figure 20.8. This menu contains settings for the style of the text. Selected options are shown by a tick next to them. Options can be combined, for example, Bold, Italic and Outline can all be selected at the same time.

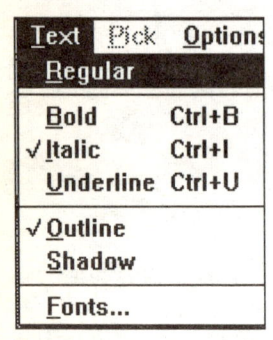

```
Text   Pick   Options
  Regular
  Bold        Ctrl+B
√ Italic      Ctrl+I
  Underline   Ctrl+U
√ Outline
  Shadow
  Fonts...
```

Figure 20.8

Click on TEXT then on FONTS to display the Font box shown in figure 20.9.

Fonts are styles of lettering. The fonts in the Font list will depend on the fonts which have been installed in the copy of Windows you are using. If you have Windows 3.1 then you will have some TrueType fonts. These are indicated by the T symbol to the left of the font name. Chapter 8 contains more details on using fonts.

Select the required font from the list. Select the required size. A sample of the text will be shown in the sample area at the bottom right of the window. Styles such as Bold, Italic, Underlined, etc. can be selected in the same way as from the Text options.

ACCESSORIES 1

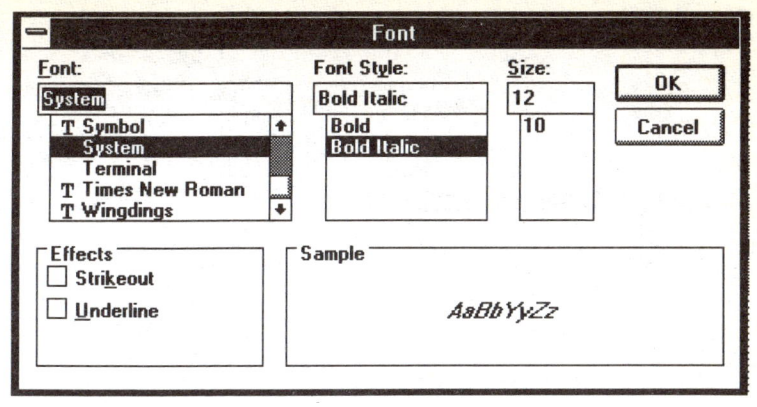

Figure 20.9

Editing the picture

Most pictures will require editing in some way after they are drawn. You may wish to remove elements of the picture, add new elements, or change some parts of the picture. Paintbrush provides a variety of methods for editing an existing picture.

Editing tools

There are a number of different ways to edit elements of the picture or remove any mistakes.

Method	Effect
Normal eraser	The normal eraser turns everything to the background colour effectively rubbing it out.
Colour eraser	The colour eraser turns the foreground colour to the background colour.
Undo	Undo takes back all changes since the **last** change of tool. Click on EDIT then on UNDO.
BackSpace	The BackSpace key acts as an eraser and can remove any drawing done since the last change of tool. To use it, press BackSpace. The cursor changes to a rectangle with a X on it. Click, hold down and move the tool over the area to be erased.

Cut-out tools The cut-out tools are used for selecting part of a picture. Drag the pointer so it draws an outline which completely encloses the shape(s). The enclosed area is selected and can then be changed.

Moving picture elements

To move a selected shape, click in the centre of the shape, and drag it to the new position.

Copying picture elements

- Select the shape or shapes to be copied.
- Click on EDIT then COPY to copy the shapes to the Clipboard.
- Click on EDIT then on PASTE.
- Drag the pasted shape to the correct position on the picture.

or

- Select the shape or shapes to be copied.
- Press Ctrl Ins to copy the shape to the Clipboard.
- Press Shift Ins to paste the shape from the Clipboard.
- Drag the pasted shape to the correct position on the picture.

Deleting picture elements

- Click on EDIT then on CUT.

or

- Press Shift Delete.

The deleted element is placed in the Clipboard.

The Pick menu

The Pick menu, shown in figure 20.10, is normally greyed out, which means it cannot be selected. It becomes available for selection when part of a picture has been selected using the cut-out tools described above. Click on PICK to display the menu then select the required option.

ACCESSORIES 1

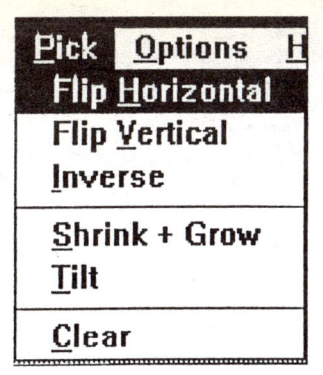

```
Pick  Options  H
Flip Horizontal
Flip Vertical
Inverse
Shrink + Grow
Tilt
Clear
```
Figure 20.10

The functions of the various options are listed below.

Option	Action
Flip Horizontal	turns selected element horizontally through 180°
Flip Vertical	turns selected element vertically through 180°
Inverse	reverses colours of selected elements
Shrink + Grow	enlarges or reduces size of selected elements
Tilt	tilts selected elements
Clear	used with Shrink + Grow and Tilt options to clear the original cut-out area

Document management

Changing drawing size

The amount of disk space needed by Paintbrush drawings can be reduced by setting the size of the picture. Click on OPTIONS then on IMAGE ATTRIBUTES. Enter the width and height of the drawing you wish to produce. Most drawings will be printed in black and white. Selecting the Black & White option will also reduce the size of the file.

Page setup

Click on FILE then PAGE SETUP to display the Page Setup options, as shown in figure 20.11.

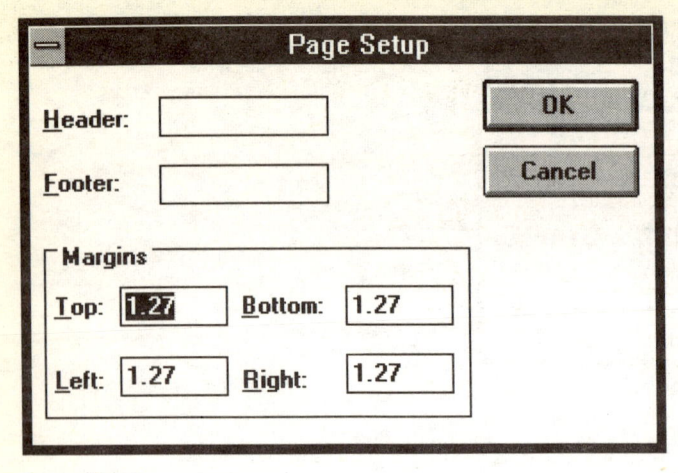

Figure 20.11

Type the text for the header and/or footer. Text will scroll in the box, allowing plenty of space for the header or footer. Standard features such as the file name, date and page number can be inserted automatically into the header or footer. These are called **field codes**. Any of the following codes can be used.

Field Code	Effect
&d	current date
&t	current time
&p	page number
&f	file name
&l	left align header or footer
&r	right align header or footer
&c	centre header or footer

Changing margins

The default margins are half an inch at the top and bottom, and half an inch at the left and right. The measurements are likely to be expressed in centimetres (1.27 cm). The margins can be changed to any required value by entering the value in the relevant box.

Changing page view

Click on VIEW to display the View menu shown in figure 20.12.

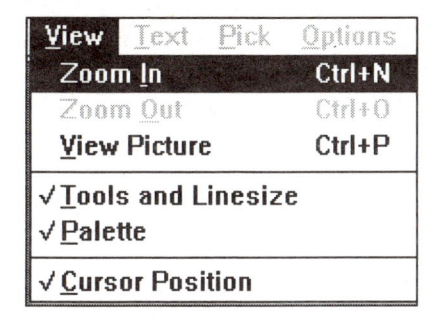

```
View   Text   Pick   Options
Zoom In                Ctrl+N
Zoom Out               Ctrl+O
View Picture           Ctrl+P
√ Tools and Linesize
√ Palette
√ Cursor Position
```

Figure 20.12

Option	Effect
Zoom In	In normal view, places a small rectangle on the screen. Move this to the area to be magnified and click. This area of the screen will be expanded to fill the whole area and individual screen points called **pixels** will be visible. These can then be coloured individually to correct fine drawings.
Zoom Out	Returns to normal view. Click on Zoom Out again to display a full page at a time.
View Picture	Displays picture only.
Tools and Linesize	Switches off display of tool box.
Palette	Switches off display of colour palette.
Cursor Position	Displays box showing co-ordinates of the current cursor position.

Exiting from Paintbrush

Click on FILE then on EXIT. You will be asked to confirm if any pictures have not been saved. Click on Yes to save the changes, No to exit without saving and Cancel to carry on working in Paintbrush.

Summary

This chapter has described

- the Paintbrush screen;
- opening existing drawing files;
- using the Paintbrush tools;
- saving and printing drawings;
- using print options;
- changing colours;
- editing drawings;
- adding text;
- changing fonts, styles and sizes;
- selecting parts of drawings;
- changing size of drawings;
- flipping and tilting drawings.

21
ACCESSORIES 2 WRITE

This chapter contains reference material for Write, the word processing program supplied with Windows.

Double click on the Write icon in the Accessories window to load the program and display the screen as shown in figure 21.1.

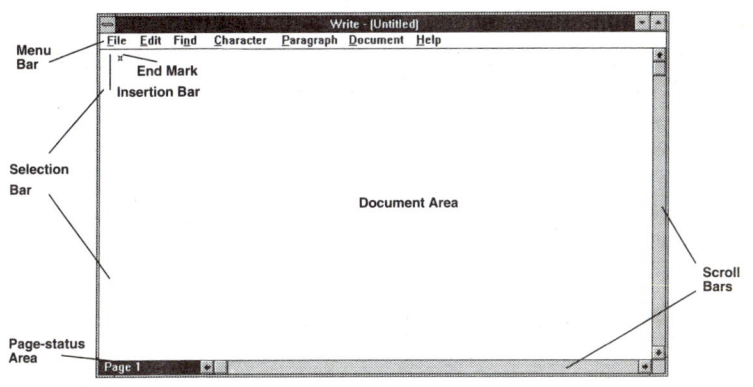

Figure 21.1

Starting a new document

Click on FILE then on NEW. Write will remind you if an existing file has not been saved and ask if you wish to save.

Opening an existing document

Click on FILE then on OPEN. Select the required directory and file name. By default, the Open dialog box displays all files with the WRI extension in the WINDOWS directory. The file type can be changed if required. Highlight the required file then click on OK. Write can import text files created on other word processors. The imported text may contain some strange characters, which are control codes inserted into the text by the program in which the text was typed.

Entering text

Text is typed in the document area. Lines of text will word wrap to the next line when a line becomes full.

Cursor movement

The insertion bar is the point at which the text is typed. It will move along the lines as the text is typed. Once the text has been entered the insertion bar or **cursor** has to be positioned at the place in the text where the change is required. The cursor can be moved around the document in several ways.

- Click with the mouse at the required place to make a new insertion point.

or

- Using the scroll bars and arrows.

or

- Using keys.

Key	Action
←	one character left
→	one character right
↑	one line up
↓	one line down
Ctrl ←	one word left
Ctrl →	one word right

Home	start of line
End	end of line
Page Up	one screen up
Page Down	one screen down
Ctrl Home	top of text
Ctrl End	bottom of text

Saving

Click on FILE then on SAVE. If this is a new file, type a file name. By default, Write files are given an extension of WRI and saved in the WINDOWS directory.

Printing

Click on FILE then on PRINT to display the Print dialog box shown in figure 21.2.

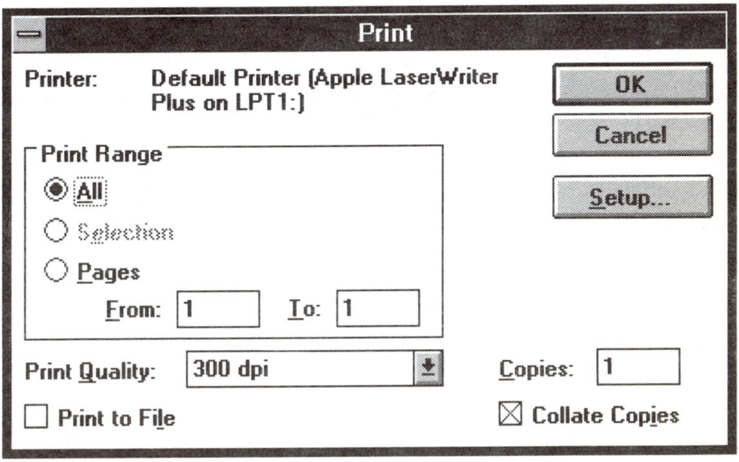

Figure 21.2

WINDOWS

The options on the Print menu control the printing of the text.

Option	Effect
All	prints all pages
Selection	prints selected text

3.1 only

Pages	prints a range of pages between first and last page numbers
Print Quality	sets 'blackness' of text in dots per inch. (300 dpi is the normal laser printing setting)
Setup	selects Printer, Paper Size and Tray and Orientation. In 3.0 these options are found on the Printer Setup menu
Copies	sets the number of copies, collated if required.

Correcting the text

Incorrect characters can be removed using the editing keys. Click to make an insertion point or use keys to move the cursor to the required location.

BackSpace	deletes character left of cursor
Delete	deletes character right of cursor

Selecting text

Words or blocks of text can be highlighted or selected so that they can be edited or their appearance changed. Text can be highlighted using the mouse or the keys.

Mouse methods

Action	Effect
Click in Selection Bar	highlights the current line of text
Click and drag in Selection Bar	highlights complete lines
Click in text and drag left or right	highlights characters left or right

Click in text and drag up or down	highlights lines up or down
Ctrl + click in Selection Bar	highlights all text
Ctrl + click in text	highlights the current sentence

Keyboard methods

Action	Effect
Shift + left or right arrow	highlights characters left or right
Shift + up or down arrow	highlights lines above or below
Shift, Ctrl + left or right arrow keys	highlights words left or right

Cut and paste

Once the required area of text is selected, it can be deleted, moved or copied anywhere within the current document or placed in the Clipboard to be used by other Windows programs. Click on EDIT to display the Edit menu then select the required option.

Option	Effect
Cut	removes selected text and places it in the Clipboard
Copy	copies selected text to the Clipboard
Paste	pastes text from the Clipboard at the current cursor position
Undo	undoes last edit
Delete	removes selected text from the document without placing it in the Clipboard
Shift + Delete	cuts selected text to the Clipboard
Shift + Insert	pastes contents of the Clipboard at the current cursor position
Ctrl + Insert	copies selected text to the Clipboard
Ctrl + Z	undoes last edit

Character formatting

Click on CHARACTER to display the Character menu, shown in figure 21.3.

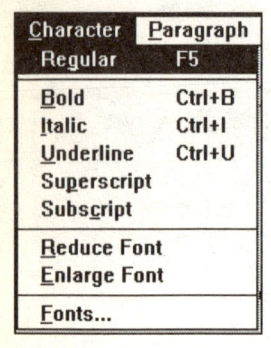

Figure 21.3

The options on the Character menu determine the appearance of the text.

Printing styles

Normal	Normal text
Bold	**Bold text**
Underline	Underlined text
Italic	*Italic text*
Superscript	Raised text, as in 100°
Subscript	Lowered text, as in H_2O

Fonts

The Font option displays the Font box, shown in figure 21.4, from which you can select any of the fonts installed on your system and use any available type size. A sample is displayed as the options are selected. There is more information about using fonts in chapter 8.

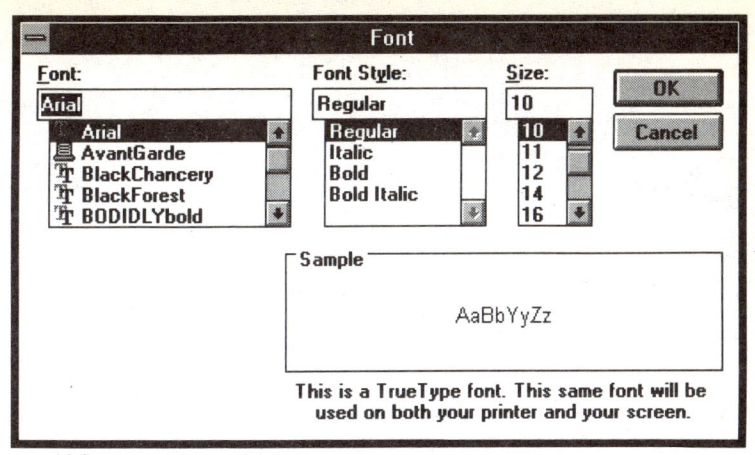

Figure 21.4

Paragraph formatting

Click on PARAGRAPH to display the Paragraph menu, shown in figure 21.5.

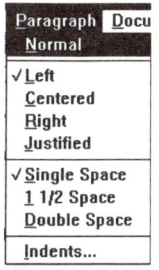

Figure 21.5

The options on the Paragraph menu determine the layout of the text on the page.

Text alignment

Left aligned   This small
                        section of text is
                        left aligned.

Centred   This small
                                    section of text is
                                         centred.

Right Aligned   This small
                                                     section of text is
                                                         right aligned.

Justified   This small section of
                        text is justified. It
                        has a straight right
                        hand edge. This is
                        achieved by padding
                        the line with spaces.

Spacing

Single   This section of
                        text is single
                        spaced.

One and a half   This section of

                        text is spaced at

                        one and a half

                        line spacing.

Double   This section of

                        text is double

                        spaced.

Indents

An **indent** is an inset from the current margins. Write allows text to be indented from both left and right margins. Click on INDENTS to display the Indents option box, shown in figure 21.6. Select Left Indent or Right

Indent to indent from the left or right margin. Select First Line to indent only the first line of each paragraph. Type the required indent in inches or centimetres.

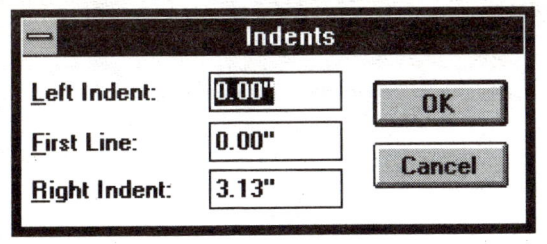

Figure 21.6

Inserting Page Breaks

Some word processors, including Write, do not automatically divide the text into pages as it is being entered. In Write, page breaks can be manually inserted as you type, or the text can be **paginated** when complete. Pagination is the process of splitting a piece of text into pages ready for printing.

Inserting manual page breaks

Hold down Ctrl and press Enter to start a new page. A dotted line is drawn across the page.

Using the Repaginate option

Click on FILE then on REPAGINATE to display the Repaginate Document box, shown in figure 21.7. If Confirm Page Breaks is checked, Write will divide the text into pages and pause at the place where it intends to start the next page.

These page break positions are indicated by arrows.

With Confirm Page Breaks checked, the Dialog box shown in figure 21.8 will be displayed. From this, you can confirm the suggested position, or

Figure 21.7

move the page break position up or down until it is in a suitable place. This process has to be repeated for each page break in the text.

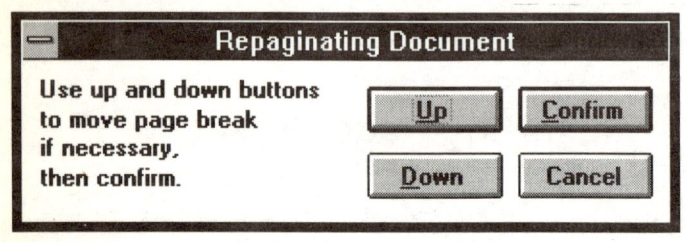

Figure 21.8

Document layout

Click on DOCUMENT to display the Document menu, shown in figure 21.9. The Document menu controls the page layout, tab stops and headers and footers.

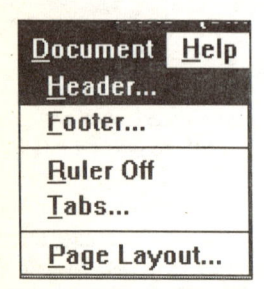

Figure 21.9

Headers

A header is a section of text which appears at the top of every page. Click on HEADER. Write opens the header box as shown in figure 21.10 for you to type the text required for the header. Any of the available formatting options can be used, so the header could be printed in a different font or size and emboldened or underlined as required.

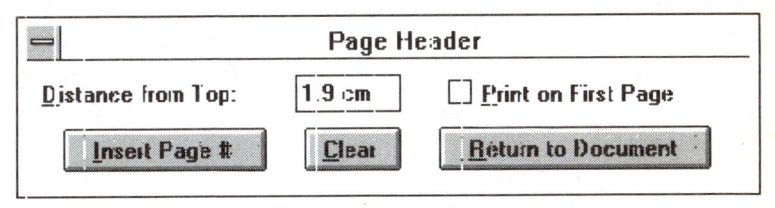

Figure 21.10

The Page Header settings control the printing of the header on the page.

Option   **Effect**
Distance from Top   sets the distance from the top edge of the paper in current units
Print on First Page   determines whether the header starts from the start of document or from the top of the second page
Insert Page #   inserts the current page number at the cursor
Clear   removes an existing header
Return to Document   closes the header window and returns to the main text

The header is not shown in the main text. It can be viewed or edited by re-opening the Header window as described above.

Footers

A footer is a section of text which appears at the bottom of every page. Click on FOOTER. Write opens the Footer box for you to type the text required for the footer. The Footer is set up in the same way as the Header. As for the header, the footer is not shown in the main text. It can be viewed or edited by re-opening the Footer window as described above.

The ruler line

A ruler line can be found in most word processors. It shows the settings of the right and left margin and any tab stops which have been set. It may also show formatting options such as bold or underlined, text alignment and line spacing. The various settings on the ruler line can be changed by clicking on the relevant icons instead of using the menus. This is usually faster and easier to do. In Write, the ruler line is not normally displayed. Click on DOCUMENT then on RULER ON to display the ruler line, as shown in figure 21.11. The ruler line has icons to represent tabs, line spacing and alignment, and has arrows indicating the left and right margin positions.

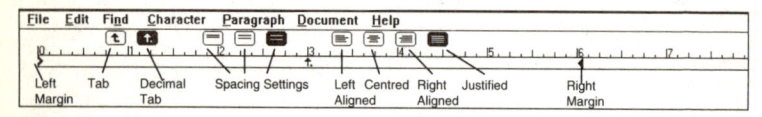

Figure 21.11

Operation	Method
Setting margins	drag indicators to required positions
Setting tabs	click on left tab or decimal tab then click on ruler line at required place
Moving tabs	drag tab stop to required position
Selecting line spacing	click on Single/One and a half/Double icon
Selecting text alignment	Click on Left/Centred/Right/Justified icon

Tabs

Tab stops are used to move the cursor directly to a pre-set position on the line. They are very useful for typing columns of figures. Click on DOCUMENT then on TABS to display the Tabs box shown in figure 21.12.

Click in one of the spaces on the Positions line and enter the required tab stop position in the current units. Write allows up to 12 tabs to be set. The default tab stop is a left aligned tab stop, where the columns of text are lined up at the leftmost character of each entry as shown at the left of the table in figure 21.13. Click on Decimal to set a decimal tab where the

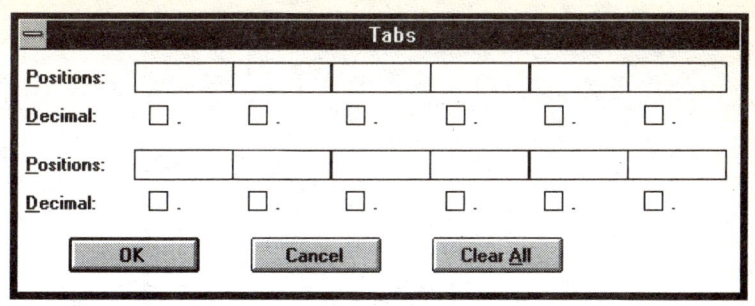

Figure 21.12

figures are lined up by the decimal points as shown in the right-hand column in the table.

12.90	12.90
314.08	314.08
2.00	2.00
0.83	0.83
100	100

Figure 21.13

Repeat the process for any other tabs required. Click on OK and the tabs will appear as upward pointing arrows in the required places on the ruler line.

To type the tabulated text, press the Tab key to move the cursor to the tab stop and then type the text.

Once typed, a tab stop can be moved to a new location. Highlight the tabulated text then click on the tab arrow on the ruler and drag it to the new position. As you move the tab stop, the text will move as well.

Clearing tab stops

Click on DOCUMENT then TABS then on the Position of the Tab stop to be cleared. Delete the tab setting. Click on Clear All to remove all the tab stops.

Page layout

Click on DOCUMENT then on PAGE LAYOUT to display the Page Layout box shown in figure 21.14.

WINDOWS

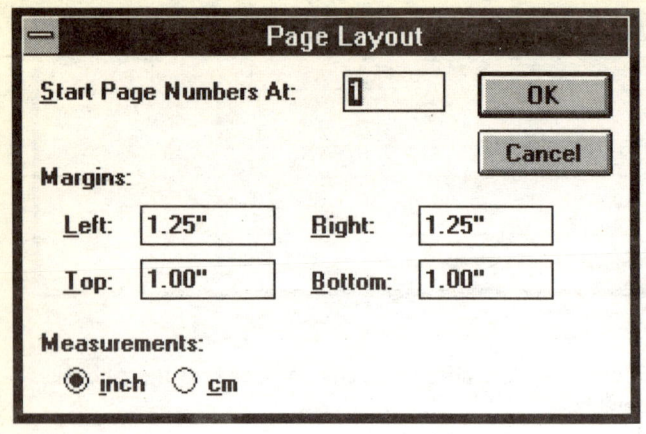

Figure 21.14

The Page Layout options determine the layout of the text on the page.

Option	Action
Start Page Numbers At	starts page numbering at any required value
Margins Left	sets Left margin
Margins Right	sets Right margin
Margins Top	sets Top margin
Margins Bottom	sets Bottom margin
Measurements	sets Write to use inches or centimetres

——— Search and replace ———

Search

3.0 only
3.1 only

Click on SEARCH to display the Search menu.
Click on FIND to display the Find menu shown in figure 21.15.

Click on the FIND option to display the Find box, shown in figure 21.16. This enables the text to be searched for particular words or parts of words. Enter the text to be searched for. Click on Find Next. The first occurrence of the search text will be highlighted. Click on Find Next to

Figure 21.15

find the next occurrence. Repeat until all occurrences have been located and the Search complete dialog box is displayed.

Figure 21.16

Replace
3.1 only

The Replace option finds the search text but can also replace this with another word or words. Click on REPLACE to display the Replace box, shown in figure 21.17. Enter the search text in the Find What box. Enter the text to be inserted in the Replace With box.

Figure 21.17

The options are as follows.

Option	Action
Find Next	finds the next occurrence of the search text
Replace	replaces the highlighted occurrence
Replace All	replaces all occurrences of the search text

Version 3.0 has the Change menu instead of the Replace menu described above. The same options are available but with different names.

Go To

The Go To option is particularly useful when you have a long Write document as it makes moving around the document much easier and faster. Click on FIND then GO TO PAGE to display box shown in figure 21.18.

Enter the required page number.

Figure 21.18

Inserting pictures and objects into Write documents

Write can insert pictures, graphics and objects created in a variety of Windows programs into its text files.

3.1 only

Click on EDIT then on INSERT OBJECT. Select the type of object to be inserted. This will open the selected application, where you can create a new drawing or object or open an existing one. Click on EXIT and RETURN TO THE WRITE document to insert the object into your document.

3.0 only

In Windows 3.0 there are no object embedding facilities as described above. Graphics can only be inserted into the document by copying them to the Clipboard, then pasting them into the Write document.

Once the graphic is inserted in the document, it can be manipulated. Click on the graphic so it is highlighted. This means the picture is selected. Click on EDIT to display the Edit menu. The version 3.1 Edit menu is shown in figure 21.19. The options at the bottom of the menu which have previously been greyed out are now available for use.

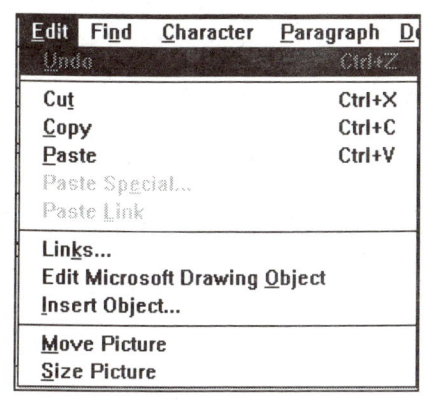

Figure 21.19

These options allow the picture to be manipulated in the document. Click to select the picture to be manipulated then select the required option.

Option	Effect
Edit Drawing Object	This returns to the drawing screen for you to edit the picture

3.1 only

Move Picture	This option allows the picture to be moved to any desired position in the document. Click to fix the new position.
Size Picture	This allows the picture to be sized to any required dimensions. Click to fix the new size.

Exiting from Write

Click on FILE then on EXIT. You will be asked to confirm if any pictures have not been saved. Click on Yes to save the changes, No to exit without saving and Cancel to carry on working in Write.

Summary

This chapter has described
- the features of the Write screen;
- starting a new document;
- opening existing Write files;
- entering text;
- editing text;
- saving the document;
- printing;
- using print options;
- selecting text;
- cut and paste;
- print styles;
- fonts and sizes;
- alignment;
- spacing;
- indents;
- page breaks;
- headers and footers;
- tabulated text;
- page layout;
- search and replace;
- inserting and manipulating pictures.

22

ACCESSORIES 3
NOTEPAD, CLOCK, CALENDAR AND CALCULATOR

This chapter describes the Windows Accessories: Notepad, Clock, Calendar and Calculator.

Notepad

Notepad is a small text editor which can be used for noting down messages and notes which do not require the features of a word processor. It can also be used to edit any short text files. The maximum size of a Notepad file is around 50,000 characters. A warning will be given if the text is approaching the maximum value.

Double click on the Notepad icon to display the Notepad window as shown in figure 22.1.

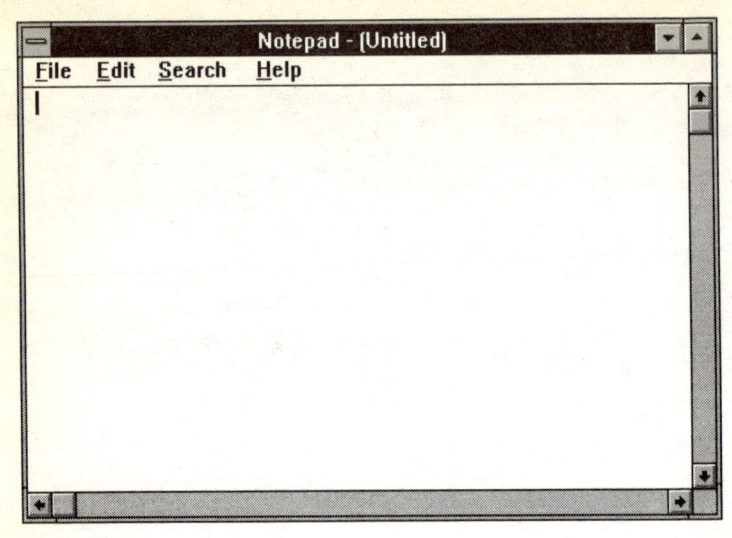

Figure 22.1

Starting a new file

Click on FILE then on NEW. Notepad will remind you if an existing file has not been saved and ask if you wish to save.

Opening an existing file

Click on FILE then on OPEN. Notepad will display all files with the extension TXT in the WINDOWS directory. Select the required directory and file name. Click on OK.

Entering text

Enter the text onto the working area. By default, Notepad does not word wrap from one line to the next. This may be convenient for a list of notes when you would start each item on a new line. For longer pieces of text, it will be more convenient to switch word wrap on. To do this, click on EDIT then on WORD WRAP.

Saving the file

Click on FILE then on SAVE or SAVE AS. If the file has not yet been given a name, type a file name. By default, Notepad files are given an extension of TXT and saved in the WINDOWS directory.

Printing a file

Click on FILE then on PRINT. The output is sent directly to Print Manager. The Print Setup option, shown in figure 22.2, allows the printer and page size to be changed and the output to be printed in **landscape** orientation (sideways) if required.

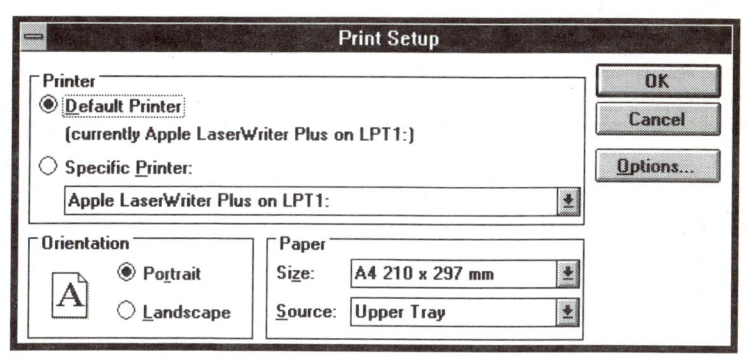

Figure 22.2

Adding date and time

Click on EDIT then TIME/DATE or press F5. This adds the date in the format defined in Control Panel. A time and date inserted into a Notepad file is likely to look like the example shown in figure 22.3.

```
15:32   11/04/93
```

Figure 22.3

Changing the page setup

Click on FILE then PAGE SETUP to display the Page Setup options as shown in figure 22.4. These allow you to set up text to be used for headers and footers, and allow the margins to be changed.

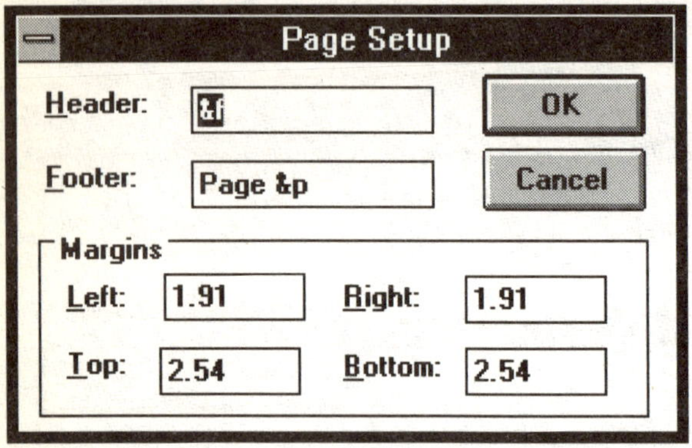

```
┌─────────────── Page Setup ───────────────┐
│                                          │
│  Header:  [&f]              [   OK   ]   │
│                                          │
│  Footer:  [Page &p]         [ Cancel ]   │
│                                          │
│  ┌Margins──────────────────────────────┐ │
│  │ Left:  [1.91]    Right:  [1.91]     │ │
│  │ Top:   [2.54]    Bottom: [2.54]     │ │
│  └─────────────────────────────────────┘ │
└──────────────────────────────────────────┘
```

Figure 22.4

Adding a header

The default header in Notepad is the file name shown in the Title Bar. Click in the Header box. The symbol **&f** represents the file name. Remove the file name entry if not required and enter the text of the header in this box. The line will scroll if the text is longer than the box.

Adding a footer

The default footer in Notepad is the page number. Click in the Footer box. The symbol **&p** represents the page number. This can be changed as for the header if required.

Changing margins

The default margins are one inch top and bottom and three quarters of an inch left and right. The measurements are likely to be expressed in centimetres (2.54 cm and 1.91 cm). Enter the required margin settings in the appropriate boxes.

Searching

Notepad provides searching facilities. It can search for whole words or parts of words, and can match case if required. Click on FIND to display the Find dialog box shown in figure 22.5. Enter the text to be found. This can be a whole word, part of a word or a number of words. Click on Find Next. Notepad will check for occurrences of the search text. If it is found, the text will be highlighted. Click on Find Next to locate any further occurrences.

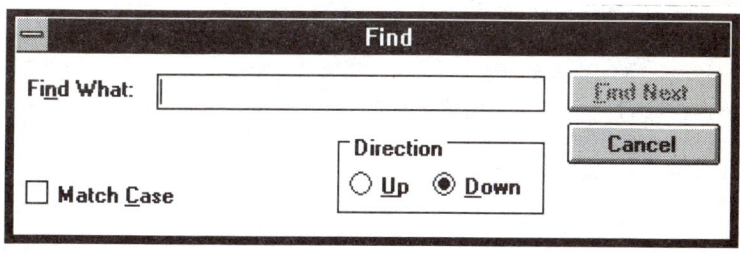

Figure 22.5

Exiting from Notepad

Click on FILE then on EXIT to exit from Notepad. You will be reminded if there is unsaved work.

Clock

To open the Windows Clock, double click on the Clock icon. This opens a window and displays the clock. The default display is an analogue clock with moving hands, as shown in figure 22.6.

The only option on the Menu Bar is the Settings option shown in figure 22.7. The options on this menu are explained below.

Option	Effect
Analog	displays clock with hands
Digital	displays clock showing numerals

WINDOWS

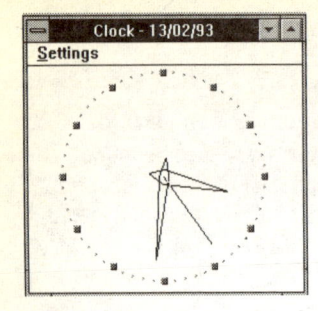

Figure 22.6

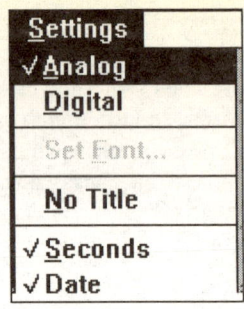

Figure 22.7

3.1 only

Set Font changes the font of the digital display

No Title removes the Title Bar from the Clock window

Seconds removes the seconds display

Date removes the date display

A Windows 3.1 digital clock display with no title, no date and a font set is shown in figure 22.8. If the time shown is incorrect, use Date/Time from the Control Panel to correct the time.

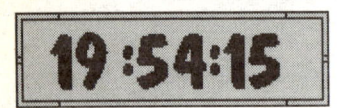

Figure 22.8

Displaying Clock on the desktop
3.1 only

In Windows 3.1, Clock can be permanently displayed on the desktop. The best way to do this is to reduce the size of the Clock window, remove the Title Bar and any elements not required and position the clock in a convenient corner of the desktop. Click on the Clock Control Menu and then on the Always on Top option. Figure 22.9 shows an example of Clock being used in this way.

Exiting from Clock

Click on the Control Menu box and select Close.

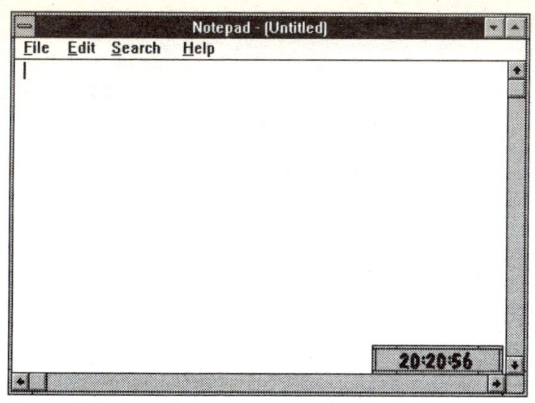

Figure 22.9

Calendar

Double click on the Calendar icon to display a diary for the current date, as shown in figure 22.10. The default settings show hourly intervals between 07:00 hours and 20:00 hours, using the 24 hour clock. Use the scroll bars to scroll to earlier or later times. The lower area of the screen is a space for making reminders and general notes.

Entering details

To enter an item for the current day, click on the line containing the required time or use the up and down arrow keys to move the cursor. Type the required entry.

Removing entries

To remove an entry from the Calendar, highlight the text to be removed. Click on EDIT then on CUT to remove the text. To erase a whole day click on EDIT and select REMOVE. Enter the dates to be removed from the Calendar. To remove a single day, only the From date needs to be entered.

WINDOWS

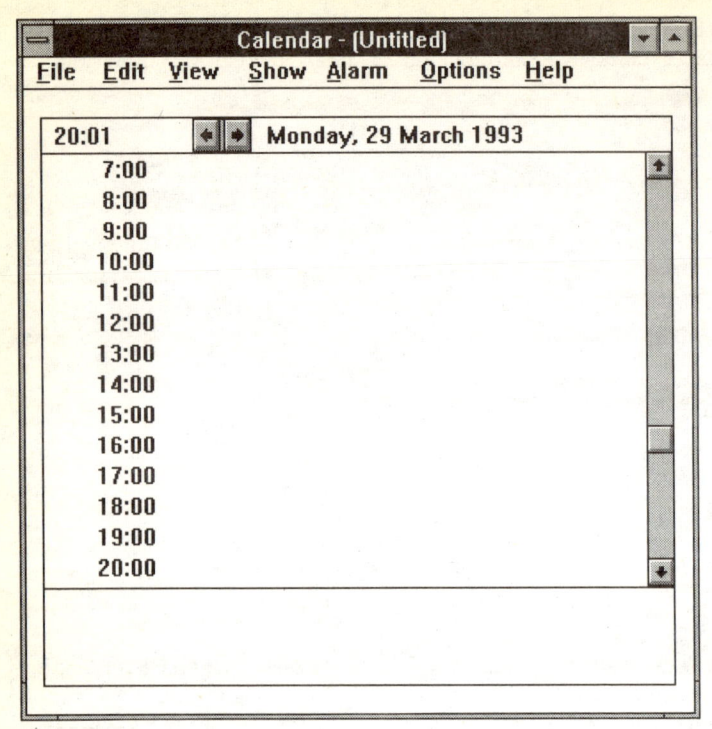

| 20:01 | ← → | **Monday, 29 March 1993** |

```
7:00
8:00
9:00
10:00
11:00
12:00
13:00
14:00
15:00
16:00
17:00
18:00
19:00
20:00
```

Figure 22.10

Changing the time interval

The standard interval on the Calendar is an hour. This can be changed to 30 minutes or 15 minutes. Click on OPTIONS then on DAY SETTINGS to display the Day Settings menu as shown in figure 22.11.

Day Settings

Interval: ○ 15 ● 30 ○ 60
Hour Format: ○ 12 ● 24
Starting Time: 7:00

[OK]   [Cancel]

Figure 22.11

— **264** —

Select the required time interval. The other settings allow you to change the time of the first appointment and to change the clock from 24 hour to 12 hour.

Changing the view

To look at the whole month, click on VIEW to display the View menu, then choose MONTH to display the Calendar for the current month, as shown in figure 22.12. The current date is indicated by > < symbols on each side of the date. The highlighted date indicates the date that was last opened.

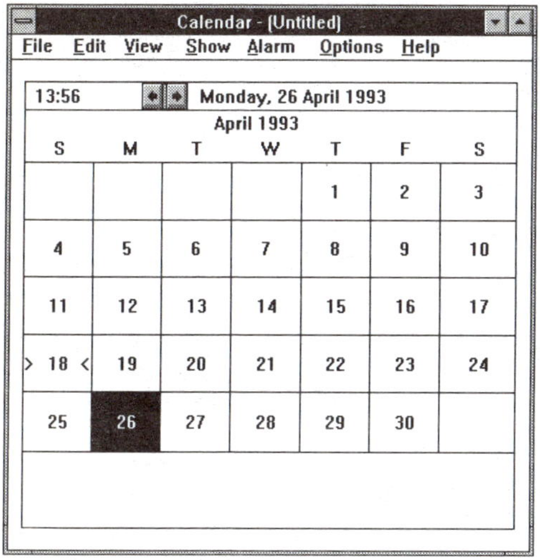

Figure 22.12

Changing to a different date

- Click on the arrows in the day view mode

or

- Click on the required date in month view

or

- Click on SHOW and select NEXT, PREVIOUS or TODAY.

or

- Click on SHOW then on DATE, and enter the required date in the format DD/MM/YY.

Saving the file

Click on FILE then on SAVE or SAVE AS. If the file has not yet been named, type a file name. By default, Calendar files are given an extension of CAL and are saved in the WINDOWS directory.

Opening an existing file

Click on FILE then on OPEN to display the CAL files in the directory. Select the required directory and file name. Click on OK.

Starting a new file

Click on FILE then on NEW. Calendar will remind you if an existing file has not been saved and ask if you wish to save.

Printing a file

The Print Setup option allows the printer and page size to be changed, and the output to be printed in landscape orientation if required. Click on FILE then on PRINT to display the Print dialog box shown in figure 22.13.

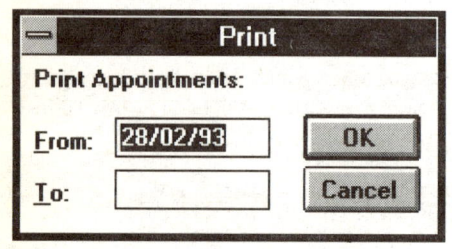

Figure 22.13

Enter the start and end dates to be printed and click on OK. For a single day, only the From date is required.

Adding a header

The default header is the file name shown on the title bar. Click on FILE then PAGE SETUP. The page setup options are the same as for Notepad and are shown in figure 22.4. Click in the Header box. The symbol **&f** represents the file name. Remove the file name entry if required and enter the text of the header in this box. The line will scroll if the text is longer than the box.

Adding a footer

The default footer is the page number. Click on FILE then PAGE SETUP. Click in the Footer area. The symbol **&p** represents the page number. This can be changed as for the header if required.

Changing margins

The default margins are one inch at the top and bottom and three quarters of an inch at the left and right. These measurements may be expressed in centimetres. Click on FILE then on PAGE SETUP and enter the required margin settings.

Special times

Appointments can be also entered at times which do not coincide with the normal time intervals. Click on OPTIONS then select SPECIAL TIME to display the dialog box shown in figure 22.14.

Figure 22.14

Enter the time required in the format HH:MM and click on AM or PM.

Setting the alarm

Select the required appointment, click on ALARM and then on SET. This will place an alarm bell symbol at the side of the appointment. An appointment which has an alarm set is indicated by an asterisk next to the appointment on the printed schedule.

Alarm options can be changed by choosing CONTROLS.

Sound determines whether Calendar sounds an audible tone.
Early Ring determines the number of warnings that will be given before the appointment time. If Calendar is minimised, the icon will also flash to indicate the alarm warnings.

Defining Special Days

Special Days could include events such as public holidays, annual leave dates, birthdays to remember, etc. Up to five different categories of events can be recorded in advance using Calendar.

Switch into Monthly View. Select the date to be marked. Click on OPTIONS then on MARK to display the Day Markings box as shown in figure 22.15. The five different categories are represented by different symbols. A symbol is assigned to each type of event. Make a note of the symbols you have chosen! Click on the required symbol then on OK. The date will be marked by placing the symbol in the date square.

Figure 22.15

Exiting from Calendar

Click on FILE then on EXIT to exit from Calendar. You will be reminded if there is unsaved work.

Calculator

Double click on the Calculator icon to load the Windows Calculator. Calculator has two forms, standard and scientific. Calculator will load in the same form as when it was last used. The standard calculator, shown in figure 22.16, is a simple left to right calculator.

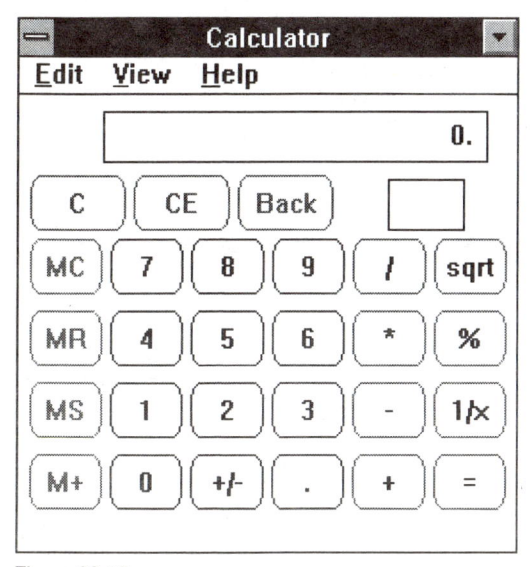

Figure 22.16

Standard calculator

To enter numbers or use functions, click on the correct box using the mouse. The functions of the various buttons are shown in the table in figure 22.17.

WINDOWS

Button	Function
0--9	adds this digit to the display
+/-	changes the number in the display from positive to negative
.	adds a decimal place at the end of the number
/	divides the current number by the next number
*	multiplies the current number by the next number
-	subtracts the next number from the current number
+	adds the current number to the next number
sqrt	gives the number, which when multiplied by itself, gives the previous number
%	calculates percentages
1/x	divides 1 by the current number, ie.finds the reciprocal
=	gives the answer to the current sum
MC	clears the memory
MR	recalls the number in memory
MS	stores the current number in memory
M+	adds the current number to the number in memory
C	completely clears the display
CE	just removes the current number from the display, useful if you have made a mistake on a number
Back	removes only the last digit keyed in

Figure 22.17

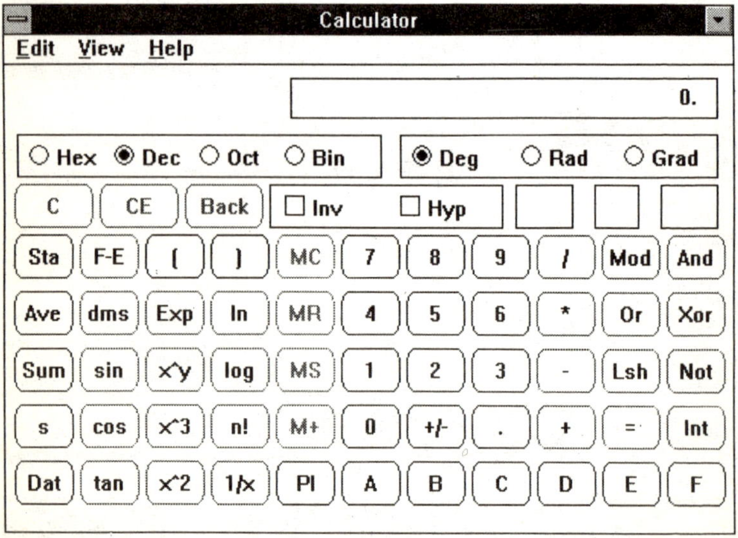

Figure 22.18

ACCESSORIES 3

Button	Function
Dec	calculates in decimal (base 10) numbers
Hex	calculates in hexadecimal (base 16) numbers
Bin	calculates in binary (base 2) numbers
Oct	calculates in octal (base 8) numbers
Deg	angles input in degrees (0 -- 360)
Rad	angles input in radians (0 -- 2π)
Grad	angles input as gradients (0 -- 400)
Dword	32 bit representation of the number
Word	lower 16 bits of displayed number
Byte	lower 8 bits of displayed number
Inv	sets inverse trig and exp functions
Hyp	sets hyperbolic trig functions
F--E	switches between Fixed and Exponential display
dms	degree-minute-second format
sin	calculates value of sine
cos	calculates value of cosine
tan	calculates value of tangent
(	opens brackets
)	closes brackets
Exp	displays number in exponential format
ln	calculates the natural logarithm
x^y	calculates x to the power of y
x^3	calculates x to the power 3
x^2	calculates x squared
log	common (base 10) logarithm
n!	calculates factorial of n
PI	value of π
A -- F	hexadecimal numbers equivalent to 10 -- 15
Mod	remainder of division
And	logical AND
Or	logical OR
Xor	logical exclusive OR
Lsh	shifts to left
Not	logical NOT
Int	integer portion of number
Sta	opens the Statistics box
Ave	calculates average of numbers in sample
s	calculates standard deviation of sample
Sum	sums numbers in sample
Dat	enters the displayed number to the statistics box

Figure 22.19

Scientific calculator

The scientific calculator has several modes of operation. The normal mode is shown in figure 22.18, where calculations are done in decimal (base 10) numbers and any angles are entered in degrees.

The functions of the various additional or different buttons are shown in the table in figure 22.19.

Statistics

The scientific calculator offers a range of statistical functions. The values to be analysed are stored in an area known as the **Statistics Box**, from where they can be summed or averaged. Calculator is also able to calculate the standard deviation of the numbers. Figure 22.20 shows a statistics box containing eight numbers. Only six of the numbers are visible due to the size of the Statistics Box.

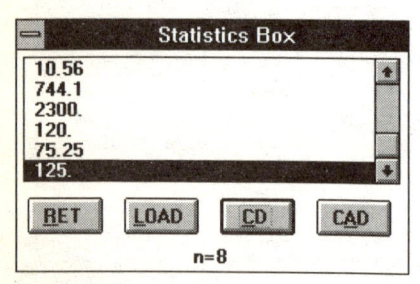

Figure 22.20

Button	Function
RET	switches to calculator and retains the contents of the Statistics Box
LOAD	changes the value in the Calculator display to the selected number in the Statistics Box
CD	deletes the selected value from the Statistics Box
CAD	deletes all values from the Statistics Box

Using the Clipboard

Whenever you use Calculator to perform a calculation, the answer can be copied to the Clipboard. The result can then be pasted into any other Windows application. Click on EDIT then on COPY.

Summary

This chapter has described the use of the Windows accessories:

- Notepad;
- Clock;
- Calendar;
- Calculator.

23

ACCESSORIES 4 CARDFILE AND TERMINAL

This chapter looks at the Cardfile and Terminal accessories.

Cardfile

Cardfile is a small database application which enables files of data such as might be kept on index cards to be built up, and stored in the computer for faster access and ease of use. Cardfile offers a number of features to facilitate use of the file, for example, good searching facilities, the ability to add pictures and graphics to the cards, printing of cards and index lists, merging of data files, and for those fortunate enough to have a modem, Cardfile can dial telephone numbers automatically.

Double click on the Cardfile icon to display the Cardfile working area shown in figure 23.1.

ACCESSORIES 4

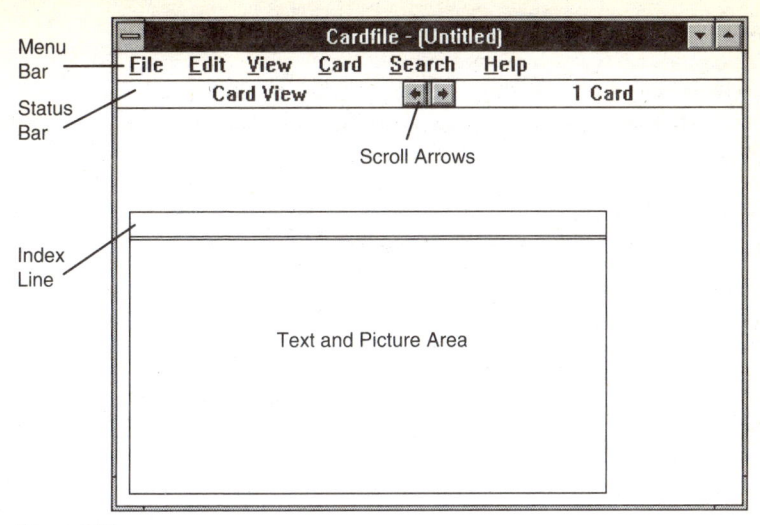

Menu Bar
Status Bar
Index Line
Scroll Arrows
Text and Picture Area

Figure 23.1

This consists of an index card divided into the text and picture area, and a line at the top of the card called the **Index Line**. Text on the Index Line is used when the cards are listed in summary form and for searching. The maximum numbers of characters on the Index Line is 40. Above the card area is the Status Bar which indicates the current view and the current card. Cardfile can be viewed in Card View, shown in figure 23.2, or in List View, shown in figure 23.3, where only the Index Lines are shown.

Figure 23.2

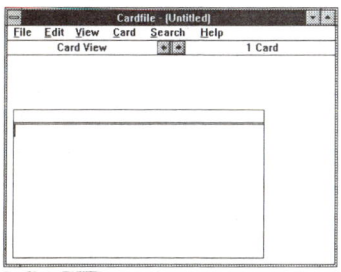

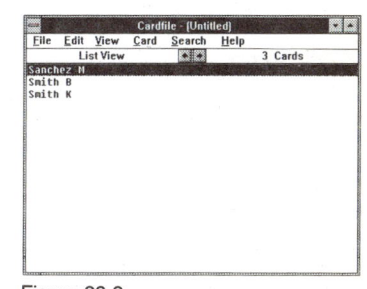

Figure 23.3

Starting a new file

Click on FILE then on NEW. Cardfile will remind you if any work has not been saved.

— **275** —

Opening an existing file

Click on FILE then on OPEN. Cardfile will display all the CRD files in the current directory. Select the required directory and file name. Click on OK.

Entering information

Click in the text area and type the required text. Lines of text are 40 characters long. Text longer than this is word wrapped to the next line. Click on EDIT then INDEX to enter text for the Index Line or press F6.

Moving through the cards

The current card is the one at the front of the stack. More cards can be seen at the same time by enlarging the Cardfile window. The number of cards in the file is indicated at the right of the Status Bar. Figure 23.4 shows a card file containing seven cards but only five cards are visible because of the size of the Cardfile window. If the required card is visible on the screen, click on the Index Line to select the card. This works in either Card view or List view. Otherwise, use the arrows on the Status Bar to move through the card file.

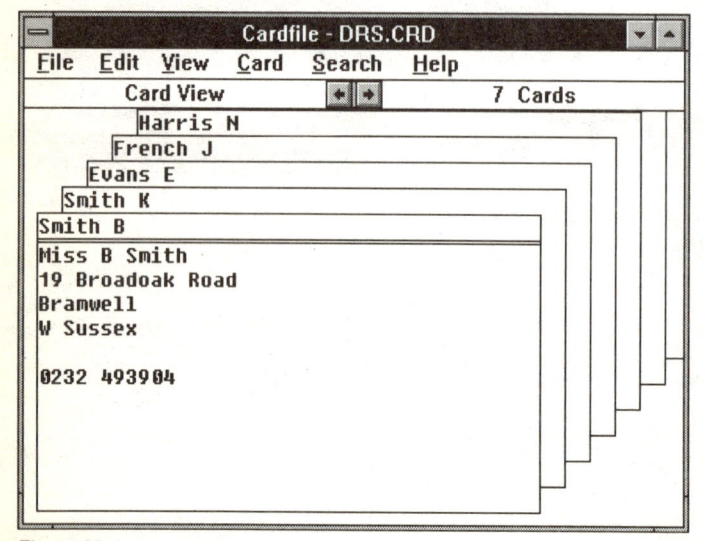

Figure 23.4

Changing view

Click on VIEW then on CARD to view the full card or on to LIST to view only the Index Lines.

Adding a new card

Click on CARD then on ADD or press F7 to display the Add card box shown in figure 23.5. Type the text for the Index Line and press Enter or click on OK. The card is then displayed ready for you to add the text.

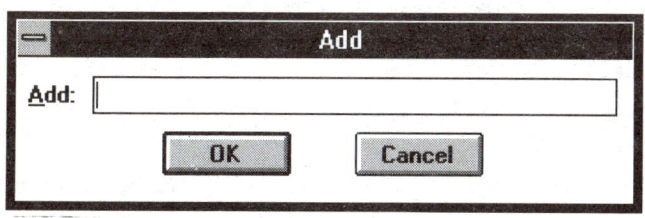

Figure 23.5

Editing the Index Line

Make the card to be edited the current card. Double click on the Index Line or click on EDIT then on INDEX to display the Index dialog box shown in figure 23.6. Correct the index entry.

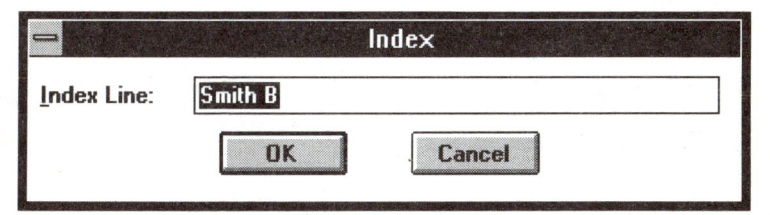

Figure 23.6

Deleting a card

Click on the card to be deleted or move through the file until it is the current card. Click on CARD then on DELETE. Click on OK to confirm the removal of the card.

Duplicating a card

Often many cards in a Cardfile will be nearly the same. A card can be duplicated and the new card then edited to reduce the work involved in typing the same data many times. Click on CARD then DUPLICATE. Edit the data to create the new card. Don't forget to edit the Index Line.

Saving the file

Click on FILE then on SAVE. If the file has not yet been named, type a file name. Cardfile files are given an extension of CRD and saved in the WINDOWS directory by default.

Printing a file

Cardfile can print a single card, all the cards, or the list of index entries. In List View it is only possible to print all the entries. They will be printed one per line down the page. In Card View, there are two print options, Print which prints the current card only, and Print All which prints all the cards, four to a page of A4 paper.

Click on FILE then on PRINT. The output is sent directly to Print Manager. The Print Setup option allows the printer and page size to be changed and the output to be printed in landscape orientation if required.

Adding a header

The default header in Cardfile is the file name shown on the Title Bar. Click on FILE then PAGE SETUP. The Page Setup options are the same as for Notepad and are shown in figure 23.7. Click in the Header box. The symbol **&f** represents the file name. Remove the file name entry if not required and enter the text of the header in this box. The line will scroll if the text is longer than the box.

Figure 23.7

Adding a footer

The default footer in Cardfile is the page number. Click on FILE then PAGE SETUP. Click in the Footer box. The symbol **&p** represents the page number. This can be changed as for the header if required.

Changing margins

The default margins are one inch top and bottom and three quarters of an inch left and right. The measurements are likely to be expressed in centimetres (2.54 cm and 1.91 cm). Click on FILE then PAGE SETUP and enter the required margin settings.

Searching

Click on SEARCH to display the Search menu shown in figure 23.8.

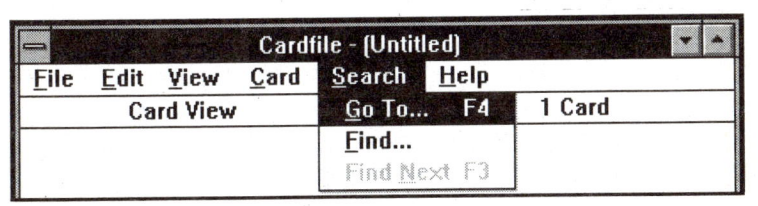

Figure 23.8

Cardfile provides fairly sophisticated searching facilities. It can search for whole words or parts of words, and match case if required. Click on FIND to display the dialog box shown in figure 23.9. Enter the text to be found in the Find What box. This can be a whole word, part of a word or a number of words.

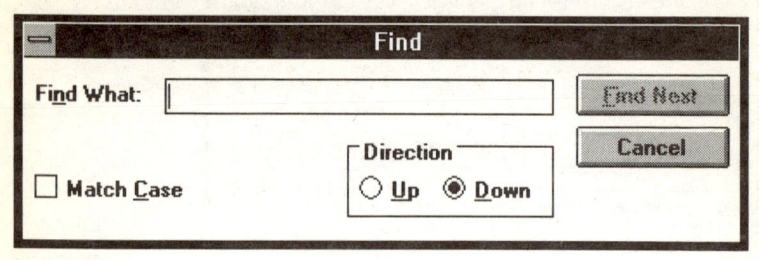

Figure 23.9

Click on Find Next. Cardfile will check for occurrences of the search text. If it is found, the card containing the text will be moved to the front of the stack and the text will be highlighted. Click on Find Next to locate any further occurrences.

The Go To option searches the Index Lines for matching entries. Click on GO TO or press F4 to display the Go To box shown in figure 23.10. Enter the word or part of a word to be searched for.

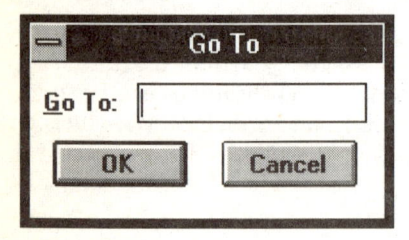

Figure 23.10

Merging Cardfiles

One Cardfile can be merged with another Cardfile. Each card from the merge file is added to the original file. Click on FILE then on MERGE. Cardfile will display all the CRD files in the current directory. Select the file to be merged.

Cardfile does not check for duplicate entries in the merged file.

ACCESSORIES 4

Adding pictures

Pictures can be added to cards from a variety of sources. Cardfile can only import graphics from the Clipboard. Click on EDIT to display the Edit menu, shown in figure 23.11. Click on PICTURE to switch Cardfile into Picture mode. A picture contained in the Clipboard can then be pasted onto the current card.

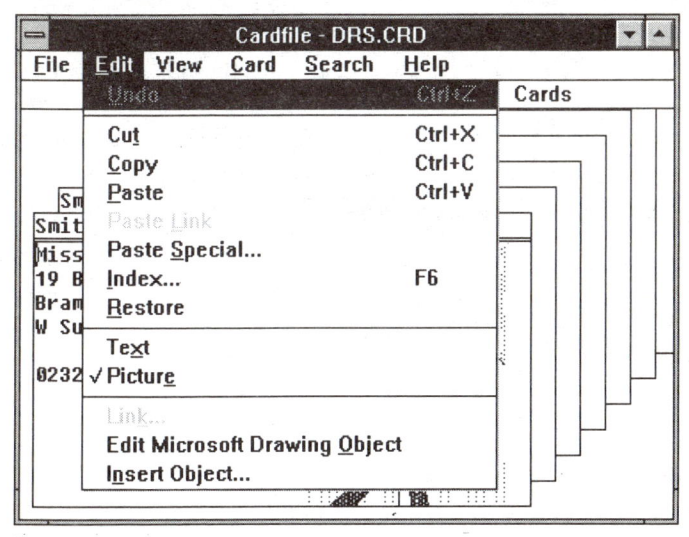

Figure 23.11

Once placed on the card, the picture can be moved around until it is in the required place. Version 3.0 has limited picture capabilities. In version 3.1 the picture will be sized to fit on the card. Version 3.1 is also able to import other objects such as sound files. Click on INSERT OBJECT to display a list of the objects that can be inserted, as in figure 23.12. Select the type of object from the list and specify the file to be inserted.

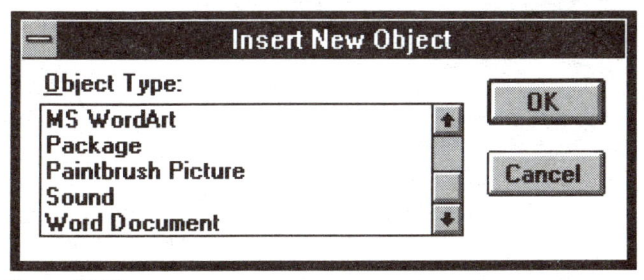

Figure 23.12

— 281 —

Auto dialling telephone numbers

This feature requires a suitable modem.

Select the card containing the required telephone number. Click on CARD then on AUTODIAL. Cardfile examines the card and displays the first possible telephone number in the box shown in figure 23.13. Edit this number if it isn't correct. Check the Use Prefix box and enter the prefix being used, if you do not have a direct external telephone line. Click on Setup and select the serial port and speed of the modem you are using. Click on OK to dial the number. You will hear Cardfile dial the number and a box will be displayed asking you to pick up the phone. Click on OK and you will hear the other telephone ringing.

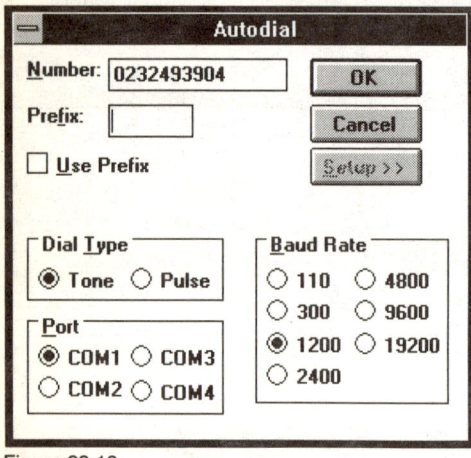

Figure 23.13

Exiting from Cardfile

Click on FILE then on EXIT to exit from Cardfile. You will be reminded if there is unsaved work.

Terminal

To use Windows Terminal, you need a modem connected to the serial port of your computer and to a telephone line.

ACCESSORIES 4

Terminal is a program which allows your computer to communicate with another computer via a **modem**. A modem is a device which converts digital signals from a computer to an analogue signal which can be sent down a telephone wire. A second modem at the other end converts the signal back into digital impulses for use by the other computer. A modem can be used to access information services which contain on-line databases and offer electronic mail facilities. There are also **bulletin boards** set up by various organisations and individuals. A subscription is normally payable for using the bulletin board service, particularly if software is available which can be downloaded by people using the service. Using modems can be expensive because you must also consider the telephone costs.

Double click on the Terminal icon to display the Terminal window, as shown in figure 23.14.

Terminal

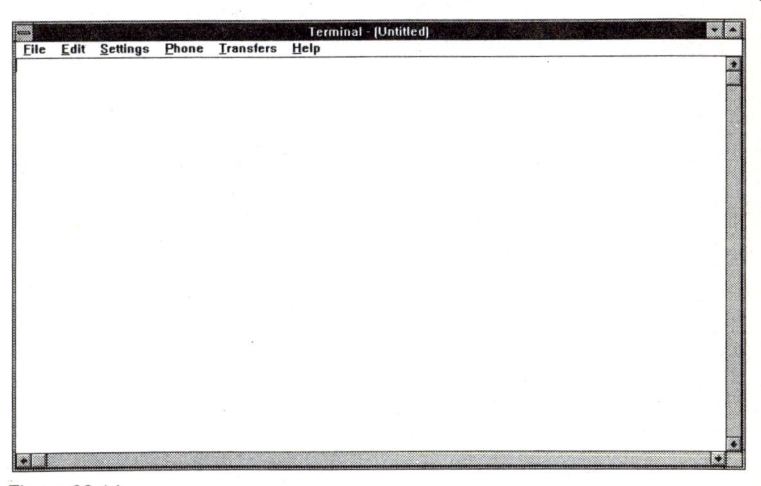

Figure 23.14

There are three steps to using Terminal:

- setting up the communications parameters;
- making the connection;
- transferring the data.

The most important parameters are the phone number, the communications port, the speed of transmission (baud rate) and the characteristics of the data being sent (data bits/stop bits/parity). These details will

— 283 —

WINDOWS

normally be supplied by the operators of the service you are trying to access.

Setting up the communications parameters

The communications parameters are set up from the Settings menu. Click on SETTINGS then on COMMUNICATIONS to display the Communications box shown in figure 23.15. This shows the Windows default settings. Terminal expects the modem to be on COM2 as your mouse will normally be on COM1. The default settings will work with most modems. If you experience any difficulties in connecting to the external computer, you would need to check the communications settings and change them where necessary.

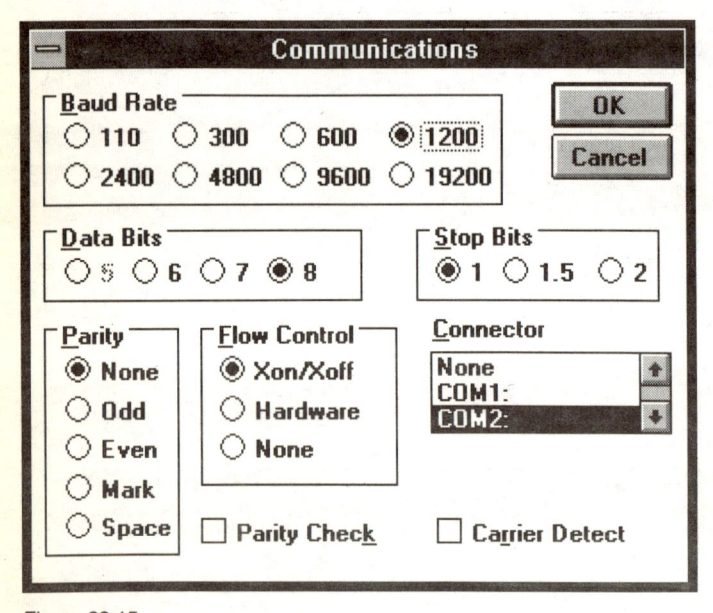

Figure 23.15

Once all the settings have been selected, click on PHONE then on DIAL to display the Phone Number box shown in figure 23.16. This enables you to dial the number. Terminal will display messages as to whether connection has been established. After a certain time without establishing a connection, you will be timed out. Check the settings and dial again.

Figure 23.16

Transferring data

Data can be transferred to and from the other computer using the Transfers menu, shown in figure 23.17.

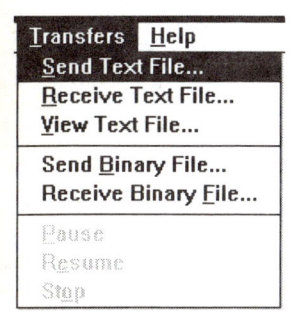

Figure 23.17

Data can be sent to or received from the other computer as text files or as binary files. Text files are easier to handle. The text file should be created in a text editor or word processor without any formatting. Click on TRANSFERS then on SEND TEXT FILE to display the Send Text File dialog box shown in figure 23.18. Select the required file. Click on OK to send the file.

Terminal displays the progress of the transmission as the file is being sent. An example of this is shown in figure 23.19. Files can be received from external sources in a similar way. Click on TRANSFERS then on RECEIVE TEXT FILE to display the Receive Text File dialog box.

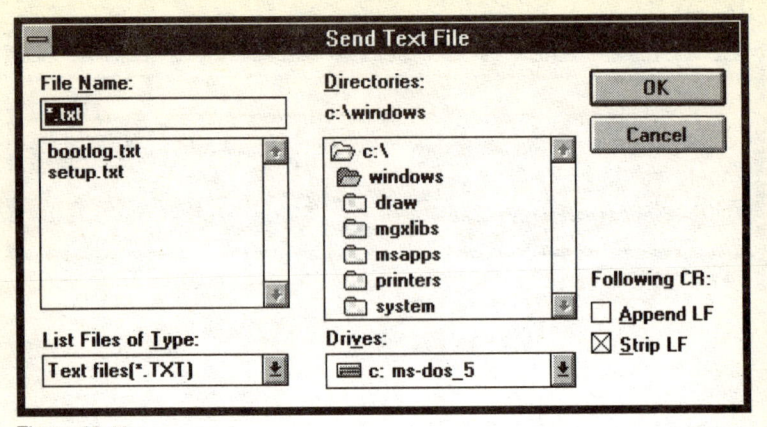

Figure 23.18

Figure 23.19

Exiting from Terminal

Click on FILE then on EXIT to exit from Terminal. You will be reminded if there is unsaved work.

Summary

This chapter has described the use of the Windows accessories:
- Cardfile;
- Terminal.

24

ACCESSORIES 5 CHARACTER MAP, SOUND RECORDER, MEDIA PLAYER AND RECORDER

This chapter looks at the remaining programs in the Windows Accessories group. These are Character Map, Sound Recorder, Media Player and Recorder.

Character Map

3.1 only

Many of the fonts that you use within Windows have characters and symbols which are not available from the normal keys on the keyboard. Character Map enables these characters to be extracted from the font and used within any Windows application.

Double click on the Character Map icon in the Accessories group. When Character Map has loaded, the screen shown in figure 24.1 will be displayed.

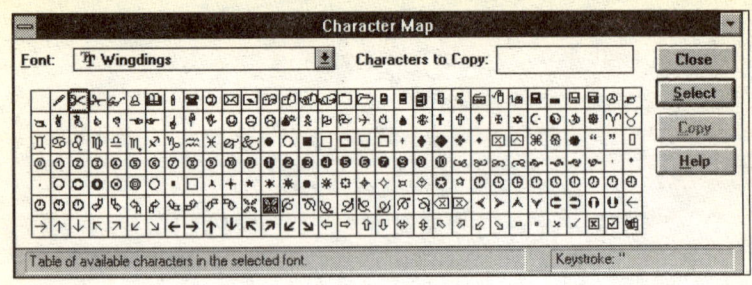

Figure 24.1

Figure 24.1 is showing the Wingdings font. Wingdings is a TrueType symbol font supplied with Windows version 3.1 which contains a good range of symbols. Some fonts contain only the normal characters, some have foreign characters or special characters such as a copyright sign. The Font list box gives access to all the fonts installed on your system. The Keystroke box indicates how you can obtain the selected symbol.

Viewing symbols

- Click on the required symbol and hold down the mouse button to see an enlarged picture of the symbol.

or
- Click in the symbol area. Use the arrow keys to move around the characters. As you move, the currently selected character is displayed in a larger size as shown in figure 24.2.

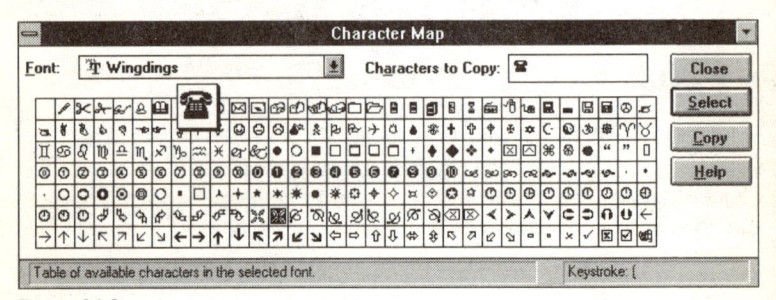

Figure 24.2

Copying symbols

Click on the Select button to place the selected character into the Characters to Copy box. Repeat until all required characters have been selected then click on Copy. The symbols will be pasted into the Clipboard, ready for use in any Windows application.

Characters may appear differently when they are pasted into some applications. It is a good idea to select the required font from within the application **before** pasting in the symbols from the Clipboard.

Closing Character Map

Click on the Control Menu box and select Close to exit to Program Manager.

Sound Recorder

3.1 only

Double click on the Sound Recorder icon to display the screen shown in figure 24.3. The horizontal line in the display shows the pattern of the sound sample currently in memory. The buttons at the bottom of the window perform the same functions as on a tape recorder.

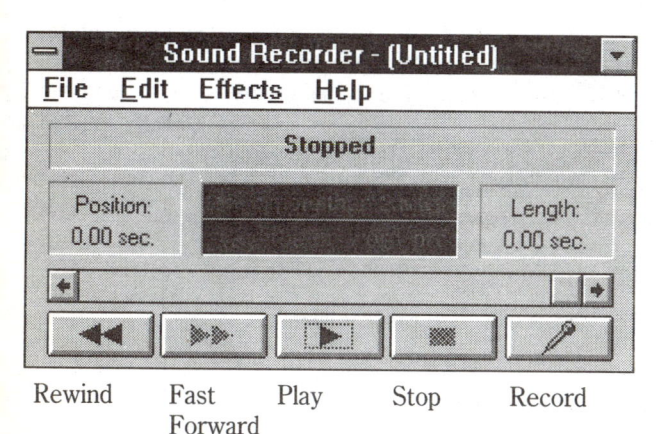

Rewind Fast Forward Play Stop Record

Figure 24.3

Loading a sound file

To load a sound file, click on FILE then on OPEN. This will display the Open box showing a list of the sound files in the WINDOWS directory. The Windows format for sound files is the WAV format. Select the required sound file.

The screen after a WAV file has been displayed can look as shown in figure 24.4. The horizontal green line has changed to a pattern of different thicknesses. This represents the volume and frequency of the sounds in the sample.

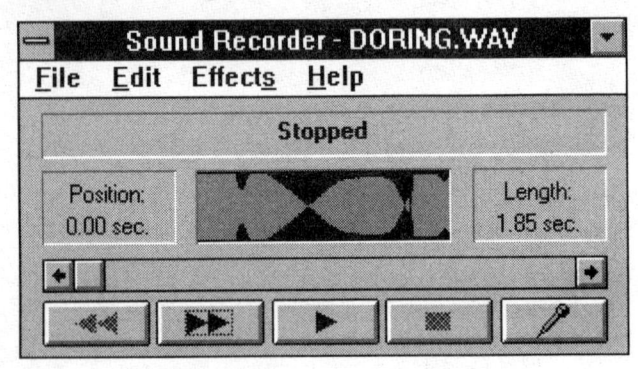

Figure 24.4

Special effects

Sound Recorder allows you to change the sound in a number of different ways. Click on EFFECTS to display the Effects menu as shown in figure 24.5. The available effects enable you to change the volume, change the

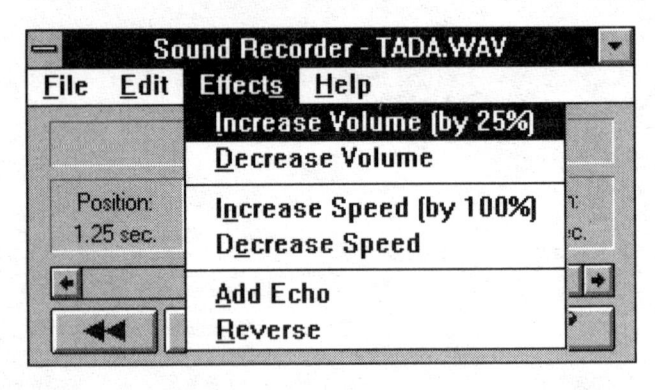

Figure 24.5

— 290 —

speed, add an echo and reverse the sample. Select the required option. A selection can be repeated, perhaps to increase volume for a second time. Selections can be combined, for example, you can change the speed of a sample and add an echo.

Editing the sample

You can also change the sample from the Edit menu. This allows you to delete parts of the sample and insert and mix the sample with other files. The Edit menu is shown in figure 24.6.

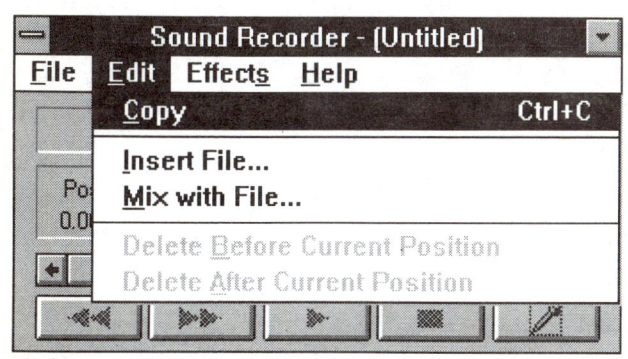

Figure 24.6

Deleting part of a file

To delete part of a sample, first position the file at the correct place in the sample using the Play and Stop buttons. Click on EDIT then on DELETE BEFORE OR DELETE AFTER CURRENT POSITION.

Inserting files

To insert another file into the current one, move to the place where you want the new sample to be inserted. Click on EDIT then on INSERT FILE to display the Insert File box shown in figure 24.7. Choose the file to be inserted from the list box and click on OK. This sample should now be inserted into the existing sound file.

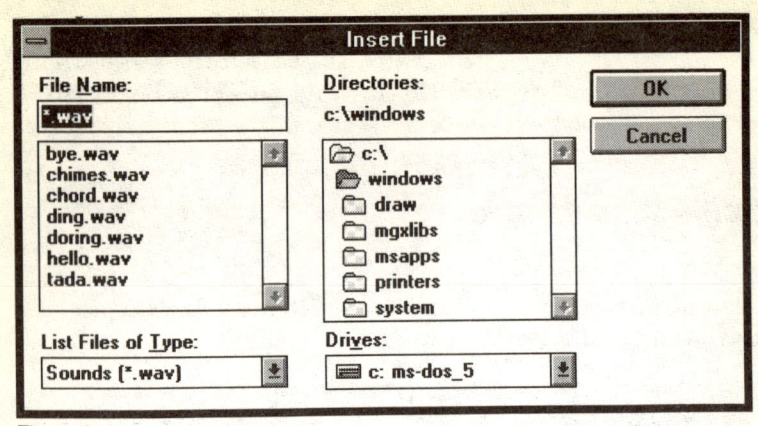

Figure 24.7

Mixing files

When two samples are mixed, both of the samples are played together. The sample is mixed at the current place. Mixing is useful when the tune and lyrics are recorded in separate files. To mix the samples, click on EDIT then on MIX WITH FILE to display the Mix With File box. This is identical to the Insert File box shown in figure 24.7. Select the file to be mixed. If the sample which is being mixed is longer than the current sample, the length of the sample will be increased to match.

Embedding a sound

Sounds can also be placed in the Clipboard. This makes them available to other applications. Click on EDIT then on COPY to copy the sound to the Clipboard. Go into the other application and click on EDIT then on PASTE. This will insert the embedded sound icon into the document. It can then be played by double clicking on the icon.

Saving a sound file

Click on FILE then on SAVE. If the file has not yet been named, type a file name. By default, Windows sound files are given the extension WAV and saved in the WINDOWS directory.

Recording your own samples

If your sound card has the facility to plug in a microphone, electronic keyboard or hi-fi system, you can record your own sounds and play them back through the computer.

Recording music and sounds can require large amounts of memory and disk space. **NB**

Click on the Record button and then either play on the keyboard or start the music playing. Once recorded, the sound can then be edited using the Special Effects menu.

Exiting from Sound Recorder

Click on FILE then on EXIT to exit from Sound Recorder. You will be reminded if there is unsaved work.

Media Player

3.1 only

Media Player is a program which can play files which contain sound or video elements and can control external audio devices, such as CD players. This has become known as **multimedia**.

Double click on the Media Player icon to display the Media Player Control Panel, shown in figure 24.8.

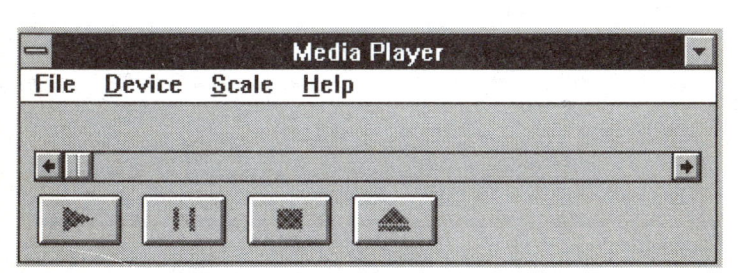

Media Player

Play   Pause   Stop   Eject

Figure 24.8

Media Player supports simple devices such as CD players and compound devices such as MIDI sequencers. The necessary hardware and drivers must be installed on the computer before Media Player can be used. Once the driver has been installed, the device is controlled from this panel. This has the normal controls for starting and playing the devices. More details of the use of Media Player can be found in the Windows User Guide.

Exiting from Media Player

Click on FILE then on EXIT to exit from Media Player.

Recorder

Recorder is a facility which enables frequently used sequences of keystrokes or mouse operations to be recorded so they can be performed much faster. The sequence of keystrokes is called a **macro**.

Double click on the Recorder icon to display the Recorder windows as shown in figure 24.9.

Figure 24.9

ACCESSORIES 5

Creating a macro

Macros are very useful but require a little planning to get the most out of the technique. A suitable example for a macro could be pasting the result of a calculation within Calculator into another application, for example, Write.

Each macro should be assigned a shortcut key as this enables the macro to be started without loading Recorder. It is important that you start recording from the correct place. ☺

Check that you are in the correct application. In the example above, the macro would be started from within Calculator after the result of the calculation had been obtained. The Write window would be visible on the screen behind Calculator.

Use Ctrl Escape to display the Task List and switch to Recorder. Click on MACRO then RECORD to display the Record Macro box, as shown in figure 24.10. Enter a name for the macro or assign a shortcut key. This can be any key combined with Ctrl, Alt or Shift. Shortcut keys are combined with the Ctrl key by default, because Windows has fewer selections activated by the Ctrl key than the Alt key.

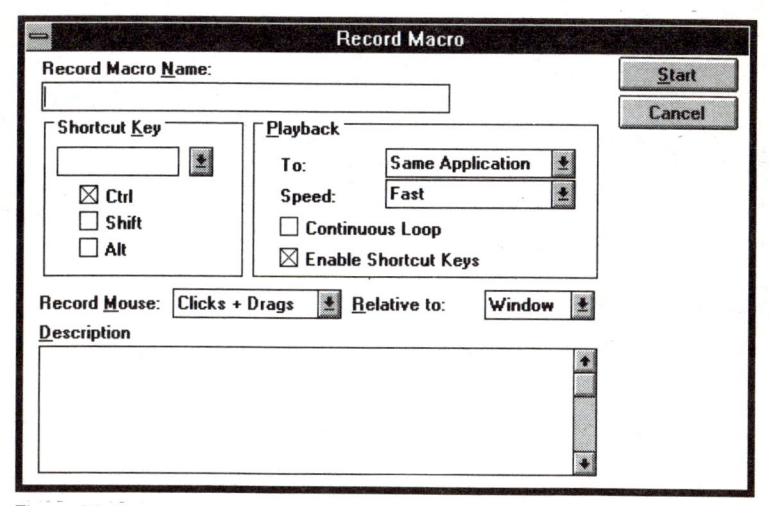

Figure 24.10

Click on Start to start recording. The Recorder icon will flash while it is recording. The mouse movements to be recorded are those to execute the following sequence of operations:

Action	Effect
Click on Edit	pull down Edit menu
Click on Copy	copy the result to Clipboard
Click on Write	open Write
Click on Edit	pull down the Edit menu
Click on Paste	paste the answer into the Write text
Click on the Recorder icon (if the recorder icon is visible) *or* Press Ctrl Break	stop recording

Recorder will display a dialog box, as shown in figure 24.11. Click on Save Macro to store your macro for future use. Click on Cancel Recording to try again. Click on OK. Recorder will report any errors that occur during the recording or execution of your macro.

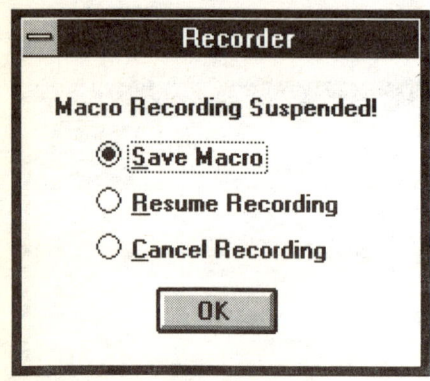

Figure 24.11

Running the macro

If you have assigned a shortcut key to your macro, it can be run from within any application. Hold down the Ctrl key and press the key which you used as the macro shortcut key. If the macro has been named, it has to be run from within Recorder. Open the Recorder window. Click on MACRO then on RUN. The most likely cause of errors in running the macro is that a window which the macro expected to be open was not available. Try recording the macro again.

The more advanced features of creating macros are outside the scope of this book. Readers are referred to the Windows User Guide for further information.

Exiting from Recorder

Click on FILE then on EXIT to exit from Recorder. You will be reminded if there is unsaved work.

Summary

This chapter describes the facilities provided by:

- Character Map;
- Sound Recorder;
- Media Player;
- Recorder.

25
INSTALLING WINDOWS

This chapter describes the installation and setting up of Windows on your computer.

Installing Windows

Windows is supplied on several floppy disks. Disk 1 contains a **Setup** program, which makes it very easy to install Windows.

- Insert Windows Disk 1 into your floppy disk drive.
- Type A: and press Enter to log on to the disk drive.
- Type Setup and press Enter to start the installation process.

The screen will be as shown in figure 25.1. Setup provides full instructions and reports on progress as it is installing Windows. Follow the on-screen instructions to insert the disks as required and you should not have any problems.

Setup performs the following tasks:

- Installs Windows programs, accessories and groups.
- Detects the configuration of your system and sets Windows up so as to optimise performance on your hardware.
- Alters the system files to include device drivers to make Windows run more efficiently.

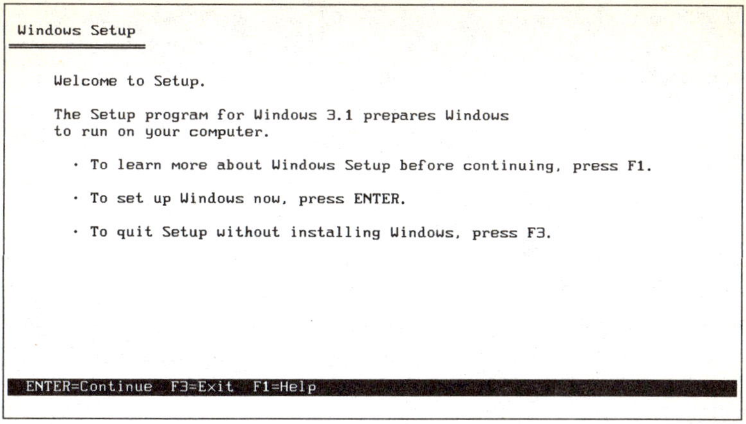

```
Windows Setup

    Welcome to Setup.

    The Setup program for Windows 3.1 prepares Windows
    to run on your computer.

      · To learn more about Windows Setup before continuing, press F1.

      · To set up Windows now, press ENTER.

      · To quit Setup without installing Windows, press F3.




ENTER=Continue  F3=Exit  F1=Help
```

Figure 25.1

- Installs printers.
- Checks the hard disk for existing DOS programs and attempts to set those programs up so they will run under Windows.

In the unlikely event of something going wrong during Setup, it is always possible to change your Windows installation at a later stage from the Windows Setup program and Control Panel. These are described in chapters 18 and 19 respectively.

Optimising your system

Optimising is setting up your system so it runs in the most efficient manner. In Windows, this entails considering the features of your system and using its strengths to achieve the best performance. There are three main factors, the processor speed, the memory and the available disk space. These factors all influence the way that Windows runs. Appendix 2 considers the factors which have to be taken into account when buying a computer to run Windows applications.

Processor speed

The speed of the processor determines how long it takes to load applications, carry out commands, redraw the screen, etc. Another consideration is that at least a 386 processor is needed to operate in 386 Enhanced mode. This mode makes your Windows applications run faster and supports multi-tasking.

Memory

The amount of memory in your computer is the most important factor in determining the efficiency of Windows on your system. One of the strengths of Windows is its ability to have many programs active at the same time, and to switch easily and quickly between them. To do this, Windows uses all the available memory in the computer plus extra memory, which it creates by using disk space. There are four types of computer memory:

Base or Conventional Memory Normally 640 Kilobytes (KB) in size. Used by DOS and DOS applications. Any memory resident 'pop-up' programs you use will run in this memory and reduce the amount available for Windows. Such programs should be removed for optimum Windows performance.

Extended Memory Additional memory above 640 KB. Many computers now have 2 Megabytes (MB), 4 MB, 8 MB or more. Extended memory needs a memory manager to control its use. Windows uses extended memory through its HIMEM.SYS memory manager.

Expanded Memory Memory separate from conventional and extended memory. Expanded memory is needed by some applications but not generally used by most applications. Installed on a separate board and needs an expanded memory manager.

Virtual Memory Disk space Windows uses for temporary storage of the data files it needs as it is working. Windows calls this storage space the **swap file**. The disk space used for the swap file is several Megabytes. Windows uses this space as if it were a memory, thus enabling more programs to be run than if Windows was only using the actual memory of the computer. Swap files are important because they influence the speed at which Windows is able to move programs in and out of memory as you are working.

Disk storage

The amount of available space on your hard disk has an effect on the way Windows runs. Windows uses part of the disk as storage space for its swap files. If you are short of space, the swap files will be restricted to temporary files, and may be smaller than the optimum. Windows applications will then run more slowly. The performance of Windows on your system can be improved by using disk utilities which defragment the disk so that all the free space is in one area. Windows 3.1 provides the facility of removing some of its components so you can make more disk space available. This is described in chapter 19.

Running Windows

When you type WIN, Windows checks your system configuration and loads in the most appropriate mode for your system. The most important factors are the type of processor and the amount of memory in the computer.

Processor	Memory	Mode
8086	any	Real
286	less than 1 MB	Real
286	more than 1 MB	Standard
386	less than 1 MB	Real
386	more than 1 MB but less than 2 MB	Standard
386 or better	more than 2 MB	386 Enhanced

Real mode

Real mode is the only mode which will run on computers with less than 1 MB of memory. This mode is compatible with Windows version 2 and programs designed to run under this version.

Standard mode

Standard mode is the normal Windows mode. It is able to use any extended memory installed in the computer.

386 Enhanced mode

386 Enhanced mode is only available on 386 or better computers with sufficient memory. It is able to use the extended memory installed in the computer, and in addition, is able to use virtual memory to increase the number of applications that can be active at the same time. This is the only mode which supports multi-tasking.

Using swap files

Application swap files

In standard mode, Windows uses applications swap files for non-Windows applications. The available disk space determines the amount of space available for swap files, and therefore limits the number of non-Windows applications which can be open.

386 Enhanced swap files

In 386 Enhanced mode, Windows uses swap files to increase performance and allow more applications to be open at the same time. Windows Setup will have created a swap file on your disk according to the type of disk and amount of free space. The minimum size of the swap file is 1024 KB. Setup always tries to create a permanent swap file, as this is much faster in operation. A temporary swap file has to be created each time Windows is loaded.

Setting up swap files

In Windows 3.1, swap files are maintained through the 386 Enhanced option in Control Panel. In Windows 3.0 there is a separate utility program for this purpose called SWAPFILE.

3.1 only

Double click on the 386 Enhanced icon to display the 386 Enhanced option box, as shown in figure 25.2.

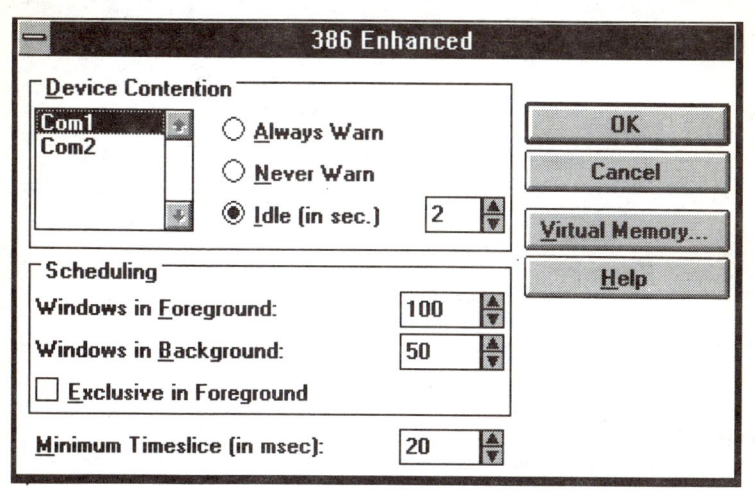

Figure 25.2

Windows Setup will have created a swap file during installation. Click on Virtual Memory to display the top part of the Virtual Memory box, showing the type and size of the current swap file. Click on Change to extend the box to the complete box shown in & figure 25.3. Windows has now looked at the space available on the hard disk, and has recommended a type and size of swap file. The maximum recommended size for the swap file will be less than half of the available disk space.

The Type box has three settings: Temporary, Permanent and None. Selecting None will make the maximum amount of disk space available, but will reduce the number of applications which can be opened before running out of memory. A permanent swap file requires a large area of contiguous disk space, which it uses permanently, and is therefore not available for you to use for other files. A permanent swap file enables Windows to run much faster because the disk space being used is not fragmented. You may find that you are unable to create a permanent swap file on your system because of a lack of suitable disk space. Selecting Permanent will produce a dialog box with a message such as shown in figure 25.4.

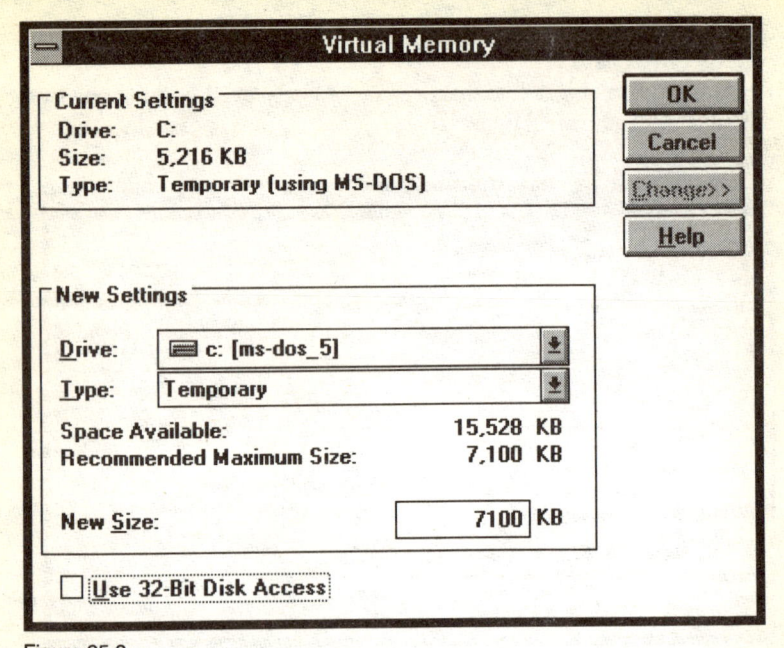

Figure 25.3

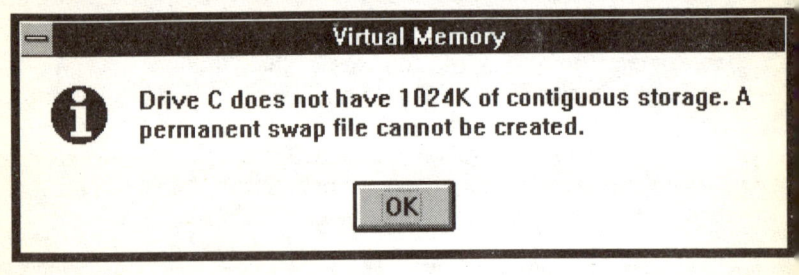

Figure 25.4

A temporary swap file is created each time that Windows is loaded. This means that Windows will take longer to load. It is also slower in operation than a permanent file because the disk space will not be in a single area of the disk.

As a rule, you should accept the suggestions made by Control Panel. You can always change them at a later stage if you find Windows is not performing as well as before.

During installation, Windows Setup will have checked your system as to whether your hard disk controller is able to use the 32 Bit Disk Access feature. It will probably be checked if you are using a permanent swap file. This option can increase the performance of non-Windows applications and speed up the access from Windows to DOS prompt. It is only worth changing this option if you use DOS applications frequently.

3.0 only

If your computer is able to run in 386 Enhanced mode, Setup will have created a swap file during installation. This will either be a permanent swap file or a temporary swap file as discussed earlier. In version 3.0 there is a program called SWAPFILE which allows you to create or alter a permanent swap file. From Program Manager, click on FILE then on RUN. Type the file name SWAPFILE. SWAPFILE will examine your disk to see if a swap file already exists and inform you of its current size. This can then be removed and a new one created. If you do not have a swap file on the disk, SWAPFILE will check whether it is possible to create a suitable permanent swap file and will recommend the amount of disk space to be used. This will always be less than half of the available free disk space. In general, you should accept the recommendations. If you are unable or do not wish to create a permanent swap file, Windows will use a temporary swap file. This is created automatically each time Windows is loaded. The file is normally created in the Windows directory.

Summary

This chapter has discussed:

- installation of Windows;
- factors affecting the running of Windows;
- setting up of swap files.

APPENDIX 1
— KEYBOARD EQUIVALENTS OR —
SHORTCUT KEYS

This appendix lists only those keys which have general application throughout Windows. The keys which perform specific tasks within Windows programs are not included. They can often be found in the relevant chapters.

Arrow keys	moves cursor one space in direction of arrow
F1	accesses Help contents
Shift F1	accesses context sensitive Help
Tab	cycles round elements of a window
Enter	selects highlighted option
Ctrl Tab	cycles group windows
Alt tab	cycles and restores open programs
Alt Esc	cycles open programs
Ctrl Esc	displays Task List
Alt SpaceBar	displays application Control Menu box
Page Up	moves cursor one screen up
Page Down	moves cursor one screen down
Home	moves cursor to top of window
End	moves cursor to bottom of window
Ctrl plus Arrow keys	moves cursor one word left or right
Ctrl Home	moves cursor to top of text

APPENDIX 1

Ctrl End	moves cursor to bottom of text
BackSpace	deletes character to left of cursor
Delete	deletes character to right of cursor
Shift and Arrow keys	selects text
Shift Delete	cuts highlighted element from window to Clipboard
Shift Insert	pastes contents of Clipboard into window
Ctrl Insert	copies highlighted element to Clipboard
Alt Backspace	undoes last operation
Alt plus initial letter	pulls down menu
Alt Hyphen	pulls down Control Menu box of group window
Alt F4	closes active window
Ctrl F4	closes group window
Print Screen	copies screen to Clipboard
Alt Print Screen	copies active window to Clipboard
F2	starts new game

APPENDIX 2
CHOOSING A COMPUTER TO RUN WINDOWS

The minimum configuration to run Windows 3.0 is an 8086 computer with at least 640 Kilobytes (KB) of memory, a suitable graphics adaptor and at least 6 Megabytes (MB) of hard disk space. With this minimum configuration, Windows will only run in real mode. Real mode provides compatibility with previous versions of Windows and is the only version of Windows which can run in a computer with only the basic 640 KB of memory.

To run Windows 3.0 in standard mode, the minimum system configuration required is a 286 computer with at least 1 MB of memory, a suitable graphics adapter and at least 6 MB of free disk space. In practice, disk space of 9 MB or more will be required to enable you to operate, save files, install fonts, etc. Standard mode does not support multi-tasking, which means that you cannot run more than one application at the same time. To run Windows 3.1 in standard mode, the minimum configuration is the same as that described above for Windows 3.0.

To run Windows 3.1 in 386 Enhanced mode, the minimum configuration is a 386 computer with at least 2 MB memory, and 8–10 MB hard disk space.

To run Windows 3.11, the minimum configuration is a 386 computer with 4 MB memory and 10 MB hard disk space.

This book assumes you have at least a 286 computer with sufficient memory to run Windows in standard mode. Those operations which require 386 Enhanced mode are clearly indicated in the text. The book does not cover real mode as this is no longer available in Windows 3.1. Chapter 25 gives more information about standard and 386 Enhanced modes and how to set up Windows to run most efficiently.

Memory

The minimum configuration of a 286 with 1 MB RAM will be pretty slow when running Windows applications. Many of the major Windows packages are very large programs which will not all fit in memory at the same time. The computer handles this by loading the part of the package currently being used into memory and leaving the rest stored on the hard disk. This means that to use another part of the package, for example to print a document, the section in memory has to be replaced with a new section from the disk. Clearly this will take a finite amount of time. The more memory in the computer the larger the proportion of the program which can be stored in memory at once. There will be a reduction in the need to access information on the disk, making the program work faster. In practice, the amount of memory makes a considerable difference to the speed of operation of the program. On the plus side, Windows is able to use extended memory in the computer, so it will use as much memory as is available to it.

This problem gets worse with each new release of the software package because as the developers increase the functionality of the package, its size increases, as does the amount of disk space required. In practice, 2 MB of memory is adequate but still slow with some applications. Increasingly, 4 MB or 8 MB (or even more) are needed.

Disk storage

Applications like Microsoft Word, Excel, Micrographx Draw and Aldus PageMaker all make heavy demands on the hardware, and can create very large files making demands on your valuable hard disk space. For example, a typical chapter of this book written in Microsoft Word and including the embedded graphics for the illustrations can produce a file of approximately 2 MB. You can see that a 40 MB hard disk will soon be full if you are using Windows frequently. Hard disks in Windows machines are now a minimum size of 80 or 100 MB, and machines with at least 200 or 300 MB are needed for professional users.

Processor speed

The processor is the heart of the computer that processes the information and carries out all the commands. The speed of the processor determines the rate at which the commands are carried out by the computer. Processor chips have gone through four major generations. The fifth generation, the aptly named Pentium, was unveiled in March 1993. The first computers containing the new chip were appearing on the market at the time this book went to press.

The first generation was the 8086 processor, which powered the original IBM PC, XT and compatible computers. The next generation was the 286 processor, which worked much faster than the previous processor. The third generation was the 386 processor which worked considerably faster than the 286. The current standard is the 486 processor which runs at over twice the speed of the 386. The Pentium promises to run at least twice as fast as the 486. Within these generations, the processor chips can be obtained with different clock speeds, such as 25 MHz, 33 MHz, etc. As the size and requirements of Windows applications increases, the 486 processor is becoming essential for Windows machines. The basic rule for Windows performance is the faster the better!

Another important factor is that at least a 386 processor with a minimum of 2 MB of memory is needed to operate in 386 Enhanced mode. This mode makes your Windows applications run faster and supports multi-tasking. You are strongly recommended to purchase a reasonably fast (33 MHz or more) 386 computer if you are planning to use Windows a lot. If you can afford it, you should invest in the extra speed of the 486 processor.

This section has probably made you realise that Windows computing can hit you hard in the pocket. The faster and bigger the computer, the better Windows will run. The price of computer hardware has been falling steadily for some while, but a top end computer is still going to cost well over £1,000. Added to that you need to think about the output from your system. The graphic capabilities of Windows software require printers which are capable of doing them justice. You can get Windows to print graphics on a cheap dot matrix printer but it is slow, alarmingly noisy and the quality is often poor. A laser or ink jet printer is essential if you are going to print good quality graphics. This will set you back another £400 upwards. The best advice is to go for as good a system as you can afford. You will also need to be prepared to update the hardware if necessary, buy extra devices if you want to explore Windows multi-media or communicating features, and update the software as new versions are released. Having said all that, Windows computing is an exciting and rewarding environment which is easy and fun to work in, and your expenditure will bring many benefits in terms of the results you are able to produce from your system.

GLOSSARY

Accessory: a utility program supplied with Windows.
Application: a computer program
Arrow keys: cursor movement keys.

Backing store: storage of information on external devices such as hard or floppy disks.
Backup: duplicate data file which provides security against loss of data.
Browse: a method of selecting files.
Button: a box which can be clicked on to perform an action.
Byte: the amount of storage needed to store one character.

Calendar: one of the Windows accessories which allows you to schedule your day.
Cardfile: one of the standard accessories supplied with Windows which is a simple database.
CD-ROM: a compact disk which can store large amounts of data.
CGA: Colour Graphics Adapter – one of the first standards for colour monitors.
Character: a letter, number or symbol.
Character field: field which stores any alphanumeric characters.
Check box: a small box which can be switched on or off, indicated by an X in the box.
Clip art: pictures stored on disk in digitised form.
Clipboard: an area of memory available to all Windows applications for exchange of data.
Click: press and release a mouse button, usually the left button.
Close: exit from a program or remove a window from the desktop.
Command: an instruction given to the computer.
Command line: a space where instructions are entered.

GLOSSARY

Control Panel: a Windows program which is used to change the default system settings.
Copy: to duplicate data from an application into the Clipboard.
Cursor: a block or line which indicates the current typing position.
Cut: to remove data from an application into the Clipboard.

Database: a collection of data stored in files and records.
Default: the standard settings built-in to Windows.
Default drive: the drive containing the program files, usually drive C.
Desktop: the screen and all the windows, applications and icons within Windows.
Dialog box: a box giving or asking for information.
Directory: the list of files on a drive or an area of the disk which is used to store the files connected with particular applications.
Directory tree: the directory structure of the disk.
Diskette: a magnetic medium for storing information. There are two main types: 5.25" floppy disks and the smaller, more rigid 3.5" disks.
Disk drive: a backing storage device which reads and writes to magnetic disks.
Double click: clicking the mouse button twice in quick succession.
DOS prompt: the place at which DOS commands are typed.
Drag: click and hold down the mouse button while moving the pointer.
Drop down list box: a box containing an arrow which can be clicked to display the list of items.

Edit: the alteration of a document, Cardfile or drawing, etc.
EGA: Enhanced Graphics Adapter – another standard for colour and monochrome monitors giving better resolution than CGA.
Electronic mail: facility for communicating over a computer network or using modems.
Embedded object: data created in one application and used in a different application.
Enhanced mode: Windows multi-tasking mode.
Extended memory: the portion of the computer's RAM above the 640 K base memory. Windows uses the extended memory to store files it needs to work and runs faster if there is more memory available.

File: any data stored on magnetic media.
File name: the name given to the file. Maximum length is eight characters.
Floppy disk: a transportable magnetic storage medium which is cheap and widely available.
Font: a type style. Many different fonts are available for use in Windows.
Footer: a section of text which appears at the bottom of each page.
Format disk: prepare disk for receiving data by marking out tracks and catalogue.
Function keys: the keys marked with F1, F2, etc. at the left or top of the keyboard, used as shortcuts to commands.

Graphical User Interface (GUI): an environment such as Windows which uses pictorial representations instead of commands.
Graphics: computer pictures.
Group: a related set of icons.

Hard disk: magnetic storage device built into the computer.
Hardware: physical devices like the computer and printer.
Header: a section of text which appears at the top of each page.
Help screens: the basic components of the extensive Windows Help facilities.
Hercules: a monochrome graphics display standard giving better resolution than CGA and EGA.
Highlight: a technique where the selected area is colour reversed.
Hotlinks: a quick way of jumping between help topics.

Icon: a pictorial representation of a computer program.
Icon Bar: the area at the bottom of the screen where minimised programs are displayed.
Index Line: in Cardfile, the top line of each card used to index or sort the cards.
Input device: any device used to get information into the computer.
Insertion point: an I bar defining the point at which text will be typed, made by clicking with the mouse.

Kilobyte (K): the amount of storage space needed for 1024 characters.

LAN (Local Area Network): a network of connected computers sharing files and devices.
Landscape: printer orientation where the data is printed sideways on the paper.
List box: a box with scroll bars containing items that can be selected.
Load: the operation of transferring a file from a disk into the memory of the computer.
Logged drive: the drive from which you start Windows.

Macro: a stored series of operations which can be executed by a shortcut key.
Maximise: expand the current window to fill the whole screen.
Media player: one of the Windows accessories which allows the playing of CDs and sound files.
Megabyte (Mb): the amount of storage needed for 1,048,576 bytes.
Memory: the internal storage area of the computer.
Menu: a list of options.
Menu Bar: a line at the top of the window containing the menu titles.
Minimise: to collapse the current window so it appears as an icon at the bottom of the screen.
MIS: Management Information System.
Modem: a device which enables a computer to communicate with another computer via a telephone line.
Mouse: a pointing device attached to the computer.

GLOSSARY

MS-DOS: Miscrosoft Disk Operating System – the commonest PC operating system.
Multimedia: the use of CDs, sound and video within a computer application.
Multi-tasking: the ability to run more than one program at the same time.

Network: a collection of linked computers sharing files and devices.
Non-Windows application: a program which does not use the facilities of Windows but can be run under Windows.
Notepad: a Windows accessory which allows you to edit the files.

Open application: a program which is active although it may be minimised.
Open file: to load a file from disk into memory.
Operating system: the set of utility programs which enables the computer to operate.
Option: a selection from a command menu.
Output device: any device used to display information from a program.

Paste: to copy the data from the Clipboard into an application. The data is pasted in at the current cursor position.
Paintbrush: a Windows program which allows you to paint pictures.
Path: the full file name of a file, including all levels of directory and the file name.
Pointer: an arrow which is moved around the screen by moving the mouse.
Pixel: an individual point of colour on the screen.
Portrait: printer orientation where the data is printed with the shorter side of the paper at the top.
Printer driver: a file containing instructions to enable Windows to print on a particular printer.
Processing unit: the part of the computer which takes the information input, processes it according to the program instructions and outputs it to the output device.
Program: the set of instructions which determines how the data is processed.
Program Information File (PIF): a file which contains instructions as to how to run non-Windows applications.
Public Domain (PD) Software: computer programs which are uncopyrighted and can be distributed free of charge.

Radio button: a circular option button, only one of which can be selected.
RAM: Random Access Memory. The memory of the computer which is available for programs to use.
Recorder: an accessory which allows you to create macros for use within Windows.
Restore button: returns the window to its previous size before it was maximised.
Ruler line: a bar at the top of the screen in Write which controls the text for formatting.

WINDOWS

Save: the operation of storing a file on the disk for future use.

Scanner: a hardware device which can scan graphics, photographs or text and convert the images to a digitised format suitable for processing by a computer.

Screen saver: a program activated when the computer has not been used for a pre-determined period which clears all the elements from the screen and displays some moving pictures.

Scroll bar: grey bars down the right hand side and along the bottom of the screen which are used to scroll the screen when the full area is too large to be displayed all at once.

Shareware: Computer programs which are distributed free on a trial basis. Payment is normally made direct to the author.

Software: computer programs.

Sound card: a printed circuit board which can be slotted into the computer to give it added sound capabilities.

Sound recorder: an accessory which plays and records sound files.

Split bar: a bar dividing a screen window into two parts.

Super VGA (SVGA): a new colour graphics standard offering higher resolution and 256 colours.

Swap file: a file used by Windows to move data between memory and the disk.

Task list: a window which shows all the open applications.

Terminal: an accessory supplied with Windows which will drive a modem.

Text file: a file which can be read by a word processor.

Title Bar: the top line of every window containing the window title.

True Type font: a font which prints exactly as it appears on the screen.

VGA: Video Graphics Array – a colour and monochrome graphics standard giving higher resolution than EGA or CGA.

Virtual memory: the space on the hard disk that Windows uses for its swap files.

Wallpaper: the background to the Windows desktop. Any bit-mapped file can be used. Several are supplied with Windows.

Wildcard: a character which can stand for any character in a file name. Wildcards are used in searching for types of files.

Window: an area on the screen in which an application runs or a document is held.

Windows: Microsoft's graphical environment which uses a mouse, a pointer and icons for invoking and controlling program applications.

Windows applications: programs specifically designed to make full use of the graphical features of Windows.

Word processor: a program that manipulates text data.

Write: one of the standard accessories which is a word processor.